Life Is CHANGED, Not ENDED

An Introduction to Christian Eschatology

Robin Ryan, CP

Paulist Press
New York / Mahwah, NJ

Cover and book design by Lynn Else

Library of Congress Cataloging-in-Publication Data
Names: Ryan, Robin, author.
Title: Life is changed, not ended: an introduction to Christian eschatology / Robin Ryan, CP.
Description: New York; Mahwah, NJ: Paperback, [2024] | Includes bibliographical references and index. | Summary: "A comprehensive overview of the Church's teaching on eschatology"—Provided by publisher.
Identifiers: LCCN 2023054194 (print) | LCCN 2023054195 (ebook) | ISBN 9780809156979 (paperback) | ISBN 9780809188604 (ebook)
Subjects: LCSH: Eschatology. | Christianity.
Classification: LCC BT821.3 .R84 2024 (print) | LCC BT821.3 (ebook) | DDC 236—dc23/eng/20240416
LC record available at https://lccn.loc.gov/2023054194
LC ebook record available at https://lccn.loc.gov/2023054195

ISBN 978-0-8091-5697-9 (paperback)
ISBN 978-0-8091-8860-4 (e-book)

Published by Paulist Press
997 Macarthur Boulevard
Mahwah, NJ 07430
www.paulistpress.com

Printed and bound in the
United States of America

CONTENTS

PREFACE

In the Roman Missal, the first Preface for Mass for the Dead includes these words:

> Indeed for your faithful, Lord, life is changed not ended,
> And, when this earthly dwelling turns to dust,
> An eternal dwelling is made ready for them in heaven.[1]

These words, familiar to practicing Catholics, express a fundamental hope of all Christians: death—as powerful force as it may be—does not have the final word for human beings or for the cosmos itself. Death gives way to "change"—a transformation of earthly realities that can only be imagined on our side of death. This is an expression of faith that is rooted in belief in the death and resurrection of Jesus Christ. It is at the core of Christian faith.

This book is a study in Christian *eschatology*—a term derived from the Greek word *eschata*, meaning last or ultimate things. Jeannine Hill Fletcher describes eschatology as "the area of belief that speaks of the final destiny of humankind and the world, and articulates a vision of the ultimate aim toward which creation tends."[2] Eschatology is about the future—the future of the individual person, the future of humankind, and the future of the cosmos. We are headed somewhere, or better, we are directed ultimately to Someone, and eschatology explores the destiny that awaits each of us. In his encyclical On Christian Hope (*Spe Salvi*), Pope Benedict XVI wrote, "Here too we see as a distinguishing mark of Christians the fact that they have a future: it is not that they know the details of what awaits them, but they know in general terms that their life will not end in emptiness."[3] What we know "in general terms" is rooted in God's self-revelation in Christ.

Eschatology, however, is not only about the future—the "not yet." The future impacts upon the present, giving people a vision and an impetus for the decisions they make in the here and now. Fletcher observes, "Dwelling on what is to come in the ultimate future, eschatology is simultaneously an assessment of the here and now as it is illuminated by the life and person of Jesus Christ."[4] The impact of the future on the present is particularly evident in Jesus's proclamation of the reign (kingdom) of God. In his public ministry Jesus not only proclaimed the future coming of the kingdom, he made it present in his healings, exorcisms, and table fellowship. Through his teaching he inculcated in his disciples the values of the reign of God. The twentieth century recovery of the centrality of Jesus's proclamation of God's reign was a source of renewal for Christian eschatology. Theological reflection on the expectation of the kingdom, and what that means for Christian praxis, has been emphasized in a focused way in political and liberation theologies.

Eschatology entails, then, reflection on the language and vision of human hope. This theme of hope will be developed at greater length in the next chapter. Here we can simply observe that each of us is driven by hopes that lie deep within: the hope to establish loving relationships within our families and among friends; the hope to be successful in the work in which we are involved; the hope to have good health; the hope that our lives will make a genuine difference to other people, and so on. Honest reflection on these "earthly" hopes can move us to inquire whether these hopes are driven by an absolute hope—a dynamism toward ultimate fulfillment, toward happiness that will not end.

In the neo-Scholastic theology that was dominant in the late nineteenth and early twentieth centuries, eschatology entailed consideration of the four "last things": death, judgment, heaven, and hell. To these four were added purgation, the general resurrection, and the Parousia of Christ. This approach to eschatology entailed a kind of "mapping" of the next world, and it sometimes lost sight of the limitations of our concepts and images in our efforts to depict life beyond death. The French theologian Yves Congar said that before the mid-twentieth century, seminary textbooks treated eschatology as colorful objects.[5] Commenting on this theological approach, Thomas O'Meara observes that life after death was presented like life on earth, and judgments about a person appeared arbitrary and extrinsic.[6]

After 1950, the approach to eschatology began to shift. Zachary Hayes identifies two major shifts leading up to the Second Vatican Council.[7] The first happened in the aftermath of the dogmatic definition of the Assumption of Mary, with theologians taking up the question of the theology of death. Karl Rahner's work on death was particularly influential. Eschatology came to be seen as inextricably linked to anthropology—the understanding of the human person in relation to God, self, other people, and the natural world—and to Christology, reflection on the person and saving work of Christ. "This anthropological shift gave eschatology a tone decidedly different from that of the earlier physical style."[8] A second turn involved focus on the relationship between eschatology and human history. It explored the connection between Christian hope and the humanistic and technological projects of the modern world. This focus is evident in *Gaudium et Spes*, the Pastoral Constitution on the Church in the Modern World. Sensitive to the Marxist claim that religion is the opium of the people, Vatican II tried to show that hope in the coming of God's reign inspires, rather than discourages, work to improve the world. Addressing the relation between the divine gift of the kingdom and human efforts to build a more just and peace-filled world became a pivotal issue in the years after Vatican II.

In recent years, another shift of emphasis has come to characterize Christian eschatology. This shift entails renewed focus on the future of the cosmos. In his encyclical *Laudato Si'* and in other writings, Pope Francis repeatedly reminds us of the intrinsic human connection with the natural world. Everything is interconnected. In this vein, Christian theologians accentuate the principle of sacramentality, which is central to Christian faith and practice: the world is a reflection of God; created things mediate the presence of the Creator. Some theologians argue that in the incarnation of the Word of God, God became forever connected with flesh—with the fragile, finite, perishable world of matter.[9] This means that eschatology must explore the hope that Christians have for the cosmos. Here theology enters into dialogue with scientific cosmology, which paints a rather bleak picture of the ultimate future of the earth and of the universe in its totality. This focus on the future of the cosmos as a whole will be further discussed in chapter 7.

CONTEMPORARY PERSPECTIVES ON THE AFTERLIFE

I embark on this study of Christian eschatology as a Catholic Christian who lives and works in the United States. The context in which I theologize, then, is an increasingly secularized society, as is true in much of North America, western Europe, and some other parts of the world, like Japan and Australia. As Charles Taylor has demonstrated, life in these societies reveals that we live in a "secular age"—a time when religious faith is one option among others for finding meaning and discovering purpose in one's life.[10] Studies of religious practice in the United States repeatedly show high rates of disaffiliation from some religious groups, including the Catholic church. There has been a significant increase of the so-called Nones—those people, both young and old, who profess to have no religious affiliation.[11] These trends of disaffiliation, and the overall climate of secularization, strongly influence people's approach to death and to life after death. Anecdotally, this is evident in the fact that a significant number of Catholics forego the church's full funeral rites for their beloved dead, opting instead for private or scaled-down gatherings to remember those who have died.

Two German theologians who have written extensively about Christian eschatology pay close attention to this secularized context. The Catholic Gerhard Lohfink begins his book on the topic with a section titled "What People Think."[12] He notes the skepticism about any belief in life after death on the part of many people today. Lohfink cites the poem by Bertolt Brecht (d. 1956) titled "Lucifer's Evening Song." The poem contains the line, "Don't let them get your hopes up! Today is all there is." Lohfink proceeds to chronicle and to critique some modern perspectives on death and eternal life. He adduces the idea of survival in one's descendants, a belief that was prominent in ancient Israel. Modern versions of this idea affirm that one's life and accomplishments are remembered and continue in those one has left behind. Lohfink observes, however, that the good one has done can easily crumble. Lohfink also adduces belief in continual reincarnation, a tenet of Eastern religions and a belief held by some contemporary Christians. In a 1992 statement on eschatological themes, the International Theological Commission devoted an entire section to expounding and critiquing modern belief in reincarnation (transmigration of souls).[13] Lohfink concedes that the truth in reincarnation is the justified longing for purification and the insight that human existence is not simply extinguished in death. But he argues that these aspirations are fulfilled much better in Christian faith. A third contemporary perspective on death is dissolution into the universe. Here the meaning of death is deliverance from the burden of one's ego and dissolution into the natural world. This idea is sometimes given expression in the practice of scattering the ashes of the deceased on the sea. Lohfink also discusses the longing for extinction among some contemporaries, sometimes evident in those who die by assisted suicide.

The German Protestant theologian Jürgen Moltmann has made eschatology a point of departure for his entire theological project.[14] Moltmann observes that contemporary Western society tends to avoid death and to ignore the effects of loss on loved ones. He reflects on the way in which authentic love makes one vulnerable to the deep pain of grief when we lose those we love. But, he argues, modern societies provide few rituals for dealing with dying, death, and mourning. Moltmann asserts, "Modern society has no time for mourning, and no space, so it has no respect and no protection for mourners either."[15] The dead are simply gone from sight, and their loved ones are left to deal with their grief alone. Moltmann's observations are reminiscent of a passage in one of Karl Rahner's early essays: "Have we not really lost sight of our own deceased relatives? We pray for them perhaps, because this is the done thing and because we would otherwise have a bad conscience about it. But apart from that, if we are honest, they have ceased to exist for us."[16]

So the context of contemporary Western cultures is one in which there are a variety of perspectives on death and afterlife as well as an inclination to avoid the reality of death and its painful effects on those left behind. At the same time, pastoral experience reveals that many Christians do grapple with the mystery of death and dying and that they desire and appreciate the rituals of faith that the church offers. Though not as extensive as it once was, the practice of giving "Mass cards" to the bereaved is still followed, as a way of comforting them with the knowledge that their loved one will be remembered in the prayer of the church. Mourners often express their gratitude for the rites for those who have died that are found in the Order of Christian Funerals: the Vigil for the Deceased, Funeral Mass, and Burial. These rites contain some of the most tender and hope-filled texts in the entire liturgical tradition, and it is my experience as a priest that mourners find them to be consoling. The doctrine of the communion of saints, to be explored further in chapter 7, can also be a source of consolation for those suffering the loss of a loved one. They are strengthened by the belief that death is not powerful enough to sever the bonds of faith and charity that they have forged with others. It is also the case that the approach to death and afterlife in African, Asian, and some Latin American cultures is distinct from that of Western societies. The reverence offered to ancestors in these cultures opens a space for connection with the beloved dead, and it situates the reality of death as part of life.

An example of these non-Western rites is the observance of the Day of the Dead (*Día de Los Muertos*) in some Latin American cultures, including among Latino/a peoples in the United States. Day of the Dead rituals began thousands of years ago among Indigenous peoples in southern Mexico and parts of Central America. When the Spanish missionaries arrived at the time of colonization, this tradition became linked with the Catholic observance of All Saints and All Souls days. A major feature of this tradition is the construction of altars (*ofrendas*) that honor the deceased. Photos of the deceased, their favorite foods and drink, tributes to their accomplishments as well as reminders of death like sugar skulls fill these altars. Carmen Nanko-Fernández names this practice of ordinary people an example of "performative theologizing."[17] She observes, "The practices surrounding the days of the dead serve as resistance to US customs that sanitize death and the process of dying."[18] She adds, "The days of the dead are performed eschatology. They point toward a divine reign that is present and still in process, to relationships sustained beyond death, to a communion of saints."[19] This practice of popular devotion shows that the context for engaging in eschatological reflection is more complex than if one attended to Western society alone.

INTERPRETING A TRADITION

This study of Christian eschatology is an endeavor of faith seeking understanding (*fides quaerens intellectum*). This way of doing theology, famously named by Anselm of Canterbury, has its starting point in divine self-revelation—God's self-communication in creation, in the history of Israel, and in an unsurpassable way in and through Jesus Christ. What we know about life with God after death is only available to us through God's self-revelation. Lohfink observes, "What happens to us after death is something we can only know in faith, and it is only from faith that we can ultimately speak of it....I want to emphasize again that as regards what happens to us after death we can know nothing except through God's own self and out of a listening faith."[20] We can reason about our eschatological beliefs through the use of analogy and metaphor, with the aim of giving reasons for our hope (1 Pet 3:15). But this reasoning is grounded in what has been revealed to us by God, who has given of self as one to be known and loved.

Christians believe that God's self-communication is most fully present in the life, death, and resurrection of Jesus Christ, whom they profess to be the Word of God made flesh. Dermot Lane expresses this point clearly: "The person of Jesus reveals who God is, who we are, and who we are called to become in the future. In particular, the person of the crucified and risen Christ is the focus, or better the paradigm, for interpreting eschatological statements."[21] The affirmation of the resurrection of Jesus is the foundation of Christian hope for life with God beyond death. That will become evident in our exploration of the eschatology of the New Testament. So Christology is at the heart of Christian eschatology: "Given the centrality of the Christ-event we can say that eschatology is about the application of christology to the self, society, history and creation in the mode of fulfillment."[22]

This starting point means that I will not be exploring and analyzing near-death experiences. Some studies of eschatology do include such exploration, suggesting that these experiences offer at least indirect evidence of life after death.[23] Studies of these experiences are indeed intriguing, and they seem to show that some people have a profound experience of the divine—or the transcendent—at a moment when they have found themselves to be on the brink of death. But these individuals did not actually cross the threshold of death; they remained among the living, able to recount their experiences to others. Thus, they do not provide direct evidence of life after death.

Karl Rahner wrote a famous essay on the hermeneutics—principles of interpretation—of eschatological statements in 1960, which he summarized and revised in his later book *Foundations of*

Christian Faith.[24] Rahner's principles will be studied in more detail in chapter 5. It is, however, helpful to mention two of those principles at the beginning of this study. The first of these involves the kind of knowledge that we have of the eschatological future. Rahner thinks of Christian eschatology as a forward look from the experience of the grace of Christ in the present. This is true of the eschatological statements found in Scripture and in the theological tradition. Rahner articulates this principle in these words:

> Now if we want to read the eschatological statements of the New Testament correctly, because of the very nature of man [*sic*] they are necessarily conclusions from the experience of the Christian *present*. What we know about Christian eschatology is what we know about man's present situation in the history of salvation. We do not project something from the future into the present, but rather in man's experience of himself and of God in grace and in Christ we project our Christian present into its future.[25]

Rahner does admit that our present is impinged upon by our future, as it is by our past, but he emphasizes that we begin with the present experience of grace. This principle leads Rahner to be critical of eschatological statements that purport to be "eyewitness reports" of what is going to happen in the future. He insists that Christians know as much about their future as they know of themselves and their redemption in Christ through divine revelation.

Some theologians argue that beginning with the present means starting with the status quo and thus ignoring the radical transformation that God's future will effect in creation and the conversion to which we are called by this future. Jürgen Moltmann, for example, asserts that primacy should be given to the future rather than the present: "Christianity is wholly and entirely confident hope, a stretching out to what is ahead, and a readiness for a fresh start. *Future* is not just something or other to do with Christianity. It is the essential element of the faith which is specifically Christian."[26] Moltmann proceeds to argue that Christ is already in the process of coming and his coming already acts on the present, leading believers to open themselves for Christ's future.

This focus on the future foregrounds discontinuity over continuity in imagining the future, and it highlights prophetic criticism of the present. Nevertheless, I find Rahner's approach to be more compelling than that of Moltmann. While we have the promise of God's future and of life with God in that future, our only direct knowledge of this future is knowledge based on our present experience of God's self-communication Christ—the experience of grace. We extrapolate from that present experience and project it into the future. I think that Rahner is correct in saying, "Eschatological knowledge is knowledge of the eschatological present."[27]

This discussion of eschatological knowledge leads into a second principle of interpretation proffered by Rahner. This is the principle of "the hiddenness of the last things."[28] The New Testament tells us that God has not revealed the day of the end (see Mark 13:32). For Rahner this means more than just our ignorance of the *date* of the end. It points to the truth that the end, the condition of final fulfillment, has for us the character of hiddenness that is essential and proper to it. God is incomprehensible mystery, and if God in God's very self is our ultimate end, then there is a hiddenness that is essential to our end. Rahner asserts that "the God who alone is supposed to be man's absolute future remains the incomprehensible mystery to be worshipped in silence." Therefore, Rahner says, "as Christians we do not have to act as though we knew all about ourselves in heaven."[29]

Other theologians echo Rahner's salutary reminder of the limitations inherent in eschatological knowledge. In his encyclical *Spe Salvi,* Benedict XVI points out that throughout history Christians have attempted to express a "knowing without knowing" about the future, developing images of heaven that remain far removed from what can only be known negatively, via unknowing.[30] Dermot Lane adduces the well-known principle enunciated by the Fourth Lateran Council (1215) concerning the limitations of language about God: "No similitude can be expressed without implying a greater dissimilitude." He finds this fundamental principle to be particularly applicable to the relationship that exists between human experience and eschatology.[31] Further along in this study, we will see that in recent years some theologians have argued that we need to move beyond abstract theological concepts and articulate Christian hope for the eschatological future in images and narrative. While there may be some truth in that position, one must continue to keep in mind Rahner's principle of the hiddenness of the last things and thus of the limitations of images and stories that are employed to depict the eschaton.

I proceed in this study according to what might be called a hermeneutics of critical appreciation. I perceive the Judeo-Christian tradition to be fundamentally trustworthy in what it discloses about our future in God. This is true even though this tradition is always subject to the limitations of particular contexts and, as we have seen, to the limitations inherent in all talk about God and our future with God. Though I do not adopt a hermeneutics of suspicion in this study, adherents of that approach offer us salutary reminders of the possibility of distortions in any tradition. Thus, I must be alert to theological assumptions and assertions that I judge to be distortions of the gospel of Jesus Christ. I will attempt to situate eschatological narratives and statements found in the Bible and the theological tradition within their historical and cultural contexts. And I will try to unfold the meaning of these stories and statements, noting what I believe to be their relevance or irrelevance for contemporary Christian belief, worship, and praxis. I approach this endeavor as a white, male, Roman Catholic priest who was born and lives in the United States, with all of the limitations entailed in my social location.

The order of procedure of this book is relatively straightforward. Because eschatology is so closely linked with theological anthropology, the first chapter will address anthropological foundations. Chapters 2 and 3 will explore the hope for a future in God found in the Old Testament and the New Testament. In chapters 4 and 5, we will examine major developments in eschatology from the early church to the twenty-first century. Chapter 6 will be a systematic treatment of teaching about the destiny of the individual, as expressed in the Christian tradition and contemporary theology. In chapter 7, we will explore what the Bible and the theological tradition disclose about the corporate future of humankind and of the cosmos. The epilogue will consist of some final reflections on eschatology and the mystery of suffering.

ACKNOWLEDGEMENTS

There are many people who offered their encouragement and support during the writing of this book. Among them were Fr. Donald Senior, CP, and Donna Crilly. My Passionist confrere, Don Senior, died before I finished the book. But he encouraged me from the beginning and offered helpful comments, especially for the chapter on New Testament eschatology. Donna Crilly, senior academic editor at Paulist Press, invited me to take up the project and was very faithful in her support throughout the entire writing process. I am most grateful to both Don and Donna.

1

ANTHROPOLOGICAL FOUNDATIONS

In the introduction we saw that Christian eschatology is intimately linked with Christology and theological anthropology. The foundation for the ultimate hope of Christians is the life, death, and resurrection of Jesus Christ. And the Christian vision of final fulfillment is directly related to the understanding of the human person—the person in relation to God, others, self, and the natural world. Dermot Lane observes that eschatology is not something additional or extrinsic to anthropology. Drawing on the work of Karl Rahner, Lane affirms that eschatology is anthropology in a mode of fulfillment—"anthropology conjugated in the future."[1] Lane proceeds to assert, "To this extent, eschatology is about the full flowering of the gift and grace of historical existence in eternity."[2]

If this is true, then we need to say something about the Christian understanding of the human person, which is the subject of this chapter. Thus, I will explore several dimensions of being human that eschatology must address. This exploration will in no way entail the development of a comprehensive theological anthropology. Crafting a systematic theological anthropology is beyond the scope of this book. I will simply attempt to elucidate some of the foundational aspects of human existence in the world.

CREATURES OF THE EARTH

The second story of creation in the Book of Genesis (Gen 2:4b—3:24) is known for its simplicity and earthiness. This (Yahwist) account abounds with anthropomorphic imagery for God and God's action in creating. And the story depicts the origin of humanity as profoundly linked with the rest of creation. The Yahwist author tells us that "the LORD God formed the man [*adam*] out of the dust [*adamah*] of the ground and blew into his nostrils the breath of life, and the man became a living being" (2:7). Here God is depicted as a potter fashioning the human being out of the very dust of the earth, from which God will also fashion the other creatures in the primordial garden. Then God settles the human being in this garden to cultivate and care for it (2:15). The Hebrew word employed here is *abad*, which can also mean "to serve." The human serves God by serving the ground. The human creature who has been taken from the ground will in turn work the ground that has been watered by God. Then God gives the *adam* the task of naming the animals that God forms out of the ground. As Anne Clifford observes, "Naming is a way in which humans relate to nonhuman creatures."[3] And this activity suggests the importance of community: the *adam* is not to be a solitary creature but a communal being essentially in relationship to others.[4]

This creation story, then, elucidates the close connection between human beings and the rest of the natural world. Ecologically minded theologians highlight this biblical affirmation in the light of what they perceive to be a deficient understanding of the human person as separate from other creatures and from the earth itself. They argue that theological emphasis on human uniqueness has sometimes obscured the truth that to be human is to be a creature of the earth, inextricably linked with other earthbound creatures.

In Pope Francis's encyclical *Laudato Si'*, he accentuates this truth about the bond between human beings and the rest of creation. In the opening section of the letter, the pope laments, "We have forgotten that we ourselves are dust of the earth (cf. Gen 2:7); our very bodies are made up of her elements, we breathe her air and we receive life and refreshment from her waters" (2). In a part of the encyclical in which he addresses the theme of communion, Francis quotes a statement he had made in his earlier apostolic exhortation

Evangelii Gaudium (The Joy of the Gospel): "Here I would reiterate that 'God has joined us so closely to the world around us that we can feel the desertification of the soil almost as a physical ailment, and the extinction of species as a painful disfigurement'" (LS 89; EG 215). At the end of *Laudato Si'*, in a section on the sacraments, the pope declares, "The sacraments are a privileged way in which nature is taken up by God to become a means of mediating supernatural life. Through our worship of God, we are invited to embrace the world on a different plane. Water, oil, fire and colors are taken up in all their symbolic power and incorporated in our act of praise" (235). Thus, even in the sublime act of worshipping God, we remain connected to the earth.

Daniel Horan adverts to anecdotal experience of the Catholic liturgy for Ash Wednesday as a way of demonstrating that we are not always comfortable in perceiving ourselves as creatures of the earth. He notes that some ministers who distribute ashes in that liturgy prefer to recite the formula, "Repent and believe in the Gospel" rather than the formula, "Remember that you are dust and to dust you shall return."[5] While the former formula is legitimate for liturgical use, Horan suggests that the discomfort ministers have with the latter formula derives from a feeling that it is "grim and death centered" and also that "it sounds too pedestrian, material and creation focused in the literal face of the dignity and uniqueness ascribed to human beings."[6] Horan contends that we should embrace the fact that we are dust, a fact that is supported by both science and the Bible. Making a strong argument against a separatist view of human existence, he asserts, "That we are animals, material creatures made up of the same elements as all other creatures and as interdependent and interrelated as any of God's other animals, should not detract from the inherent dignity and value of each person."[7]

We will explore the concept of deep incarnation in chapter 7, when we discuss corporate and cosmic fulfillment. But here it is helpful to consider that this relatively recent idea highlights the intrinsic connection of Jesus, the incarnate Word of God, with the entirety of creation. Originally proposed by the Danish Lutheran theologian Niels Gregersen, the concept of deep incarnation has been adopted and developed by a number of thinkers, including the late Australian theologian Denis Edwards and the U.S. American theologian Elizabeth Johnson. Gregersen focuses on the verse in the

Prologue to the Gospel of John that affirms that in Jesus the Word (*Logos*) became "flesh" (*sarx*; John 1:14). Gregersen argues that the term *sarx* links the Word of God not only with the human nature of Jesus but with all "flesh," that is, with all that is finite and perishable, with the matter that extends throughout the universe. Gregersen says that deep incarnation means "that God became flesh for the purpose of reconciling humanity with God, and of conjoining God and the world so intensely together that there can be a future for a material world characterized by decomposition, frailty and suffering."[8] Gregersen asserts that "the incarnate Christ cannot be at all the incarnate Logos, unless he is intrinsically related to the cosmos at large."[9] Gregersen's interpretation of John 1:14 is not unlike the statement made by Pope John Paul II in his encyclical on the Holy Spirit, *Dominum et Vivificantem*: "The Incarnation of God the Son signifies the taking up into unity with God not only of human nature, but in this human nature of everything that is 'flesh': the whole of humanity, the entire visible and material world. The Incarnation also has a cosmic significance, a cosmic dimension" (50).

The recognition that we humans are creatures of the earth has implications for Christian eschatology. If as creatures we are inextricably linked to the earth and even to the cosmos at large, then the affirmations that we make about final fulfillment should include the fulfillment of all of creation. As Christians, we believe that salvation in Christ is the salvation *of* the world, not salvation *from* the world. John Haught, a theologian who has dialogued extensively with science, affirms that our human lives are caught up with the whole universe in a mysterious movement toward meaning, truth, beauty, and love.[10] We will see that theologians past and present have differed in their vision of which elements of the world will participate in God's final salvation. But the affirmation that human beings are creatures of the earth provides a principle for judging whether a particular account of eschatology is adequate to the experience of humans and other creatures alike.

SELF-TRANSCENDENCE

Human beings are creatures of the earth, and we are also beings of self-transcendence. The movement of self-transcendence pulsates through our being and through the cosmos itself. Our desires are so deep and strong that they can never be satisfied by anything created. Our yearnings impel us toward the infinite. Augustine of Hippo expressed this truth in the famous statement found at the beginning of his *Confessions*: "Nevertheless to praise you [God] is the desire of man [*sic*], a little piece of your creation. You stir man to take pleasure in praising you, because you have made us for yourself, and our heart is restless until it rests in you."[11] Augustine's experience of his own restless heart convinced him that his desires would be fulfilled only by God.

Thomas Aquinas echoes Augustine's insight in his discussion of human happiness in the *Summa Theologiae*.[12] He argues that there must be an ultimate end, or final goal, of human desire; there cannot be endless ends. And he discusses possible candidates that might make for true happiness: riches, honors, fame, pleasure, and so on.[13] Predictably, he concludes that none of these finite goods can serve as an ultimate end for human beings. He asserts that nothing short of God can satisfy us completely:

> The object of the will, that is the human appetite, is the Good without reserve, just as the object of the mind is the True without reserve. Clearly, then, nothing can satisfy our will except such goodness, which is found, not in anything created, but in God alone. Everything created is a derivative good.[14]

As Brian Davies explains, for Aquinas the one thing that makes human beings distinctive is our ability to understand; this for him is the characteristic activity of people. This means that our ultimate goal must be to understand the source and goal of all things, that is, God. Aquinas speaks of this goal as "the joy of seeing God 'as he is.'"[15] That will happen only through the grace of God empowering our vision. Aquinas asserts that this knowing and enjoying of God constitutes *beatitude*, which is the ultimate fulfillment of human desire.

The modern theologian who has written most extensively about self-transcendence is Karl Rahner. He extends the dynamic of self-transcendence beyond human beings to the universe itself. This is the way in which he envisions God creating the universe by means of evolution.[16] Rahner proceeds from the assumption of an evolving universe, that is, "that there is a development which determines the entire cosmic reality and continues on through it."[17] He conceives of belief in creation as the transcendental origination of all being from absolute being. Everything that exists bears the stamp of the one primordial ground of being, God. Rahner envisions a uniquely close relationship between God and creation. God is distinct from creation, but God establishes this distinction and in so doing keeps creation with God's self in a unique way.[18] Created beings are subject to the constant "pressure" of divine being. This "pressure," or immanent presence and activity of God, gives creatures the capacity for *active self-transcendence.* God confers on creatures not only their existence but also their capacity to evolve into something radically new.[19] This enduring divine activity is not something that could be detected or measured by natural science. It makes possible a *becoming* in creation that is a becoming *more.*

Hydrogen atoms that appeared more than 13 billion years ago eventually develop into reflective human beings. God's immanent presence within creation, God's self-bestowal to creation, makes possible an increase in being that is related to what was there before but not simply accounted for by what was previously existent. God's immanent presence enables creature *A* to surpass itself and become creature *B*, though God does not do this as an innerworldly cause but as the primary cause who is indescribably close to creation. Drawing on Rahner's argument, and speaking in terms on the Spirit of God, Denis Edwards says that "the Creator Spirit can be understood as enabling the new to emerge from within creation itself, by means of the processes, relationships and causal connections that can be studied in the natural sciences."[20]

Rahner's account of the most fundamental activities of the human person in knowing and willing also features self-transcendence.[21] He invites readers to reflect upon their experience of endless questioning. We question everything. And every answer leads to further questions. In Rahner's words, "Every answer is always just the beginning of a new question. Man [*sic*] experiences himself as infinite possibility because in practice and in theory he necessarily places every sought-after result in question. He always situates it in a broader horizon which looms before him in its vastness."[22] Human beings are characterized by a dynamism toward unrestricted truth. Rahner uses the metaphor of the *horizon* in his account of human knowing and choosing in freedom. The infinite horizon of Being is what contextualizes and makes possible our knowledge of finite objects. He argues that in every act of knowing there is a preapprehension—an anticipatory grasp—of this horizon of Being, "an unthematic but ever-present knowledge of the infinity of reality."[23] Rahner identifies this infinite horizon with mystery—the inexhaustible mystery of God. This horizon of mystery draws the dynamism of the human spirit toward itself. Elizabeth Johnson observes that for Rahner God is "the ineffable plenitude toward which we are journeying, the goal which summons and bears our thirsty minds and desiring hearts."[24]

Johnson's mention of "desiring hearts" indicates that for Rahner this same dynamism of self-transcendence also makes itself known in our willing—our choices for the good in freedom. Every choice for the good implies a longing, a preapprehension of absolute goodness, that is, God. As such, God can be named not only as mystery—the infinity of Being—but as *holy* mystery—absolute goodness. This longing for absolute goodness tells us something about the meaning of human freedom. Freedom includes freedom of choice but is something more profound and enduring than freedom of choice. For Rahner, freedom has to do with the disposition of ourselves as free persons. Freedom is the capacity for an enduring act of self-transcendence—the capacity for definitive self-disposal toward God. It is the God-given capacity to give oneself over to God in a lasting way. The self-transcendence of freedom entails authentic self-actualization: "When freedom is really understood, it is not the power to be able to do this or that, but the power to decide about oneself and to actualize oneself."[25] Acts of true human freedom bear the mark of the eternal.

Thus, for Rahner, just as the universe itself is characterized by active self-transcendence, so human existence evinces the self-transcendence of the human spirit. In every act of knowledge and freedom we "run up against" the mystery of God. As transcendent beings, we always have to do with God, even in our most ordinary activities. The original experience of God is not found in properly religious activities but in our everyday encounter with the world. For Rahner, we are always embraced by mystery. The presence of holy mystery—the mystery of God—ceaselessly impinges upon our existence.

The unavoidable question is whether this mystery remains the horizon that is distant from the world of trees and animals and human beings, or whether it draws close to the world, and whether it gives itself to human beings. It is in respect to this question that Rahner develops his theology of grace and Christology. He will argue that the revelation of God to Israel and through Jesus Christ discloses that what was always "on God's mind" was to give of self in love to the world and in a most personal way to human beings. This is the ultimate reason for the existence of creation in the first place. The goal of the history of creation is God's self-communication to it. Rahner will call Jesus the "absolute savior" because in his divinity he is the climax of God's self-communication to the world, and in his humanity he is the climax of human acceptance of God's self-communication to the world.[26]

The phenomenon of self-transcendence of the universe and, in a particular way, of the human person, offers an opening, a point of connection between the experience of life in the world and what Christians believe about final fulfillment. The world both comes from God and is radically oriented to God. The story of the cosmos is an evolving one that has its goal in God. Thinkers like Augustine, Thomas Aquinas, and Karl Rahner bear witness to the fact that God alone, and nothing less than God, can fulfill the ultimate aspirations of the human person and of the universe itself. In an essay titled "A Faith That Loves the Earth," Rahner writes, "The earth births children of immense appetites, and what she gives them is too beautiful to be ignored by them and too little ever to satisfy them."[27]

CREATED FOR COMMUNION

From a Christian standpoint, the God who alone can fulfill the desires of the human person is the triune God. In light of the revelation of God in Christ and the Spirit, we believe that God is, in God's very self, a dynamic personal communion of life and love. God is an eternal communion of mutual giving and receiving among three divine persons traditionally named Father, Son, and Holy Spirit. Classical theology envisions each of these divine persons to be a "subsistent relation." The Trinity, then, is all about relationship. If human beings have been created in the image and likeness of this Triune God (Gen 1:26), then they are inherently relational—they are "hardwired" for relationship.

This relational understanding of human existence is found within the Hebrew Scriptures and the New Testament. For the Jewish people, true life entailed communion—communion with God and others. To be cut off from communion, as experienced, for example, by those suffering diseases like leprosy, was to be as good as dead. When Jesus heals the leper who approaches him with a pleading request (see Mark 1:40–45), he not only restores him to physical health, he restores him to communion with others. Jesus raises him from spiritual death. In his landmark book *A Theology of Liberation*, Gustavo Gutiérrez built on this biblical theme by describing salvation as communion with God and with other human beings and sin as a breach of communion with God and others.[28]

Dermot Lane emphasizes this relational understanding of the person as essential for understanding what Christians believe about final fulfillment. Lane asserts that "there is no self without relationships, no self apart from other selves, no self without being constituted by the actions of other human subjects."[29] Noting the reciprocal relationship between individuality and relationality, he argues that it is relational existence that begets individual existence—as happens, for example, in the conception and birth of a child. It is necessary for the individual self to go beyond itself by relating to others in order to sustain itself and to experience growth in maturity. Lane quotes the well-known statement made by the Jesuit paleontologist Teilhard de Chardin about true union with others: "True union does not fuse the elements it brings together; by mutual fertilization and adaptation it gives them a renewed vitality. It is egoism that hardens and neutralizes human stuff. Union differentiates."[30] Lane extends this intrinsic relationality of the human person beyond the realm of fellow human beings to the universe itself. He speaks of a strong sense of solidarity "on a wider cosmic scale in the light of the emerging common-creation story."[31]

Pope Francis has made the theme of communion a key building block in his teaching on theological anthropology, ecclesiology and ecology. In *Laudato Si'* he quotes the *Catechism of the Catholic Church* in describing the human person as someone who "is capable of self-knowledge, of self-possession and of freely giving himself [herself] and entering into communion with other persons."[32] Referring to the Genesis stories of creation and fall, he says that these ancient, symbolic stories "bear witness to a conviction which we today share, that everything is interconnected, and that genuine care for our own lives and our relationships with nature is inseparable from fraternity, justice and faithfulness to others."[33] Ecclesiologically, Francis builds upon the view of church as an ordered spiritual communion, which is found in Vatican II's *Lumen Gentium*. He exhorts believers to commit themselves to building communion in the church and in the world: "It is necessary to build communion, to teach communion, to get the better of misunderstandings and divisions, starting with the family, with ecclesial reality, in ecumenical dialogue, too. Our world needs unity. We need reconciliation and communion, and the Church is the home of communion."[34] Near the end of *Laudato Si'* the pope extends this call to communion to include all creatures, and he connects it with the mystery of the Trinity:

> The human person grows more, matures more and is sanctified more to the extent that he or she enters into relationships, going out from themselves to live in communion with God, with others and with all creatures. In this way, they make their own that Trinitarian dynamism which God imprinted in them when they were created. Everything is interconnected, and this invites us to develop a spirituality of that global solidarity which flows from the mystery of the Trinity.[35]

It is clear that the Christian view of the human person is inherently relational. We are created for communion. This understanding gives an opening to a vision of final fulfillment that embraces our relationships with other humans and nonhumans as well. Eternal blessedness is not a matter of the individual alone with God. I will explore this topic further in the discussion of the communion of saints in chapter 7. For now, we can simply make note of an observation made by Elizabeth Johnson in an essay on the communion of saints: "'Communion in the holy,' then, embraces holy people and a holy world in interrelationship."[36]

BODY AND SOUL

The standard description of the human person that developed through the centuries in Catholic theology is that of a union (or unity) of body and soul. This anthropological understanding is found in the current official teaching of the church. In a 1979 letter on certain questions concerning eschatology, the Congregation for the Doctrine of the Faith spoke of the soul as a "spiritual element" that survives and subsists after death; it is "an element endowed with consciousness and will, so that the 'human self' subsists, though deprived for the present of the complement of its body."[37] The Congregation conceded that the word *soul* has various meanings in the Bible, but it asserted that there is no valid reason for rejecting it. The *Catechism of the Catholic Church* offers a similar, though somewhat more detailed, description of the person.[38] The person is "a being at once both corporeal and spiritual." The soul refers to "the innermost aspect of man [*sic*]"; it is the "spiritual principle" of the human person. The human body is a human body precisely because it is animated by a spiritual soul. Building on the theology of Thomas Aquinas and citing the teaching of the Council of Vienne (1312; DS 902), the *CCC* affirms that the unity of the soul and body is so profound that one has to consider the soul the "form" of the body (*anima forma corporis*). The *Catechism* proceeds to declare that each soul is created immediately by God and, drawing on the teaching of the Fifth Lateran Council (1513; DS 1440), that the soul is immortal.

There have been a number of critiques of this understanding of the "makeup" of the human person. Protestant theologians have argued that the notion of the immortality of the soul derives from Greek philosophy (particularly Plato) rather than from the Bible, which focuses on the resurrection of the body. Some Protestant thinkers oppose the idea of an innate immortality residing in the human person because they conclude that such a characteristic would give the human person autonomy vis-à-vis the Creator God, thereby obscuring our total dependence on God.[39] Theologians in dialogue with the findings of neuroscience raise questions about the relationship of the soul to the mind and, in turn, of the mind to the brain. More generally, some theologians argue that the conception of a duality of body and soul, even when qualified by affirmations of the unity of the person, inevitably leads to a *dualistic* anthropology. For example, the Catholic theologian Dermot Lane argues that body-soul and spirit-matter anthropologies, "though they be defensible in certain forms...run the risk of being understood dualistically."[40] Drawing on the findings of feminist theology, ecology, and cosmology, Lane prefers the language of "embodied self-consciousness" or simply "embodied self" as descriptors of the human person. He states, "An anthropology that emphasizes the self as an embodied self is much more available to an eschatology of bodily resurrection."[41]

Joseph Ratzinger (later Pope Benedict XVI) forcefully argued for the appropriateness and relevance of the traditional anthropology. He made his positions known in a debate about the intermediate state, which will be discussed in chapter 6.[42] For our purposes here, we can just note that Ratzinger asserts that the body-soul anthropology developed gradually in the history of Christian thought, culminating in the work of Thomas Aquinas. It succeeded in offering a distinctive account of the makeup of the human person. It drew upon elements in thought and language of diverse kinds but "purified and transformed these in the light of faith, and fused them into a new unity."[43] This theological anthropology did not entail an uncritical borrowing of Greek anthropology, and it resonates well with the biblical teaching of the resurrection of the body/flesh. It envisions the soul as both personal and the form of matter, able to survive death but always oriented to its union with the body. Ratzinger argues that this traditional view of the relationship between body and soul, if understood correctly, is not dualistic.

There have been other recent attempts to craft a theological anthropology that resonates with the contemporary experience of being human. For example, the theologian and scientist John Polkinghorne draws on the category of "information" that is used in contemporary science.[44] Rather than conceiving of the soul as a "separate spiritual component," he proposes that the carrier of continuity of living personhood is "the immensely complex 'information-bearing pattern' in which [that] matter is organized."[45] Polkinghorne likens this conception to Aquinas's understanding of the soul as the form of the body. He suggests that each individual soul carries specific elements of its patterning that are the signature of its unique personal identity. With death this information pattern is dissolved. However, from a Christian perspective one can hope that "the pattern that is a human being could be held in the divine memory after that person's death."[46] Believers can further hope that God will re-embody this information-bearing pattern in some new environment of God's choosing.

In view of the inherently interrelational quality of the human person discussed above, it seems advantageous to envision a relational or dialogical conception of the soul. Terence Nichols and Joseph Ratzinger offer helpful insights along these lines. Ratzinger envisions the immortality of the soul in relational categories. "Being referred to God" expresses the very core of the human person. "As a created being he [she] is made for a relationship which entails indestructibility."[47] Ratzinger asserts that the "soul" is "our term for that in us which offers a foothold for this relation."[48] This capacity for relatedness to God is a gift; it is not something that inheres in us, though it is given to us to be our own possession. Likewise, Nichols speaks of the soul as "Subject-in-Relation."[49] He suggests that God "elects" each emerging human person, and it is God's election that constitutes the person as person, "as a unique soul/person, with the potentiality for relationality, for free choice, and eventually for eternal life with God."[50] The creation of the soul by God means that God constitutes the newly emerging person as someone in personal relation to God. Nichols argues that the soul can survive death because of its relation to God. This ability is not due to physical nature but is a gift of God's grace.

I agree with Dermot Lane's argument that we must conceive of the human person as an embodied self. As shown above, we are creatures of the earth, ineluctably tied to matter. It is the salvation of the whole person (and the entire cosmos) that is the abiding concern of Christian faith. But this embodied self has been given the capacity and the summons to live one's whole life in relationship with—in dialogue with—God. This "foothold" for relation with God is the carrier of personal identity in and beyond death. It can survive physical death because it is a gift from God—the grace of an enduring relationship with the eternal God. From this perspective, it is the embodied self's capacity for relationship with God that constitutes the self as person.

FREEDOM

Christian eschatology has placed great emphasis on the role of human freedom in the determination of one's ultimate destiny. Freedom is a gift of God that is empowered by God, even when a particular choice is made that is contrary to the will of God. Limitations on human freedom have been recognized in antiquity and modernity. In his bitter debate with Pelagius and his followers, for example, Augustine argued that human freedom had been profoundly affected by the deleterious effects of original sin. These effects have a crippling effect on human freedom. In more recent times, the fields of psychology, sociology, and genetics have made us more aware that human freedom is conditioned by any number of internal and external factors. And there are exceptional cases in which it is difficult to know the extent of human freedom that is present, such as in persons who have profound intellectual disabilities. Still, Catholic and other mainline Christian theology has consistently challenged believers to take the gift of freedom with utmost seriousness for its impact on the kind of person they become and the destiny that they shape for themselves.

Drawing on the biblical symbol of the exodus, liberationist theologians have made freedom and the call to promote the freedom of oppressed peoples a leitmotif of their theology. Gustavo Gutiérrez proposed an understanding of liberation consisting of three levels that are intertwined with one another.[51] The first level is social and political liberation, that is, the promotion of a just economic and political order. This dimension pertains to freeing the poor from oppression. The second level of liberation might be called the psychosocial dimension. It consists of empowering people to assume conscious responsibility for their lives and their destiny. For those who are inclined to promote their own self-interest with little concern for others, this aspect of liberation entails a movement away from self-preoccupation toward concern for others. For people living in oppressive conditions, liberation means a reclaiming of personal agency, a movement toward greater self-possession and creative initiative. Gutiérrez identifies the third level of liberation as liberation from sin, which is the ultimate root of injustice and oppression. He envisions these three levels of liberation as a single, complex process that has its full realization in the saving work of Christ. The second level of liberation proposed by Gutiérrez is, I think, important for our exploration of Christian eschatology. Christians are called to assist those whose freedom has been suppressed so that they may regain their sense of personal agency in their own lives and in their commitment to building a more just social order.

We have seen that Karl Rahner envisions freedom, in its most fundamental meaning, as the capacity for definitive self-disposal before God.[52] It is the power to become a certain kind of person before others and God. Freedom does not mean absolute creativity or the absence of all conditioning factors. Our freedom must often be expressed through our active engagement of realities that must be undergone or received, above all, death itself. Psychology, sociology, and other empirical sciences can isolate the factors in our lives that condition our attitudes and behavior. But freedom in what Rahner calls its "original" sense means that I know myself as an "I"—a subject who is given over to myself and who is responsible to myself. As a being of transcendence, I can and must confront myself in my totality. Even with all my limitations and the conditioning factors in my life, I am given over to myself to become an authentic person.

This project of becoming an authentic person through freedom takes place in and through all of the finite, innerworldly choices that we make. Rahner contends that eternity is what comes to fruition from freedom exercised in time. The experience of decisions made in freedom affords us the clearest glimpse of the presence of eternity in the midst of life. He says, "Ultimate personal decisions are irrevocable, they are truly eternity coming to be in time."[53] This capacity to decide about oneself as a whole, in and through the choices we make, entails a disposing of ourselves before God. The act of freedom, like the act of knowledge, involves and is made possible by the transcendent movement of the human spirit toward the infinite horizon, God. This movement toward the Infinite is the condition of possibility of finite freedom. Even though our choices involve things that are less than God, they always have to do with God in some way. There is always present in every such act an unthematic yes or no to God:

> But since in every act of freedom which is concerned on the categorical level with a quite definite object, a quite definite person, there is always present, as the condition of possibility for such an act, transcendence toward the absolute term and source of all of our intellectual and spiritual acts, and hence towards God, there can and must be present in every such act an *unthematic "yes" or "no"* to this God of original, transcendental experience.[54]

Rahner, then, takes human freedom quite seriously, and he argues that the modern person must listen to what Christianity has to say about the gravity of freedom. Included in this message of Christianity is the awareness that we can say no to God through our free choices. Rahner speaks of an absolute contradiction that takes place in such acts—a contradiction of the very structure of oneself as a transcendent being. In saying no to God through a morally wrong choice, one is denying the movement and goal of the transcendence that made the concrete choice possible in the first place. He calls such an act "something abortive, something which miscarries and fails, something which is self-destructive and self-contradictory."[55] Rahner asserts that Christianity says that a person must take the possibility of a fundamental self-contradiction, a no to God that is ultimately a no to self, with utmost seriousness. He immediately adds, however, that Christian teaching says "nothing about whether in some people or in many people evil has become an absolute reality defining the *final end and result* of their lives."[56]

This last statement by Rahner raises the question of how powerful human freedom really is. More specifically, do we have the potential to reject God definitively and thus suffer the loss of God for eternity (a possibility traditionally named "hell")? The traditional answer to that question is in the affirmative, though always with the caveat that we do not know if that has ever happened in the life of a particular individual. The *Catechism of the Catholic Church* says, "To die in mortal sin without repenting and accepting God's merciful love means remaining separated from him for ever by our own free choice" (1033). Joseph Ratzinger observed, "Heaven reposes upon freedom, and so leaves to the damned the right to will their own damnation."[57] In its 1992 statement on eschatology, the International Theological Commission declared, "Eternal damnation has its origin in the free rejection to the very end of God's Love and Mercy."[58]

In an important essay, John R. Sachs raised questions about the capacity of human freedom.[59] First, Sachs builds upon Rahner's affirmation that human beings are created as those upon whom God freely bestows God's own self in love. God created human beings with a view to giving himself as one to be known and loved. Therefore, Sachs argues, "human freedom is simply and most radically the capacity for God, not the capacity for *either* God *or* something else."[60] Freedom can achieve finality only when it reaches the definitiveness for which it has been created, that is, when it accepts God's gift of Self. Second, Sachs appeals to the notion of final judgment. No human being is capable of making an absolute and final self-judgment. That belongs to God alone. Sachs asserts that this divine judgment is something more than God "finalizing" what a person has made of her or his life. It "can only be the final future fullness of God's forgiving, life-giving judgment in the cross and resurrection of Christ....Thus God's final act is a *life-giving* judgment which forgives, heals, purifies and bestows fullness and, *therefore*, finality upon human life, that final identity for which it was created and toward which it is directed."[61] Sachs is willing to speak of the possibility of an "indefinite" persistence in rejection of God, but not of its finality or eternity. Only human freedom that has chosen God can attain the finality for which it was created.

We will explore these questions again in chapter 6. Here it is sufficient to acknowledge the key role that human freedom plays in Christian eschatology. Because the human person is always oriented toward the mystery of God in everything he or she does, our free choices shape our relationship with God. The Christian notion of salvation and the final fulfillment that results from salvation is one in which human freedom is engaged in the most profound way. The doctrine of grace tells us that our free yes to God is made possible and empowered by the grace of God at work within us. Still, divine grace engages human freedom; it liberates human freedom so that it may attain finality.

SIN

The mention of the human capacity to accept or reject God's offer of self evokes the reality of evil and sin. When we examine the eschatologies of the Old Testament and the New Testament, we will see that visions of definitive salvation from God, especially those articulated in the genre of apocalyptic, have often been set forth in the context of oppression and intense suffering. People of faith have experienced the power of evil in the world, and they have called on God to defeat the power of evil and give them relief in their suffering. Believers have also acknowledged and lamented the tendency to radical selfishness that lurks within themselves. In his encyclical *Laudato Si'*, Pope Francis writes of the "rupture" of our relationships with God, our neighbors, and the earth. He names this rupture *sin*, and he observes that "sin is manifest in all its destructive power in wars, the various forms of violence and abuse, the abandonment of the most vulnerable, and attacks on nature."[62]

The sobering words of Pope Francis call to mind the Christian doctrine of original sin. This traditional teaching, articulated in diverse ways through the centuries, attests to the wounding of God's good creation by the wrongful actions of human beings, stretching back to the very beginnings of human history. Something has gone awry, and this situation of "rupture," as Pope Francis calls it, profoundly affects all human beings, especially in the choices that we make. There have been two main lines of interpretation of the meaning of original sin in the Christian tradition, the first associated with the late second-century theologian Irenaeus of Lyons and the second with Augustine of Hippo.

For Irenaeus, the Genesis stories of creation present Adam and Eve (whom he takes to be historical figures) as created in God's image and likeness but not created as fully mature or complete. Irenaeus sees "Adam" as a child who still had to grow to maturity. He was only given as much of the Spirit as he was able to receive in this state of childhood. Irenaeus thinks that God was capable of giving human beings perfection from the beginning, but they were incapable of receiving it because they were still infants. God created an infant humanity and asked of it only what it could bear. Then he set out to educate it in an orderly fashion and in successive stages. The sin of Adam damaged human nature, but it was somewhat excusable because he was in a childlike state and easily misled by the deceiver. Brian Daley cites a famous passage from Irenaeus's work *Against Heresies*, which expresses his view of the broad sweep of creation, sin, and redemption:

> It was necessary that the human person should in the first instance be created; and having been created, should receive growth; and having received growth, should be strengthened; and having been strengthened, should abound; and having abounded, should recover [from the disease of sin]; and having recovered, should be glorified; and being glorified should see his Lord. For God is the one who is yet to be seen, and the beholding of God is productive of immortality, but immortality renders one near unto God.[63]

Writing in the early fifth century, Augustine has a quite different take on the Genesis accounts of creation. He envisions Adam as created by God in an exalted condition in paradise. The first human being was immune from physical ills, had surpassing intellectual gifts, lacked nothing, and had the power to live this way forever. He was created with the ability to refrain from sinning. His only weakness was that he was a creature and thus changeable; he could fall away. Despite his abundant gifts and powers, Adam sinned. His fault was entirely his own and it was a grievous fault. It was a heinous crime that resulted in the ruin of the entire human race, which became a *massa damnata*, sinful itself and propagating sinners. Citing Paul in Romans 5:12, Augustine insisted that all human beings are understood to have sinned in that first human being because all were in him when he sinned. Human nature, as a result, is corrupted and is desperately in need of the healing grace of God. Writing against his opponent, Pelagius, Augustine describes this corruption in some detail:

> Behold what damage the disobedience of the will has inflicted on man's nature! Let him be permitted to pray that he may be healed! Why need he presume so much on the capacity of his nature. It is wounded, hurt, damaged, destroyed. It is a true confession of its weakness, not a false defense of its capacity, that it stands in need of. It requires the grace of God, not that it may be made, but that it be re-made.[64]

Though Augustine's view of the human person had a major impact on the Christian tradition, many contemporary theologians prefer the Irenaean strain of interpretation of creation and fall to that of Augustine. Especially in the light of the findings of evolutionary biology, they view the depiction of evolving humanity as having exalted power and living in a perfect, paradisal state to be incongruent with the scientific understanding of the appearance of *Homo sapiens* on earth. Contemporary theology finds more resonance in a vision of an imperfect humanity, created by God through the process of evolution and called by God to grow into intellectual, moral, and spiritual maturity.

Karl Rahner's reflection on the doctrine of original sin is one example of a modern approach to the teaching.[65] When he addresses the sin at the beginning of the human race, the "first sin," he speaks of it as some action (unknowable to us) in and through which human beings rejected the offer of God's self-communication. This originating sin resulted in the loss of the antecedent holiness that comes from God's self-communication. Nevertheless, God's offer of self continues to be present in the life of every person because and in view of Christ. When Rahner focuses his attention on the "state" of original sin, he elucidates the way in which the presence of sin in human history profoundly impacts the situation of human freedom. Our acts of freedom are, he says, codetermined by the guilty choices of others, both our forebears and our contemporaries. This codetermination of our freedom is not something that remains external to us; it affects our freedom from within. We make our decisions "in a world which is co-determined by guilt and by the guilty refusals of others."[66] This situation of codetermination by guilt becomes solidified in unjust structures. Rahner employs the example of the ordinary action of buying a banana. On the face of it, this is simply an innocuous act of purchasing a piece of fruit. But it can also be an action that implicates a person in supporting the structural realities of unfair trade policies and the exploitation of banana pickers.

Rahner asserts that by its doctrine of original sin Christianity teaches "that this co-determination of the situation of every person by the guilt of others is something universal, permanent, and therefore also original."[67] This doctrine reflects a certain Christian "pessimism" about reality in this world. However, this historical pessimism is actually a service to the world because it guards against the illusion that human beings can create a perfect world through their own efforts. History has taught us that such a utopian ideal "only leads inevitably to greater violence and greater cruelty than those which man [*sic*] wants to eradicate from the world."[68] This issue of the relation between human efforts to build a better world and the action of God in bringing human history and the cosmos to final fulfillment is one that will be explored throughout this book.

Christian eschatology, then, addresses human beings whose freedom is codetermined by the guilt of others and who are themselves sinners whose free choices at times impact negatively on others. As Pope Francis affirms, we live in a world where there is rupture in our relationships with God, others, self, and nature. Thus, the vision of final fulfillment offered by Christianity must include elements of judgment, healing, forgiveness, reconciliation, and God's action in overcoming the power of evil. One attempt to include the action of reconciliation in eschatology is offered by John Thiel. Thiel reads the New Testament accounts of the post-Easter activity of the risen Christ as consisting mainly of gestures of reconciliation, including reconciling the failure of his closest disciples. Thiel envisions the blessed dead (those who are "in heaven") as imitating the risen Lord through the ongoing endeavor of forgiveness and reconciliation. He says, "To be a disciple of Jesus means that, even in the afterlife, the bonds of reconciliation that unite the communion of saints must be forged in the work of forgiveness, made and remade in acts of love that grace those who forgive as much as those who are forgiven."[69]

THE MYSTERY OF SUFFERING

The human person is one who is confronted by the mystery of suffering in her or his own personal life and in the wider world.[70] This experience leads to hope for the relief of suffering and to the search to find meaning in suffering. As noted above, much of the eschatological literature in the Bible and the history of theology has been spawned by the experience of intense suffering.

In the face of this global encounter with suffering, the Judeo-Christian tradition has consistently affirmed the intrinsic goodness of creation. It has reiterated this conviction against various forms of dualism that have arisen through the centuries. Dualistic theories usually view the world and matter in a negative light, often envisioning creation as the result of a "fall" of spiritual beings in a premundane realm. In response to such accounts, Christian thinkers have insisted that the world is the good gift of a good Creator, even if it has been wounded by sin. And in Christ, the Word of God truly became flesh (John 1:14), inextricably connected with all that is "earthy." Thus the material world is the place where God's saving purposes are being accomplished.

From this perspective, suffering has been viewed as the result of evil, which is usually divided theologically into two distinct categories: moral evil and physical (natural) evil. Moral evil is the wrongdoing committed by human beings through which people inflict suffering on other people and, in so doing, upon themselves. Christian thinkers, past and present, have argued that the origin of moral evil is not to be traced to God in any sense. Having gifted human beings with freedom, God permits such evil but does not directly cause it. While Christian theology attributes the source of moral evil to those who commit it, the complexity entailed in social conditioning and psychological development can lend an air of mystery to it. It is very difficult to fathom what could have been going through the minds of the perpetrators of the Nazi war crimes, the 1994 Rwandan genocide, or the utter brutality inflicted upon enslaved peoples throughout human history.

Much of the suffering that human beings undergo originates from what has traditionally been labeled "physical" or "natural" evil: physical illness and disease; the debility and decline that accompany the aging process; the deleterious effects of genetic abnormalities; mental illness; injuries and losses due to natural disasters, and so forth. Today, scientists and theologians also point out that nonhuman sentient beings suffer from natural causes that result from the evolutionary process of natural selection, predation, death, and species extinction. The findings of evolutionary science have compelled theologians to address physical/natural evil more directly, They have probed deeply into the costs entailed in evolution for human and nonhuman beings. Many thinkers adduce the passage in the Letter to the Romans in which Paul marvels at the "groaning" of all creation, which is in "labor pains" awaiting its redemption. Elizabeth Johnson exclaims, "How stunning to think that massive death is intrinsic to the process of evolution!"[71] In dialogue with evolutionary science, some contemporary theologians argue that such loss and death have been necessary for the cosmos to attain the level of development and the intensification of beauty that are found in it. Here theologians often assert that in creating an evolving world, God limited God's self in order to allow creation to be and to develop. Just as God respects the free will of human beings in history, so God respects the free processes involved in the emergence of the universe, allowing creation to be and to develop through the subtle interplay of natural law, chance, and time. They further suggest that in the cross of Jesus we can perceive God's solidarity with and compassion for every creature that suffers. The issues related to suffering caused by natural evil have impelled theologians to rethink God's relation to creation and to expand their view to include divine concern for nonhuman animals. This is a cutting-edge issue in contemporary theology, one in which Christian thinkers struggle to find the right words. Denis Edwards cautions that "in any authentically theological approach to natural evil, we must stand with the Book of Job (chapters 38—42) before the mystery of God and God's creation, and acknowledge that there is a great deal that we do not know."[72]

Human suffering has many distinct faces. Instead of attempting to construct a precise definition of suffering that would encompass its multiple manifestations, it may be more helpful to reflect upon dimensions of suffering. Phil Zylla enumerates four dimensions of human suffering: physical pain; psychological anguish; social degradation; and spiritual despondency.[73] Chronic physical pain can be utterly debilitating for body and spirit; it can diminish the human spirit and make it difficult for the sufferer to interact positively with others. Psychological anguish is an aspect of suffering that is sometimes more intense than physical pain. As Zylla points out, at the root of the psychological dimension of suffering is fear: fear of the unknown, of pain, of a difficult future, of death. Such anguish can also be caused by the loss of a loved one. There is also a social dimension of suffering. Sometimes the physically or mentally ill, or persons with disabilities, are ignored, avoided, or even abandoned. The long-term care resident who seldom receives a visitor suffers alienation from the community. To suffer spiritual despondency is "to experience the eclipse of hope itself, which leads us to experience a growing distance from God."[74] A person may well feel that God has abandoned her or him, echoing the prayer of the suffering Jesus found in the Gospel of Mark: "My God, my God, why have you abandoned me?" (Mark 15:34). This sense of desolation can lead to a crisis of faith and of personal meaning in one's life.

It is impossible to "measure" the suffering of another, or even one's own suffering. But attention to these dimensions of suffering can provide insight into the intensity of suffering that is present, and it can inform protocols for care of the suffering person. The more dimensions of suffering that a person experiences, the greater the intensity of that suffering. Care for suffering people must attend to all the dimensions of human suffering.

There are a number of interpretations of and approaches to suffering in the Hebrew and Christian Scriptures.[75] One prominent theme is the cry of lament, as evident in Jesus's cry from the cross, quoted above. Lament is present in the Old Testament in the Psalms, the Book of Lamentations, the prophets, and the Book of Job. Of all the genres of psalms in the Bible, laments comprise the greatest number.

The Hebrew Scriptures bear direct and compelling testimony to the crying out of the one who is suffering. They show that the Hebrew ideal was not that of suffering alone or suffering in silence. Lament psalms are usually emphatic in their trust that God will hear the petitioner and respond with aid. Walter Brueggemann observes, "The world of lament speech thus is based on the premise that the speech of Israel draws God into the trouble. God will act and life will be restored."[76] At the same time, biblical laments are striking for their realistic descriptions of the experience of suffering and for the boldness with which people of faith express their complaints to God. Laments offer eloquent testimony to the fact that for the people of Israel the God of the covenant was so real, so close at hand and directly involved in their lives, that they knew they could, and even should, cry out to God. And that was precisely the way in which God remained real for them, even amid experiences of suffering that defied explanation.

Christian eschatology must address the long history of human suffering that has affected the life of every person, especially of those who have lived in situations of oppression and deprivation. Christians believe that God has heard the laments pleadingly uttered throughout a blood-stained human history. They even trust that God is attentive to the pitiful cries of a nonhuman animal whose life is slipping away. Final fulfillment in God may not resolve the mystery of suffering in human and cosmic history, but believers hope that it will reveal a God who has always been present to every suffering creature and has always been on the move from within to overcome suffering.

THE VIRTUE OF HOPE

In the introduction we saw that the discipline of eschatology entails theological reflection on the language and vision of human hope. We distinguished everyday, "earthly" hopes from absolute hope—the hope for the ultimate fulfillment of one's life, for unending happiness and completion. Hope appears to be an intrinsic dimension of the human condition. Human beings are always projecting themselves beyond the present and toward the future at every moment. The author of the First Letter of Peter exhorted the Christian community to which he was writing: "Always be ready to give an explanation to anyone who asks you for a reason for your hope" (1 Pet 3:15). In so doing he was connecting hope very closely with faith, and he was affirming that their faith in the God of Jesus Christ shaped their hope for the future.

Hope is one of the three virtues that Christians name as "theological"—along with its sisters faith and charity. In classical theology, it is considered theological because it has God in God's very self as its object or goal, and it is a gift of God. The virtue of hope is a gift of God's grace. The discussion of hope by Thomas Aquinas in his *Summa Theologiae* elucidates this classical picture.[77] Borrowing from Aristotle, Aquinas affirms that hope is a virtue because it is a quality that makes its possessor good and his or her activity sound. He says that the object of hope is a good that lies in the future and that is difficult but possible to attain. Aquinas emphasizes that the ultimate object of hope is eternal beatitude, which is the possession of God's very self: "This is simply to say that we should hope for nothing less from God than his very self; his goodness, by which he confers good upon creaturely things, is nothing less than his own being. And so the proper and principal object of hope is indeed eternal blessedness."[78] Aquinas thinks that, while one usually hopes for oneself, the bond of charity with another person(s) makes it possible to hope for the eternal happiness of another. Faith precedes hope because eternal blessedness and the assistance from God needed to attain it are revealed to us in faith. Despair, he thinks, is based on a false view of God, one that denies that God grants pardon to sinners and brings people to salvation.[79] The person who despairs has lost sight of the infinite mercy and compassion of God.

Many theologians distinguish, or even contrast, hope and optimism. Generally speaking, optimism is a "sunny" outlook on life that views future prospects as promising. Optimism is based on what we think we can accomplish through our own resources and efforts. It has confidence about what we can get done through careful planning and a positive attitude. Dermot Lane and John MacQuarrie are sharply critical of optimism. Lane asserts that "optimism tends to ignore the ambiguity of the world in which we live and the presence of so much evil within that world."[80] MacQuarrie similarly says that optimism is "a philosophy that misses the ambiguity of the world and fails to consider seriously its evil and negative features."[81] Optimism tends to overlook or even dismiss the scandalous extent of human suffering in the world, past and present.

Hope is the virtue for the times when things do not look promising at all. It is the virtue needed in our lives when it is difficult to see beyond the darkness. MacQuarrie suggests that hope is humble and vulnerable, as it lives in the awareness of the world's evils, sufferings, and lacks.[82] Hope is a fragile virtue. The virtue of hope is ultimately based not on human abilities but on God's goodness and fidelity. It is grounded in a power greater than ourselves—the power of God's grace present and effective within us and beyond us. At the same time, the virtue of hope does not lead its possessors to sit back passively, doing nothing to improve the situation. God's grace works in us and through us, empowering our good and worthy efforts.

Sometimes hope is born amid the most negative moments of life. That is spelled out in the work of Edward Schillebeeckx, who incorporated the phenomenon of negative contrast experiences into his theology. Contrast experiences entail our natural human reaction to evil and suffering in the world, to things that we instinctively know should not be. When we hear of evils like child abuse, torture, or ethnic cleansing, normal people instinctively feel revulsion and protest. We immediately realize that something has gone terribly wrong. Schillebeeckx writes,

> What we experience as reality, what we see and hear of this reality daily through television and other mass media, is evidently not "in order"; there is something fundamentally wrong. This reality is full of contradictions. So the human experience of suffering and evil, of oppression and unhappiness is the basis and source of a fundamental "no" that men and women say to their actual situation of being-in-this-world.[83]

But Schillebeeckx does not stop there, with the negativity of contrast experiences. He argues that our reaction to evil and suffering contains, at least implicitly, a positive moment. It awakens insight into something better; it occasions an intuition into goodness and value that should be realized. Schillebeeckx observes, "This human inability to give in to the situation offers an illuminating perspective. It discloses an openness to another situation which has the right to our affirmative 'yes.'"[84] Such experiences, then, can evoke hope for and commitment to the good that is willed by God.

Jürgen Moltmann argues that Christianity is unique among the world religions for its focus on human hope for the future: "Christianity is wholly and entirely confident hope, a stretching out to what is ahead, and a readiness for a fresh start."[85] In its depths, Christian hope is grounded in the memory of the life, death, and resurrection of Jesus. As such, hope can embrace the cross—the cross of Jesus and the many "crosses" that continue to be set up in the world. It can be a confident hope because it is born from faith in the God who was present to the crucified Jesus, on the move to bring new life out of death. Christians believe that this same God is lovingly present to the crucified of today.

2

THE HOPE OF ISRAEL

We turn now to the hope of the people of Israel that is expressed in the Old Testament. The Old Testament is a complex set of documents comprising many strands of tradition. They reflect nine centuries or more of written tradition and an even longer span of oral tradition. The visions of hope that are depicted in these texts manifest diverse perspectives and some significant developments. It is not possible to attend to all the nuances and complexities of Hebrew thought about eschatology in an overview such as this. I will simply highlight certain themes and some developments in the ways in which the Hebrew people articulated their hope in God.

THE GOD OF PROMISES

If *eschatology* is taken in a narrow sense, to refer just to explicit belief in and reflection on life after death, then it is clear that the Old Testament is quite limited in what it says in this regard. Belief in eternal life, resurrection from the dead, and final judgment was a late development in the writings of the Old Testament and receives limited attention. However, if eschatology is understood in a broader sense to refer to the conviction that this world of human experience is destined for a goal set for it by God, toward which God is leading it, then one can speak of the emergence of eschatology in the Old Testament.[1] John MacQuarrie observes that the history contained in the Old Testament is a history written toward the future.[2] It is a history with a forward trajectory. Though interpreted in different ways and expressed through a variety of symbols, there develops in Israel a strong belief that history is directed by God, who is the Lord of history. At the heart of this belief is the conviction that God makes promises to God's people and that God acts to fulfill those promises. This conviction is expressed in traditions that are foundational for the faith and the life of Israel.

The Story of Abraham[3]

The story of Abraham found in the Book of Genesis (chapters 12—25) is paradigmatic for the Hebrew sense of divine promise and fulfillment. The story revolves around the themes of call, promise, and covenant. Abram is called by God to go forth from his native land of Ur of the Chaldeans to the land of Canaan:

> The LORD said to Abram: Go forth from your land, your relatives, and from your father's house to a land that I will show you. I will make of you a great nation, and I will bless you; I will make your name great, so that you will be a blessing. I will bless those who bless you and curse those who curse you. All the families of the earth will find blessing in you. (Gen 12:1–3)

Abram is summoned to go forth from the old and familiar to the new and unfamiliar, to an unknown future. The narrator proceeds to tell us that "Abram went as the LORD directed him" (Gen 12:4). He is given the promise of land and innumerable progeny. The promise of descendants is humanly unfulfillable because both Abram and his wife Sarai are elderly and they are childless. Further along, in the scene of the establishment of a covenant between Abram and YHWH, Abram "reminds" the LORD that he and his wife remain childless: "Lord God, what can you give me, if I die childless and have only a servant of my household, Eliezer of Damascus?" (Gen 15:2). In the face of this objection, God renews the promise of progeny and land: Abram's descendants will be as numerous as the stars in the sky, and God will give him the land as his possession. We are told that Abram put his trust in God, "who attributed it to him as an act of righteousness" (Gen 15:6). Abram is depicted as in right relationship with God. He exhibits "a radical trust in a possibility opened solely by God's initiative."[4]

When Abraham and Sarah welcome the three mysterious visitors by the oak of Mamre, they are promised the birth of a son, a promise that causes Sarah to laugh but which she will soon see fulfilled in the birth of Isaac (Gen 18). The dramatic twist in this ancestral story of promise and fulfillment comes with the divine command to sacrifice Isaac as a burnt offering (Gen 22:1–19). Isaac is not only the beloved child of Abraham and Sarah, but he also represents the fulfillment of the divine promises and the future of the people of God. Isaac's life is saved only when the angel of God intervenes at the last minute, instructing Abraham to do no harm to the boy. While the story may reflect an underlying protest against the practice of child sacrifice, the focus of the narrative is Abraham's radical act of obedience to God. The angel speaks the words that come from God: "For now I know that you fear God, since you did not withhold from me your only son, your only one" (Gen 22:12). This is an act of faith and hope that is not able to be explained in purely human terms.

Bill T. Arnold observes that the promises of land and progeny in the Abraham story and other ancestral traditions of the Hebrew Scriptures "drive the narrative forward." He observes, "Since neither the numerical extent of the progeny as 'a great nation' (Gen 12:2) nor the geographical extent of the land promised (Gen 15:18–21) became a reality in the lives of the ancestral generations, the promises themselves are by definition projected into the future."[5] Zachary Hayes, drawing on the analysis of this Abraham tradition given by Mircea Eliade, notes that these texts imply a vision of life that breaks out of the fatalistic cycles that characterized the religious thought of the ancient world, where there was nothing new and different. The biblical vision "locates humanity in an open history which remains incomplete down to the present." God is presented as personal and free and as One who directs human history to its ultimate end. "History is a movement to a mysterious future promised by God."[6]

The Exodus Tradition

The experience and tradition of the exodus was also foundational for Israel's faith in the God who fulfills divine promises. In the later Deuteronomistic literature, the memory of their forebears' liberation from slavery in Egypt becomes a confessional statement of faith for all the people of Israel:

> Later on, when your son asks you, "What do these decrees and statutes and ordinances mean?" which the Lord, our God, has enjoined on you, you shall say to your son, "We were once slaves of Pharaoh in Egypt, but the Lord brought us out of Egypt with a strong hand and wrought before our eyes signs and wonders, great and dire, against Egypt and against Pharaoh and his whole house. He brought us from there to bring us in and give us the land he had promised on oath to our ancestors." (Deut 6:20–23)

This creedal confession affirms belief in a God who acts through events in human history, who is in fact sovereign over history. God liberates a people, forming them into a nation, and leads them to a future which God has promised. Commenting on the exodus, K. A. Kitchen observes, "Within the biblical tradition, few other events enjoyed anything like the prominence accorded so pervasively in the work of so many writers, or were deemed of such basic importance for Israel's history."[7]

The exodus tradition profoundly shaped Israel's perception of the character of God.[8] In the extended speech of God in Exodus 6:2–8, there is a seminal self-reference in which God identifies God's self as the one who has entered into covenant with Abraham, Isaac, and Jacob. Witnessing the plight of the people in Egypt, God remembers the covenant and his promises to act on behalf of this oppressed people:

> Now that I have heard the groaning of the Israelites, whom the Egyptians have reduced to slavery, I am mindful of my covenant. Therefore, say to the Israelites: I am the Lord. I will free you from the burdens of the Egyptians and will deliver you from their slavery. I will redeem you by my outstretched arm with mighty acts of judgment. I will take you as my own people, and I will be your God.... I will bring you into the land which I swore to give to Abraham, Isaac, and Jacob. (Exod 6:5–8)

Thus, to Moses is revealed the God of compassion, the one who is faithful to the divine promises. Commenting on this passage, Walter

Brueggemann says, "As much as any text in the Exodus tradition, this one invites reflection upon the character of the God of Israel." The character of God that is disclosed in this text, and in the primal event of the Exodus, "is to make relationships, bring emancipation, and establish covenants."[9]

The enduring memory of God's saving action in the exodus also served as a catalyst for the hope of Israel at later times of crisis. To the exiles in Babylon, the prophet known as Second Isaiah (Isa 40—55) spoke a word of hope that draws on this tradition. Through his instrument, Cyrus of Persia, God will again act to set God's people free. In his portrayal of this new deed of God, the prophet draws freely on the exodus and wilderness traditions: the flight from Egypt, the deliverance at the sea, the march through the wilderness, and the journey toward the promised land.[10] He blends the language of exodus with imagery drawn from creation myths, so that the new exodus represents a new creative act of God. The waters of the sea that Israel traversed represent the waters of chaos over which God is victorious:

> Awake, awake, put on strength,
>   arm of the Lord!
> Awake as in the days of old,
>   in ages long ago!
> Was it not you who crushed Rahab,
>   you who pierced the dragon?
> Was it not you who dried up the sea,
>   the waters of the great deep,
> You who made the depths of the sea into a way
>   for the redeemed to pass through?
> Those whom the Lord has ransomed will return
>   and enter Zion singing,
>   crowned with everlasting joy;
> They will meet with joy and gladness,
>   sorrow and mourning will flee. (Isa 51:9–11)

Kingship

Another tradition through which the people of ancient Israel expressed their hope was centered on the divine promises to King David. The covenant with David is recounted in 2 Samuel 7, where the prophet Nathan, speaking in God's name, says, "Moreover...the

Lord will make a house for you: when your days have been completed and you rest with your ancestors, I will raise up your offspring after you, sprung from your loins, and I will establish his kingdom" (2 Sam 7:11–12). The passage goes on to affirm the permanence of this covenant: "Your house and your kingdom are firm forever before me; your throne shall be firmly established forever" (7:16).

The tribes of Israel had no central political power from the time of the settlement (13th century BCE) to the reign of Saul (ca. 1040 BCE).[11] It was David who created a centralized political power in Israel. Despite his personal failings, he came to represent the ideal ruler who shepherded his people with strength and wisdom. But the glory days of the reigns of David and his son, Solomon, passed quickly. The kingdom was divided into two, the Northern Kingdom was conquered by Assyria in the eighth century BCE, and the Southern Kingdom overrun by Babylonia two centuries later, with many of its leading citizens forced into exile. The prophets of Israel often attributed the cause of these disasters to the corruption, idolatry, and incompetence of the kings of Israel and Judah.

The monarchy was not restored in Judah after the Babylonian exile. In some circles among the people, the hope for an ideal ruler in the line of David, through whom God would govern God's people justly, took hold. The ideal reign of this Davidic ruler is hymned in the royal psalms, for example Psalms 2, 18, 20, 21, 72, 89, 101, 110, 132, 144. In Psalm 72, the psalmist prays that God will endow the king with wise judgment so that he will be able to govern with justice. In particular, this hoped-for king is envisioned as one who will "defend the oppressed among the people, save the children of the poor and crush the oppressor" (Ps 72:4). Marinus de Jonge points out that in later times, when the monarchy no longer existed, these royal psalms "were interpreted as referring to the future Davidic anointed of the Lord, whose arrival Israel hoped for."[12]

This hope is also expressed in some of the prophetic literature. Near the end of the eighth century BCE, the prophet Isaiah promises the gift of an heir who will be a sign that God is still with God's people in the person of the Davidic king (Isa 7:14). At the time of the Babylonian invasion, the prophet Jeremiah excoriates the corrupt leaders who "destroy and scatter the flock of [God's] pasture" (Jer 23:1). He promises that God "will raise up a righteous branch for David" who will "do what is right and just in the land" (Jer 23:5). The Book of Sirach (Ben Sira), dating from the early second century BCE, contains a eulogy of the heroes of Israel that describes David as the ruler upon whom the Lord conferred the rights of royalty and whose throne God established in Israel (Sir 47:11). In a few of the intertestamental works (texts written between 200 BCE and 200 CE), the hope for an idealized Davidic ruler is expressed. For example, the Psalms of Solomon, authored in the middle of the first century BCE, look forward to a Davidic king: "Behold, O Lord, and raise up unto them their king, the son of David, at the time you have (fore)seen, O God to rule over Israel your servant" (17:21).[13] During the reign of this king, Israel will be freed from its enemies, the people in the dispersion will return, and the nations will serve God. This king will be a pious, obedient, and wise servant of God.

Marinus de Jonge observes that in the prophetic literature, the royal psalms, and other Old Testament texts, the emphasis is not on the person of the future king "but on the fact that, at last, the Davidic ideal, which no historical king (including David) ever fulfilled, will be realized."[14] At the time of Jesus, who proclaimed the nearness of the reign of God, the hope for an ideal king in the Davidic line represented one of the eschatological trajectories in the tradition of Israel, though it was not the only one and it was not prominent in the minds of all of Jesus's contemporaries.

A THIS-WORLDLY VIEW

For most of the Old Testament literature, the vision of the fulfillment of God's promises is a this-worldly one.[15] The fulfillment of God's promises consists of authentic worship of God, peace throughout the land, just leadership, an abundant yield of crops, numerous descendants and a long life. The focus is not on life after death. N. T. Wright underlines this point: "The hope of the biblical writers, which was strong and constant, focused not upon the fate of humans after death, but on the fate of Israel and her promised land. The nation and land of the present world were far more important than what happened to an individual beyond the grave."[16] Hans Schwarz makes a similar observation: "The Israelite faith emphasized, from its very beginning, life in this world, since it is there that Yahweh proved his power and faithfulness."[17]

This focus is evident in the Book of Deuteronomy and in the theological history of Israel composed by the Deuteronomistic authors, found in the Books of Joshua, Judges, 1 and 2 Samuel, and 1 and 2 Kings. As these authors look back on the roller coaster of Israel's history, they interpret the fortunes of the people as a direct result of their fidelity or infidelity to the God of the covenant. And these "fortunes" are this-worldly. In Deuteronomy 30, Moses places before the people a choice between two "ways" related to faithful worship of the God of the covenant. One way leads to life; the other to death:

> See, I have set before you today life and good, death and evil. If you obey the commandments of the LORD, your God, which I am giving you today, loving the LORD, your God, and walking in his ways, and keeping his commandments, statutes and ordinances, you will live and grow numerous, and the LORD, your God, will bless you in the land you are entering to possess. If, however, your heart turns away and you do not obey, but are led astray to bow down to other gods and serve them, I tell you today that you will certainly perish; you will not have a long life on the land which you are crossing the Jordan to enter and possess. (Deut 30:15–19)

Thus, the hope of the people of Israel, contingent on their fidelity to the covenant, is a long life on the land given by God, with many descendants. The covenant curse for infidelity is premature death and loss of the land.

Wright elucidates the significance of the family and the land for the hope of ancient Israel. "Children, and then grandchildren, are God's great blessing, and to live long enough to see them is one of the finest things to hope for" (see Ps 128 and 129).[18] To remain childless, particularly without a male heir, is a tragedy. Wright observes that to perpetuate not just the nation but one's individual family was seen as a sacred responsibility, integral to the fulfillment of God's promises to Israel. This vision of fulfillment is reflected in the Genesis account of Jacob's death, when he delivers his final testament surrounded by his sons. The biblical author concludes this account in these words: "When Jacob had finished giving these instructions to his sons, he drew his feet into the bed, breathed his last, and was gathered to his people" (Gen 49:33).

As is clear in the passage from Deuteronomy quoted above, the gift of the land is also integral to the hope of ancient Israel. We have already seen that the Abraham tradition revolves around the promise of progeny and land. Wright points out the significance of the story of Abraham's purchase of a burial plot in Genesis 23. At the time of the death of Sarah, Abraham purchases from Ephron the cave and the field of Machpelah as a place of burial for his wife. The biblical author concludes the story by writing, "Thus the field with its cave was transferred from the Hittites to Abraham as a burial place" (Gen 23:20). Further along in Genesis, in the narrative of the death of Jacob, we learn that Isaac, Rebekah, Leah, and Jacob are also buried in this place (Gen 49:31–33). Wright observes, "The point of all this was not to engage in any kind of postmortem reunion, but to make certain the promise of God, which was not at this stage for an individual life beyond the grave but for the family's possession of the promised land."[19]

The this-worldly character of the hope of Israel is also evinced in the Psalms. In these individual and communal prayers, the God of promise is acknowledged and desperately sought in very concrete ways. "Communal and individual laments, psalms of confidence, and psalms of thanksgiving are replete with cries for help, reminders of past deliverance and divine promises for the future, and gratitude for rescue realized."[20] As discussed in the previous chapter, the psalms of lament are especially compelling expressions of pleading for God's saving action in times of hardship or crisis. Starkly honest in their expression of pain and sorrow, these prayers are also imbued with a stubborn confidence that the God of promise will listen and act to save. In a time of illness, the psalmist cries out, "How long, LORD? Will you utterly forget me? How long will you hide your face from me?" For ancient Israel, the hiding of God's face—God's turning away from the people—meant utter disaster. Later in this same psalm, however, the psalmist articulates abiding trust in God's fidelity: "I trust in your mercy. Grant my heart joy in your salvation" (Ps 13:2, 6). As we saw when discussing the mystery of suffering in the previous chapter, God was so utterly real to the Hebrew people, such a vital part of their daily lives, that they knew they could, and even should, bring everything to God in prayer. And that was precisely the way that God remained such a vital force in their lives.

Even after the exile, the vision of "the new heavens and the new earth" presented in Third Isaiah is one that focuses on fullness of life in this world where there is freedom from oppression:

I will rejoice in Jerusalem
    and exult in my people.
No longer shall the sound of weeping be heard there,
    or the sound of crying;
No longer shall there be in it
    an infant who lives but a few days,
    nor anyone who does not live a full lifetime;
One who dies at a hundred years shall be considered a youth,
    and one who falls short of a hundred shall be thought
        accursed.
They shall build houses and live in them;
    they shall plant vineyards and eat their fruit;
They shall not build and others live there;
    they shall not plant and others eat. (Isa 65:19–22)

DEATH AND SHEOL

The this-worldly perspective of ancient Israel also influences the approach to death found in the Old Testament. The diversity and complexity of the Old Testament texts do not yield a single, uniform conception of death or suggest a linear chronological development in understanding of it. For example, there is a tension in the Hebrew Scriptures between an understanding of death as the natural ending to a full life and a view of death as punishment for disobedience to God. On the one hand, a "good death" is portrayed as when an individual dies with numerous offspring and at an old age. In the account of the death of Jacob, the Genesis author writes, "The length of Jacob's life was one hundred and eighty years; then he breathed his last. He died as an old man and was gathered to his people. After a full life, his sons Esau and Jacob buried him" (Gen 35:27–28). In her conversation with David, the wise woman of Tekoa reminds the king, "We must indeed die; we are then like water that is poured out on the ground and cannot be gathered up" (2 Sam 14:14). The exception to this view of death as the natural end of life is violent or premature death.

On the other hand, the second Genesis creation account (Gen 2—3) offers an etiology that attributes the cause of death to the disobedience of the primal couple, Adam and Eve. God instructs Adam, "You are free to eat from any of the trees of the garden except the tree of knowledge of good and evil. From that tree you shall not eat; when you eat from it, you shall die" (Gen 2:16–17). After the man and woman are seduced by the serpent, God says to the man, "For you are dust, and to dust you shall return" (Gen 3:19). The man and woman are banished from the garden so that they might not eat from the tree of life and live forever. This conception of death as the result of sin will be taken up in the New Testament, especially in the letters of Paul (e.g., Rom 5:12–21).

For ancient Israel, death is more than just the cessation of life; it is also personified as a force that is destructive to the well-being of the people. Kent Harold Richards speaks of the "dynamic intersection of death with life for the people of Israel." The experience of exile is a form of death. Richards observes, "Israel, maybe because of its history, is more at home in understanding death through all its faces as a radical challenge to life."[21] He notes that Israel experiences individual and communal death, which was more pervasive than biological cessation.

In the Old Testament the abode of the dead is most often called Sheol. It is depicted as a place to which one "goes down"—the lowest place imaginable.[22] Zophar, one of Job's interlocutors, says of God's perfection, "It is higher than the heavens; what can you do? It is deeper than Sheol, what can you know?" (Job 11:8). Sheol is a dark and gloomy place, devoid of real life. N. T. Wright describes Sheol as "a place of gloom and despair, a place where one can no longer enjoy life, and where the presence of YHWH is withdrawn."[23] The inhabitants of Sheol are the *Rephaim*—the "shades" of the dead who survive but with no strength, vitality, hope, or worship of God.[24] While some scholars argue that Sheol is reserved for the wicked, there are other biblical texts that see it as the meeting place of all the dead.[25]

The author of the especially gloomy Psalm 88 cries out to God:

Let my prayer come before you;
  incline your ear to my cry.
For my soul is filled with troubles;
  my life draws near to Sheol.
I am reckoned with those who go down to the pit;
  I am like a warrior without strength....
All day I call on you, Lord;
  I stretch out my hands to you.

Do you work your wonders for the dead?
Do the shades arise and praise you? (Ps 88:3–5, 10–11)

Hezekiah's prayer of thanksgiving to God for his recovery from illness refers to Sheol and its "gates":

In the noontime of life, I said,
  I must depart!
To the gates of Sheol I have been consigned
  for the rest of my years.
I said, I shall see the LORD no more
  in the land of the living.
Nor look on mortals
  among those who dwell in the world....
You have preserved my life
  from the pit of destruction;
Behind your back
  you cast all my sins.
For it is not Sheol that gives you thanks,
  nor death that praises you.
Neither do those who go down into the pit
  await your kindness.
The living, the living give you thanks,
  as I do today. (Isa 38:10–12, 17–18)

In the Book of Isaiah there is a satirical funeral lament that is a taunt song against the king of Babylon:

Below, Sheol is all astir,
  preparing for your coming;
Awakening the shades to greet you,
  all the leaders of the earth....
"You too have become weak like us,
  you are just like us!
Down to Sheol your pomp is brought,
  the sound of your harps.
Maggots are the couch beneath you,
  worms your blanket."...
No! Down to Sheol you will be brought
  to the depths of the pit. (Isa 14:9–11, 15)

In the later Wisdom tradition, Qoheleth teaches that, as it is with beasts, so death is the end for human beings. God withdraws the life breath from them:

> For the lot of mortals and the lot of beasts is the same lot: The one dies as well as the other. Both have the same life breath. Human beings have no advantage over beasts; but all is vanity. Both go to the same place; both were made from the dust, and to the dust they both return. Who knows if the life breath of mortals goes upward and the life breath of beasts goes earthward? (Eccl 3:19–21)

The passages from Psalm 88 and Isaiah 38 suggest that there is no praise of God in Sheol. That is the ultimate sign of death. Richards observes, "The most significant theme for Israel was the understanding that life provided an opportunity for the individual and community to praise Yahweh. Praise of God was the sign of life. The inability to praise was a signal of death, even in life. The Hebrew Bible is replete with the idea that death constitutes silence and that the major characteristic of life is to praise Yahweh (Ps 30:8–10; Isa 38:6–10)."

THE DAY OF THE LORD

In the course of pronouncing a series of woes against the Northern Kingdom of Israel, the eight-century BCE prophet Amos refers to the "day of the LORD":

> Woe to those who yearn
> for the day of the LORD!
> What will the day of the LORD mean for you?
> It will be darkness, not light!
> As if someone fled from a lion
> and a bear met him;
> Or as if on entering the house
> he rested his hand against the wall,
> and a snake bit it.
> Truly the day of the LORD will be darkness, not light,
> gloom without any brightness! (Amos 5:18–20)

This prophetic oracle implies that the people of Israel assumed that this "day" would be a time of blessing for them and divine judgment on their enemies. Amos challenges that assumption by warning the people of God's judgment against them for idolatry and blatant injustice. This earliest biblical reference to the day of the LORD is part of Amos's unrelenting prophetic challenge to repentance. John J. Collins suggests that the day of the LORD may have originally referred to a cultic festival that celebrated the sovereignty of God and implied that Israel would benefit from that sovereignty. The passage that immediately follows the text quoted above refers to the feasts of Israel. Collins observes, "Amos saw that Israel was not being governed by the sovereignty of God, and he wanted to undermine the assumption that the Lord would support Israel unconditionally."[26]

References to the day of the LORD and similar phrases ("the day," "that day," etc.) abound in the prophetic literature. Some of these prophetic texts express God's judgment against the people of Israel or Judah for infidelity in their covenant relationship with God. The prophet Joel (chs. 1—2) announces that the day of the LORD will take the form of a plague of locusts. Richard Hiers points out that the preexilic prophets proclaimed that God would punish Israel or Judah through oppression by other nations.[27] The late seventh-century BCE prophet Zephaniah refers to the day of the LORD extensively in pronouncing judgment on Judah and other nations. The prophet Malachi warns of the coming of God's messenger, who will refine and purify the Levites; Malachi asks, "Who can endure the day of his coming? Who can stand firm when he appears?" (Mal 3:2).

In other prophetic texts the motif of the day of the LORD is employed with reference to divine judgment against other nations, especially the enemies of Israel. During the time of the exile, Jeremiah pronounces an oracle against Babylon in which he says, "Woe to them! Their day has come, the time of their punishment" (Jer 50:27). Similarly, an oracle against Egypt attributed to Ezekiel begins with reference to this motif:

> Wail: "Alas the day!"
> Yes, a day approaches,
> a day of the Lord approaches:
> A day of dark cloud,
> a time appointed for the nations. (Ezek 30:2–3)

Other texts that speak of the day of the LORD refer to a future time when God will reestablish the fortunes of Israel/Judah.[28] For example, the passage from Isaiah 11:10–16, which probably dates from a time later than the eighth-century BCE prophet Isaiah, envisions the gathering of all the outcasts of Israel and Judah and God's leading them home in a new exodus, triumphant over their enemies. This stirring prophetic pronouncement begins, "On that day." In such passages, the promise is made that "Jerusalem and the Jewish people will experience God's special favor."[29]

Collins summarizes the development of this Old Testament theme in this way: "Amos' reinterpretation of the Day of the LORD, then, had a lasting effect on the biblical tradition. The phrase became synonymous with judgment and destruction, and increasingly came to denote a final definitive divine intervention in human affairs."[30] This prophetic motif reflects belief in God as one who is present to and active within human history, who is on the move to achieve the divine purposes.

We will see that in the New Testament the day of the LORD refers to the second coming of Christ. Paul repeatedly speaks of the day of the Lord or the day of our Lord Jesus Christ (1 Cor 1:8; 5:5; 2 Cor 1:14) to refer to the moment of definitive judgment. In his First Letter to the Thessalonians, he instructs the community, "For you yourselves know very well that the day of the Lord will come like a thief in the night" (1 Thess 5:2). The New Testament authors are strong in their insistence that it is given to no one to know the day or the hour. The biblical theme of judgment will become an integral part of the Christian eschatological tradition.

POSTEXILIC DEVELOPMENTS

In the late exilic and postexilic literature of Israel there are significant developments in eschatological perspective. First, in some texts the vision of God's definitive action of judgment and salvation becomes more universal in scope. For example, Third Isaiah, writing after the return from exile in the sixth century BCE, proclaims this oracle: "Oracle of the LORD God, who gathers the dispersed in Israel—others will I gather to them besides those already scattered" (Isa 56:8). This biblical author envisages God's definitive action as a gathering of the nations in a renewed Jerusalem: "I am coming to gather all nations and tongues; they shall come and see my glory" (Isa 66:18). Writing about a century later, the author of Zechariah 14 also envisions an assembly of all the nations in Jerusalem: "Everyone who is left of all the nations that came up against Jerusalem will go up year after year to bow down to the King, the LORD of hosts, and to celebrate the feast of Booths" (Zech 14:16). Bill T. Arnold observes, "The eschatological vision of the postexilic prophets begins to take on a transformative and cosmic dimension, resulting in descriptions of this new eon that will transcend all current experiences."[31]

Second, in Second Temple Judaism more attention is given to the destiny of the individual, especially the righteous Israelite. The Deuteronomistic view that envisions prosperity as a reward for faithful observance of the covenant and misfortune and death as a curse on those who are unfaithful is challenged in postexilic texts like the Books of Job and Ecclesiastes. Hebrew authors begin to question the view that a lifeless Sheol is the fate that awaits every person. The issue of justice comes to the fore. And there is a fluidity between the concerns for the destiny of the individual and hope for the restoration of the nation of Israel, which had suffered the degradation of exile in Babylonia and experienced further oppression under other foreign rulers.

There are several Old Testament passages that articulate God's power over Sheol, some of which suggest life after death for the individual. Biblical scholars offer a diversity of opinions in their interpretation of these passages. It is not always clear whether a text refers to: the experience of preservation from death; restoration (resurrection) of the nation of Israel; or life after death for people. These Old Testament passages include the following:

Psalm 16 rejects the worship of false gods and then reflects on the faithful presence of God. In this context, the psalmist says,

> Therefore my heart is glad, my soul rejoices;
> my body also dwells secure,
> for you will not abandon my soul to Sheol,
> nor let your devout one see the pit.
> You will show me the path to life,
> abounding joy in your presence,
> the delights at your right hand forever. (Ps 16:9–11)

Here the psalmist may well be praising God for being preserved from death. The psalm does, however, affirm that God has power over Sheol. Joseph Ratzinger comments, "Even if this text expresses no explicit faith in the overcoming of death, we hear nevertheless the accents of a ringing certitude that Yahweh is stronger than Sheol."[32] Similarly, N. T. Wright declares, "There is legitimate doubt over whether this refers to escaping death or passing through it to a life beyond, but there is no question of the basis of the hope. It is YHWH himself, the one the Psalmist embraces as his sovereign one (verse 2), his portion and cup (verse 5), the one who gives him counsel in the secret places of his heart (verse 7)."[33] The Greek (Septuagint) version of the verse about being protected from the pit will be applied to the resurrection of Jesus in the Acts of the Apostles (Acts 2:25–32; 13:35–37).

Psalm 49 is a sobering reflection on the vanity of wealth and worldly power and an affirmation of trust in the power of God. In the course of this prayer, the psalmist expresses confidence in God's ability to save him from Sheol:

> Like a herd of sheep they will be put into Sheol,
>   and Death will shepherd them.
> Straight to the grave they descend,
>   where their form will waste away.
>   Sheol will be their palace.
> But God will redeem my life,
>   will take me from the hand of Sheol. (Ps 49:15–16)

This prayer, too, appears to affirm God's power and intention to preserve the life of the psalmist from death. In so doing, it celebrates the power of a faithful God over the forces of death. Wright interprets the psalm as affirming more than just rescue from an untimely death; he argues that in this prayer we have "at least a glimmer of assurance of God's ransoming power being stronger than death itself."[34]

Psalm 73, which was a favorite of Augustine of Hippo,[35] is an extended reflection on the apparent prosperity of the wicked. The psalmist honestly admits to coming near to despair in his reflection, but then refers to an experience of God's presence in the temple that convinced him of how deluded the wicked are. This moves him to a confession of God's faithful presence and guidance:

Yet I am always with you;
you take hold of my right hand.
With your counsel you guide me,
and at the end receive me with honor. (Ps 73:23–24)

This is the translation of the psalm given in the revised edition of the New American Bible. This translation can simply convey trust in God's nearness and protection. Another, more traditional, translation of the second verse in this quotation is "receive me into glory." Ratzinger, using the traditional translation, interprets the psalmist as referring to an experience of communion with God in the temple that assured him that "such communion is more potent than the decay of the flesh."[36] Wright, who acknowledges the translation given above ("with honor") but quotes the more traditional one ("and afterward you will receive me to glory"), asserts that the psalm leaves us with "a tantalizing glimpse of life beyond the grave...a life in which those who have known God's love in the present will discover that this love is stronger than death itself, and will 'receive' them to a status of honour or glory."

Isaiah 26 is part of a section of the Book of Isaiah that is often called "The Apocalypse of Isaiah" (chapters 24—27), though scholars note the imprecision of that designation. George Nickelsburg describes this section as a collection of prophetic materials of disputed date, ranging from 500 to the third century BCE. An oft-quoted passage from this section of Isaiah is part of a prayer of praise of and trust in God as the eternal rock of Judah, in which the author petitions God to bring about the salvation for which the people long:

Salvation we have not achieved for the earth,
no inhabitants for the world were born.
But your dead shall live, their corpses shall rise!
Awake and sing, you who lie in the dust!
For your dew is a dew of light,
and you cause the land of shades to give birth. (Isa 26:18–19)

This passage may well refer to the restoration of the people after the destruction of Jerusalem by Babylonia and the deportation of a significant part of the population. Terence Nichols, however, takes it as referring to bodily resurrection.[37] Wright acknowledges that the passage may refer to national restoration, but he proceeds to say that "the wider passage, in which God's renewal of the whole cosmos is in hand, opens the way for us to propose that the reference to resurrection is intended to denote actual concrete events."[38]

There is a famous passage in Ezekiel 37:1–14 that is replete with resurrection language. It is Ezekiel's vision of the valley of dry human bones. The Lord commands the prophet to walk among the dry bones, which would have symbolized the epitome of ritual uncleanness for the Hebrew people. The Lord then instructs Ezekiel to speak words of promise and hope:

> Then he said to me: Prophesy over these bones, and say to them: Dry bones, hear the word of the Lord! Thus says the Lord God to these bones: I will make breath enter into you so that you may come to life. I will put sinews on you, make flesh grow over you, cover you with skin, and put breath into you so that you may come to life. Then you shall know that I am the Lord....I will put my spirit in you that you may come to life, and I will settle you in your land. Then you shall know that I am the Lord. I have spoken; I will do it—oracle of the Lord. (Ezek 37:4–6, 14)

This prophecy manifests a clear use of figurative language (the resurrection or recreation of human bodies) to communicate a promise of God's action to restore the people to their own land and renew their covenant relation with God. The God who created Adam by breathing life into him will act once more to recreate God's covenant people. This passage does not focus on belief in the literal resurrection of the dead. Wright observes that "the original purpose was to provide a highly charged and vivid metaphor of the way in which unclean Israel would be cleansed, exiled Israel restored to the land, and scattered Israel regathered, by a powerful and covenant-renewing act of new creation."[39] Wright points, however, that at least from the early rabbinic period, the passage was read as a prediction of literal resurrection.

The most explicit passage in the Hebrew Bible about resurrection from the dead is Daniel 12:1–3:

> At that time there shall arise Michael,
>   the great prince,
>   guardian of your people;

It shall be a time unsurpassed in distress
since the nation began until that time.
At that time your people shall escape,
everyone who is found written in the book.
Many of those who sleep
in the dust of the earth shall awake;
Some to everlasting life,
others to reproach and everlasting disgrace.
But those with insight shall shine brightly
like the splendor of the firmament,
And those who lead the many to justice
shall be like the stars forever.

The Book of Daniel is the clearest example of apocalyptic literature in the Old Testament (see below on the genre of apocalyptic). Written about 165 BCE, the book reflects the situation of the people of Israel under the hegemony of the Syrian (Seleucid) ruler Antiochus IV Epiphanes (ruled 175–164 BCE). While previous Egyptian and Syrian Hellenistic emperors had been tolerant of Jewish religious practice, Antiochus altered the policy and tried to compel Jews to accept his own version of worship. He prohibited observance of the Torah and introduced his own cult of the Most High God into the Jerusalem temple (1 Macc 1:41–61). Though some Jews acceded to this new practice, others viewed it as a desecration and resisted the demands of the king. Punishment for such disobedience included martyrdom. The military victory of Judas Maccabeus and his supporters in 164 resulted in the liberation of the temple area and greater freedom for Jews. It appears that the Book of Daniel was composed during the period of persecution by Antiochus but before the Maccabean victory. The tradition in Daniel counsels a response to persecution that is different from the Maccabean military solution. It encourages trust in God and unswerving fidelity to the covenant.

The context for the passage about resurrection in chapter 12, then, is martyrdom, or at least, the threat of martyrdom. The promise of resurrection comes near the end of a series of visions given to Daniel so that he may be able to interpret past events of history as well as God's plans for the people of Israel and for the nations. The overarching theme of these visions and the entire book is God's sovereignty over human history. God will defeat Antiochus and reign victoriously. The tyranny of evil is only temporary; before long the sovereign God will intervene in human history to vindicate the faithful and punish the wicked. In this context of brutal persecution and martyrdom, Daniel is given the promise that "many" of those who "sleep in the dust of the earth" (a biblical metaphor for death) will arise, some to everlasting life and others to everlasting disgrace. This is not an affirmation of universal resurrection. It refers to the "many" righteous who have suffered martyrdom on the one hand, and their persecutors on the other.[40] As Wright points out, this vision is a specific promise addressed to a specific situation.[41]

This same context of oppression under Antiochus is the backdrop for the stories of martyrdom found in 2 Maccabees. Second Maccabees was written probably in the second half of the second century BCE. Neither 1 nor 2 Maccabees became part of the Jewish canon of sacred books, but they were included in the Septuagint and thus were accepted by the earliest Christian community, especially because of their stories of those martyred for the faith.[42] Of particular relevance is the graphic story of the martyrdom of the mother and her seven sons, who refuse to eat pork when ordered to do so in a trial before the king, Antiochus. The second brother confronts his torturers with his belief that God will raise him up:

> You accursed fiend, you are depriving us of this present life, but the King of the universe will raise us up to live again forever, because we are dying for his laws. (2 Macc 7:9)

The third brother willingly puts forth his tongue and his hands when told to do so by his persecutors, exclaiming,

> It was from heaven that I received these; for the sake of his laws I disregard them; from him I hope to receive them again. (2 Macc 7:11)

The narrator informs the readers that the mother exhorted each of her seven sons to remain faithful to the laws of God. She is emblematic of the virtuous Jewish mother.[43] In so doing, she assured them that God would give life back to them after their cruel deaths at the hands of the torturers:

> I do not know how you came to be in my womb; it was not I who gave you breath and life, nor was it I who arranged

> the elements you are made of. Therefore since it is the Creator of the universe who shaped the beginning of humankind and brought about the origin of everything, he, in his mercy, will give you back both breath and life, because you now disregard yourselves for the sake of his law. (2 Macc 7:22–23)

It appears that the author's understanding of the resurrection, or recreation, of the dead was limited to the righteous, since the fourth brother exclaims to his torturer, "It is my choice to die at the hands or mortals with the hope that God will restore me to life; but for you, there will be no resurrection to life" (2 Macc 7:14).

These confessions of faith in the resurrection of the dead are made in the face of suffering in its most extreme form—the suffering of the martyrs. The suffering of faithful Israelites raised the question of whether they would be confined to lifeless Sheol like their persecutors, or whether the fidelity and power of a just God would gift them with a different destiny. John Macquarrie observes, "What is perhaps of special interest is that these nascent beliefs in a fuller rather than a minimal existence for the departed were motivated not by any egotistical desire to prolong the existence of oneself—the motive that is so often alleged to be the ground of such beliefs—but by the simple demand for justice that is typical of Hebrew religion throughout its history."[44]

Second Maccabees is also noteworthy for its account of Israelite prayer for the dead. When Judas Maccabeus and his soldiers go to bury fellow soldiers who had been slain in battle, they discover that their slain compatriots had been wearing amulets sacred to the idols of Jamnia, which Jews were forbidden to wear (2 Macc 12:40). They immediately pray that the sinful deed might be wiped out, and then Judas Maccabeus takes up a collection among all his soldiers to be sent to Jerusalem to provide for an expiatory sacrifice. The narrator of this account tells readers that Judas acted in a noble way, "inasmuch as he had the resurrection in mind; for if he were not expecting the fallen to rise again, it would have been superfluous and foolish to pray for the dead" (12:43–44). Robert Doran observes that what is interesting about this collection and sacrifice is that Judas believes that the community extends beyond the grave.[45] Later Christian theologians will appeal to this story as a biblical warrant for the church's practice of prayer for the dead.

The final passage for our consideration is taken from the third chapter of the Book of Wisdom, one of the latest writings in the Christian Old Testament. Wisdom was written probably in the last half of the first century BCE by a Jew who was living in Alexandria. There was a thriving Jewish community in Alexandria at the time, which was influenced by Hellenistic thought.[46] This passage from Wisdom 3 is preceded by a vivid description of the plotting and deeds of the wicked, who with violence and torture put the righteous person to the test and condemn the righteous one to death (2:19–20). The author then describes the foolishness of their thinking:

> These were their thoughts, but they erred;
>   for their wickedness blinded them,
>   and they did not know the hidden counsels of God....
>
> The souls of the righteous are in the hands of God,
>   and no torment shall touch them.
> They seemed, in the view of the foolish to be dead;
>   and their passing away was thought an affliction
>   and their going forth from us utter destruction.
> But they are in peace.
> For if to others, indeed, they seem punished,
>   yet their hope is full of immortality;
> Chastised a little, they shall be greatly blessed,
>   because God tried them
>   and found them worthy of himself.
> As gold in the furnace he proved them,
>   and as sacrificial offerings he took them to himself.
> In the time of their judgment they shall shine
>   and dart about as sparks through stubble;
> They shall judge nations and rule over peoples,
>   and the LORD shall be their King forever.
> Those who trust in him shall understand truth,
>   and the faithful shall abide with him in love:
> Because grace and mercy are with his holy ones,
>   and his care is with the elect. (Wis 2:21–22; 3:1–9)

Like the passages from Daniel and Second Maccabees, the context of this affirmation of life with God after death is the persecution and martyrdom of the righteous person. The question of what happens to those who suffer for their fidelity to God persists, and it demands a response. Ratzinger observes that for the Old Testament writers "it was suffering, endured and spiritually borne, which became that hermeneutical vantage point where real and unreal could be distinguished and communion with God came to light as the locus of true life."[47] To the surprise of their persecutors, the souls of the righteous are at peace in the hands of God. The Book of Wisdom portrays the immortality of the soul not as an innate property of the human person but as a gift of God's grace and mercy to those who attain wisdom. In this respect it is thoroughly Jewish.[48]

Some scholars view this Greek conception of the immortality of the soul to be in competition with, or even in contrast to, the biblical notion of the resurrection of the dead. Joanne McWilliam Dewart asserts that the idea of the immortality of the soul "introduced a competing understanding of the afterlife."[49] Ratzinger and Wright, however, see the two conceptions as complementary. Ratzinger argues, as was evident above, that both views derive from a spirituality of martyrdom.[50] Touching on an issue that will be discussed in modern eschatology, Wright thinks that the third chapter of Wisdom suggests that the souls of the righteous exist in a kind of "intermediate state," where they are at peace with God but await resurrection at some future time. Wright says that "it seems probable that the emerging belief in the resurrection...precipitated further reflection on the continuing identity of the people of YHWH in between bodily death and resurrection."[51] He argues that the final part of the passage quoted above, which depicts the righteous as judging nations and ruling over peoples, refers to a future resurrected state. Thus, in his mind, belief in the immortality of the soul and the resurrection of the dead come together here, as they will in later Christian theology.

Some scholars assert that these postexilic developments of belief in life with God after death derive from sustained reflection on the presence and power of God and on the nature of communion with God. Macquarrie says, "Perhaps then it was chiefly a deepening conception of God that led to a belief in the possibility of a continuing relation with him and eventually to belief in resurrection." He cites Psalm 139:8 ("If I lie down in Sheol there you are") as an expression of the belief that God's presence and rule extend everywhere.[52] Wright highlights "the emerging belief that the relationship with

YHWH would be unbreakable even by death, and the eventual belief that YHWH would raise the dead."[53] Ratzinger emphasizes the experience of communion with God as the salient factor in this emerging belief: "Communion with God is true reality and by comparison with it everything, no matter how massively it asserts itself, is a phantom, a nothing."[54] So this belief that death cannot put an end to one's relationship with God, though a minority tradition in the Old Testament as a whole, arose not from theoretical speculation but from personal communion with the God who was experienced as powerful, merciful, and faithful.

THE RISE OF APOCALYPTIC

Between the third century BCE and the third century CE, Jewish writers produced a number of works written in the symbolic language and worldview of apocalyptic. Most of these works are outside of the Jewish and Christian canons of sacred writings, though the Book of Daniel and some sections of the prophetic literature (e.g., Zech 9—14) are usually characterized as belonging to the genre of apocalyptic. John J. Collins, citing a study of this literature by a team of scholars, defines *apocalypse* as "a genre of revelatory literature with a narrative framework, in which a revelation is mediated by an otherworldly being to a human recipient, disclosing a transcendent reality which is both temporal, insofar as it envisages eschatological salvation, and spatial insofar as it involves another, supernatural world."[55] The Greek word from which *apocalypse* is derived refers to a "revelation" or "unveiling." In this literature there is an unveiling of the future of history and sometimes of the heavenly realm. Collins emphasizes that a prominent factor in Jewish apocalyptic is divine judgment: "This expectation of postmortem judgment is at the heart of apocalyptic eschatology and is the main element that distinguishes it from the eschatology of the Hebrew prophets."[56]

Brendan Byrne, drawing on the work of Philipp Vielhauer, lists five characteristics of apocalyptic eschatology.[57] First, this form of eschatology is characterized by dualism, especially in its dichotomy between the present age and the age to come. The present age is usually depicted as in the grip of evil. It will be judged and done away with. The future age, to be ushered in by divine intervention, will be transcendent and imperishable, obedient to the eternal rule of God.

Second, the present age is viewed with pessimism; it is often seen as subjugated to the dominion of Satan or other malevolent angelic powers. Third, apocalyptic eschatology is marked by universalism and individualism. It is universalist in the temporal sense because its vision spans the ages from creation to the dissolution of the present world. It is also cosmically universalist because it encompasses not only the earth but heaven and the underworld as well. And in its view of judgment there is a stress on individual responsibility before God. Fourth, apocalyptic eschatology is characterized by determinism and imminent expectation. In many of these works, there is the conviction that all has been predetermined according to the set plan of God. This is sometimes presented as the unfolding of fixed periods of history, the discernment of which is given through a privileged revelation. And there is a vivid sense of living in a critical time in which definitive divine intervention is imminent. Fifth, there is significant diversity among the works of apocalyptic eschatology. For example, the agents of salvation can vary considerably: God himself, angels, the Davidic Messiah, the transcendent Son of Man, and others. In his survey of apocalyptic works Wright highlights another feature—the raising of the dead. He observes, "Resurrection thus belongs clearly within one regular apocalyptic construal of the future that Israel's god has in store."[58] Wright concludes that these texts hold together Israel's hope for liberation from oppression by foreign powers and the hope of the individual for a newly embodied existence after death.

Daniel Harrington asserts that "apocalyptic is the literature of a dispossessed and oppressed people."[59] It reflects the Jewish experience of destruction by and subjugation to foreign powers through the centuries. While looking to the future and the heavenly realm for liberation, the intention of apocalyptic eschatology is to strengthen suffering people in the present. This genre of eschatology is "intended to interpret present, earthly circumstances in light of the supernatural world and of the future, and to influence both the understanding and behavior of the audience by means of divine authority."[60]

One of the earliest Jewish expressions of apocalyptic is the Book of Daniel. We have already considered the historical context of this biblical book—the oppression experienced by Israel under the rule of Antiochus IV Epiphanes in the second century BCE—and we saw that in Daniel 12 there appears to be a clear affirmation of the resurrection of the dead. The literary (fictive) setting of the book is the courts of the Babylonian and Persian kings in the sixth century BCE.[61] In the course of the story Daniel is given a series of visions along with instruction about these visions by heavenly beings. In chapter 8 he is given a vision of a ram and a goat. The ram represents the Medes and the Persians. It is met by a male goat coming from the west that has a great horn between its eyes. The horn represents Alexander the Great, the founder of the Hellenistic empire. The goat tramples the ram and grows "very powerful" only to have its horn broken at the height of its power. The breaking of the goat's horn refers to the untimely death of Alexander the Great. In place of this horn, four other horns arise, representing the four generals among whom Alexander's empire was divided. Out of one of these horns emerges a little horn, that is, Antiochus Epiphanes. Antiochus is portrayed as posing a direct challenge even to the powers of heaven: "It [the horn that represents Antiochus] cast down to earth some of the host and some of the stars and trampled on them" (8:10). The text alludes to the desecration of the temple and the repression of Jewish religious practice by speaking of the arrogance of Antiochus, against even "the Prince of the host" (God). The angel Gabriel helps Daniel interpret this vision, indicating that the vision "refers to the end time" (8:17). After the transgressions against God have reached their full measure through the wicked actions of Antiochus, "he shall be broken without a hand being raised" (8:25). It is God who will defeat Antiochus and reign victoriously.

Chapter 12 gives another vision of end-time events, a vision explained to Daniel by "the man clothed in linen" (12:7). The scene moves beyond the bounds of earth with its reference to Michael, "the great prince, guardian of your people" (12:1). It will be a time "unsurpassed in distress" (12:2), but everyone who is found written in the book of God's truth shall escape. It is in the context of this heavenly vision that the promise of resurrection for "many of those who sleep in the dust of the earth" is given (12:3). As noted above, the reference to resurrection and the implied judgment of the dead is characteristic of apocalyptic eschatology. Daniel is told to await the fulfillment of this vision, though he is given three different timetables for that fulfillment: "a time, two times and half a time" (12:7; probably three and a half years), 1290 days (12:11), and 1335 days (12:12). Though the timetable is imprecise, the underlying conviction is that the tyranny of evil is only temporary; before long the sovereign God will intervene in human and cosmic history to vindicate the faithful and establish the divine rule.

The Book of Daniel represents just one example of the apocalyptic eschatology that emerged late in the Old Testament and was given further expression in the time of Jesus and early Christianity. Other such works include 1 Enoch (a composite work parts of which may antedate the Book of Daniel), the Testament of Moses, and the Book of Jubilees. The Qumran community, authors and preservers of the Dead Sea scrolls, was influenced by this apocalyptic worldview. Members of this sect had "a sense of living at the close of the present age preliminary to a massive divine intervention."[62] Sometimes dubbed "the mother of Christian theology,"[63] apocalyptic influenced the preaching of Jesus, especially his proclamation of the Reign of God and his eschatological discourses. It also impacted upon the theology of the authors of the New Testament. That will become evident in the next chapter.

3
NEW TESTAMENT ESCHATOLOGY

We turn now to consider the eschatological perspectives found in the New Testament. At the close of the last chapter we saw that Jesus lived at a time in the history of Israel that was marked by a strong eschatological tonality. In a particular way, apocalyptic eschatology was in the air. This perspective on history undoubtedly influenced the ministry of Jesus, the outlook of his disciples, and the understanding of the person and work of Jesus expressed by the authors of the New Testament. In this chapter we will explore the eschatological elements that were characteristic of the public ministry of Jesus, the interpretation of his death and resurrection, the hope of sharing in his resurrection, and the expectation of his coming again (Parousia).

THE PUBLIC MINISTRY OF JESUS

John Meier underscores the eschatological overtones of the ministry of John the Baptist and the significance of Jesus's baptism by John.[1] Meier argues in favor of the historicity of Jesus's baptism by John, noting that the evangelists had to narrate this event in ways that would communicate the superiority of Jesus over John. Therefore, they would not have invented this story if the baptism had not actually taken place. John's message was an eschatological one. In Mark's version of the story, John proclaims a baptism of repentance for the forgiveness of sins and promises that a "mightier one" will soon come: "One mightier than I is coming after me. I am not worthy to stoop and loosen the thongs of his sandals. I have baptized you with water; he will baptize you with the holy Spirit" (Mark 1:7–8). Meier asserts that by submitting to John's baptism, Jesus basically accepted John's eschatological message and ritual. Through this act, "Jesus was expressing both his solidarity with a sinful Israel preparing for the final judgment and his definitive break with his past life in Nazareth."[2] Like John, Jesus uttered a warning of imminent divine judgment, "while shifting the emphasis to the joyful message of God's mercy and forgiveness available in the present moment, as he sought to regather and restore Israel in the last days."[3]

The theme of the regathering and restoration of Israel points to Jesus's calling and naming of the Twelve. Mark tells us that Jesus "appointed [or: "made"] twelve [whom he also named apostles] that they might be with him and he might send them forth to preach and to have authority to drive out demons" (Mark 3:14–15). The Twelve obviously have reference to the system of the twelve tribes of Israel, which had ceased to exist by the first century CE. But mention of the Twelve evoked the eschatological hope for the restoration of the twelve tribes through a definitive (end time) action of God.[4] So the action of Jesus in creating the Twelve was a symbolic prophetic action pointing to the inbreaking of God. The Twelve were sent out on a temporary, symbolic preaching mission to Israel that marked "the beginning of the regathering of the twelve tribes that God would complete on the last day."[5]

The eschatological character of Jesus's public ministry is most evident in his proclamation of the kingdom of God (*basileia tou theou*). Not a phrase found as such in the Hebrew Scriptures, Jesus made the kingdom of God the focus of his public ministry. It did, however, hearken back to earlier ideas of God's sovereign rule, hymned in the Psalms and some of the prophets. N. T. Wright observes that by employing the language of the kingdom, or reign, of God Jesus evoked an entire story line for the Jewish people of his day.[6] His announcement of the kingdom evoked the longing of Israel for the God of the covenant to come in power and rule the world in the way that God had always intended. The primary meaning of the phrase is dynamic, rather than spatial. It refers to an activity, that is, God drawing near to establish God's rule over creation.

The proclamation of the reign of God assumes that all is not well in God's beloved creation. It presupposes that there are powers at work in creation that are opposed to the divine purposes. The fall from God's righteous rule has resulted in a creation that is wounded by evil and the intense suffering that results from the presence of evil. "Jesus uses the phrase [the kingdom of God] to proclaim that the God who created both the world and Israel is about to bring the present time of sin, injustice, and violence to an end by coming in power to establish his rightful rule over his creation and over his people Israel once and for all."[7] Elizabeth Johnson observes that the symbol of the kingdom of God "refers to the state of the world when the will of God is finally and fully honored: compassion and kindness will abound, joy and peace will break out, and all creation will flourish."[8] As such this symbol is inherently subversive.

There is an irresolvable tension between the future and the present dimensions of Jesus's proclamation of the kingdom of God. On the one hand, the prayer that Jesus taught his disciples to say includes the petition, "Your kingdom come" (Matt 6:10), indicating that the kingdom of God is not yet fully present. In a famous saying at the Last Supper recounted in the Gospel of Mark, Jesus expresses the hope that God will vindicate him in the future: "Amen I say to you, I shall not drink again the fruit of the vine until the day when I drink it new in the kingdom of God" (Mark 14:25).[9] John Meier observes, "This future coming of the kingdom is under God's control alone, beyond human calculation or effort."[10] At the same time, there is an inescapably present dimension to Jesus's proclamation of the kingdom. A number of sayings and actions of Jesus recounted in the Gospels show that at times he spoke of the reign of God as already present in his ministry. A key verse in this regard is Luke 11:20: "But if it is by the finger of God that I drive out demons, then the kingdom of God has come upon you." When some of the opponents of Jesus suspect that his ability to expel demons comes from Beelzebul, the prince of demons, Jesus responds by assuring them that his actions manifest instead the presence of God's rule. The saying in Luke 17:21 also suggests that the reign of God is already present through the person and ministry of Jesus: "For behold, the kingdom of God is among you." Raymond Brown declares that the careful reader of the New Testament must include both the future and the present dimensions in interpreting the meaning of Jesus's proclamation: "The kingly rule of God was already making itself present in Jesus's person, proclamation, and actions, but the complete and visible manifestation of the kingdom lay in the future and would also be brought about through Jesus, the Son of Man."[11]

Jesus proclaimed the reign of God in both word and deed. As a faithful Jew, he respected the authority of the Torah. Meier observes, "Jesus never revoked the Mosaic law as such or as a whole."[12] At the same time, he felt free to deepen or interiorize a commandment, such as when he taught that angry speech is as serious as murder (Matt 5:21–22). More radically, in a couple of instances he revoked individual commandments or institutions, as when he forbade divorce and remarriage (Mark 10:11–12; Luke 16:18) and prohibited the taking of oaths (Matt 5:34–37). In his teaching Jesus implicitly makes a claim to having unique authority from God, especially when he prefaces a statement with, "Amen, I say to you...." Meier notes that this use of "Amen" as a self-affirming certification of what one is going to say is not found in the Old Testament or the intertestamental literature before the time of Jesus. Meier comments, "As so often happens with the various roles and titles Jesus assumes, he adopts the Old Testament tradition and yet adapts and transforms it to express his own special status."[13]

Jesus also teaches by means of his provocative parables. In so doing, he invites his hearers to reconsider their conception of the way in which God relates to creation. The detested Samaritan turns out to be the person who acts as neighbor to the Jew left half-dead by the roadside; workers hired late in the day receive a full day's wage from an uncommonly generous employer; the prayer of the despised tax collector is more acceptable to God than that of the righteous Pharisee; the spurned father runs out of the house and embraces his prodigal son when he spies him from a distance. There was a performative, efficacious quality about the telling of these stories. N. T. Wright comments, "The parables are not simply *information about* the kingdom, but are part of the *means of* bringing it to birth....They invite people into the new world that is being created, and warn of dire consequences if the invitation is refused. Jesus' telling of these stories is one of the key ways in which the kingdom breaks in upon Israel, redefining itself as it does so."[14]

Jesus's practice of table fellowship was also intrinsically related to his proclamation of the nearness of God's reign. Part of the eschatological imagery of Israel was a great banquet that would be celebrated by the just with God (see Isa 25:6). Jesus made use of this imagery in telling the parable of the wedding banquet given by a king for his son, in which those who are initially invited reject the invitation (Matt 22:1–14; Luke 14:16–24). A vivid memory associated with Jesus's ministry was his celebration of meals with those considered outside the boundaries of Jewish orthodoxy. The evangelists recount the harsh criticism of Jesus expressed by some of the religious leaders for his behavior in sharing meals with such people (Luke 15:1–3). Jesus's claim to have authority to forgive sins is sometimes associated with this experience of table fellowship. His communion with tax collectors and sinners was an anticipation of the eschatological banquet in which the gracious mercy of God would be extended. It was an expression of the forgiving and redeeming mercy of God. As Elizabeth Johnson observes, "The joyous fellowship of the shared table offered a foretaste of belonging characteristic of the coming reign of God."[15]

After recounting Jesus's initial proclamation that the kingdom of God is "at hand" (Mark 1:15), Mark introduces the ministry of Jesus with a fast-paced account of his healing and exorcising activity: the cure of a demoniac in the Capernaum synagogue; the healing of Simon's mother-in law; the cleansing of a leper; and the cure and forgiveness of the paralytic brought to Jesus by his friends (Mark 1:16—2:12). In the midst of this flurry of activity, the evangelist writes, "When it was evening, after sunset, they brought to him all who were ill or possessed by demons. The whole town was gathered at the door. He cured many who were sick with various diseases, and he drove out many demons, not permitting them to speak because they knew him" (Mark 1:32–34). Readers of Mark's Gospel immediately receive the impression that the announcement of the kingdom and these life-giving actions of Jesus are inextricably linked.

Scholars who sift through the layers of the New Testament to construct a portrait of the historical Jesus typically conclude that Jesus's actions as a healer and exorcist are among the most ancient recollections of his ministry. Meier asserts, "The historicity of Jesus' claim to perform miracles is supported by massive multiple attestation of all Gospel sources and many Gospel forms."[16] Wolfgang Schrage adds, "Even when one allows for a critical stance and for methodological caution toward the miracle-tradition, which in its style appropriates typical characteristics of form from ancient miracle-stories, there can be no doubt that Jesus healed sick people and drove out demons."[17]

These healings and exorcisms did cause people to marvel at the power that was displayed in them. When the restored Gerasene demoniac begins to proclaim "what Jesus had done for him," Mark tells his readers that "all were amazed" (Mark 15:20). But the Gospels make it clear that the dimension of the "marvelous" was secondary to Jesus's real intent. These deeds are described in the Synoptic gospels as "deeds of power" (*dynameis*). They are not intended as external proofs of the coming of the kingdom; rather they are "one of the means by which the kingdom came."[18] When the kingdom of God was made present in and through Jesus, people found life; they experienced *shalom*—wholeness and peace. These acts of power represented Jesus's personal warfare against the forces of evil that drained the life out of people. "The acts of power were weapons Jesus used to reclaim people and the world from the domination of evil. When Jesus healed the sick or resuscitated the dead, he was breaking the Satanic power that manifested itself in illness and death."[19]

The underlying meaning of Jesus's healings and exorcisms was the restoration of creation that Israel anticipated with the advent of God's loving rule. When the imprisoned John sends disciples to ask Jesus, "Are you the one who is to come, or should we look for another?" Jesus responds, "Go and tell John what you hear and see: the blind receive their sight, the lame walk, lepers are cleansed, the deaf hear, the dead are raised, and the poor have the good news proclaimed to them. And blessed is the one who takes no offense at me" (Matt 11:2–6). These are the deeds promised by the prophets for the end time.[20] They have eschatological significance. They indicate that the presence of the reign of God affects the whole person. The blind beggar Bartimaeus receives *insight* into who Jesus is and follows him on the road of discipleship, but he is also granted physical *sight* and, presumably, no longer has to beg for a living (Mark 10:46–52). The woman with the hemorrhage experiences salvation in her encounter with Jesus, which includes healing of the malady from which she has suffered for twelve years (Mark 5:25–34). The paralytic receives forgiveness of his sins, but Jesus also empowers him to rise from his mat and walk (Mark 2:1–12). Schrage accentuates this wholeness of body and soul that the presence of the kingdom brings to people: "Jesus cannot be charged with the interiorizing and assignment of a transcendent character to salvation, as is often the one-sided representation of Christianity; on the contrary, he is strongly committed to the view that the liberating power of the rule of God concerns the body as well as the soul."[21]

This liberating power of the rule of God is elucidated in the reflections of M. Shawn Copeland, as she chronicles the witness of enslaved African Americans. Copeland analyzes the deep Christian faith that was expressed in the Negro spirituals.[22] She affirms that for these enslaved women and men *Jesus meant freedom*. They prayed for freedom, if not for themselves, at least for their children and grandchildren. They kept hope alive for a freedom that was holistic, "at once political *and* social, psychic *and* spiritual, metaphysical *and* ontological, this-worldly *and* other-worldly."[23] Copeland speaks of the "fearless and dangerous" Jesus: "A fearless and dangerous Jesus will set the Spirit working free in the midst of those yearning to be free. A fearless and dangerous Jesus waits with God's crucified people. He knows them and they know him...they know Jesus Christ crucified."[24]

A final characteristic of Jesus's public ministry that has eschatological overtones is his apparent use of the phrase "Son of Man."[25] In the seventh chapter of the Book of Daniel (Dan 7:1–14), the prophet Daniel is given a dream vision of four grotesque beasts, each of which represents an oppressive empire. These empires are overthrown by God (the "Ancient of Days"), who appears in majesty to hold judgment. Then "one like a son of man" appears with the clouds of heaven and is given dominion over all the peoples of the earth. The phrase "one like a son of man" is a description rather than a title: it means that the one who appears with the clouds has a human form rather than the form of a beast. The identity of this figure is disputed among biblical scholars. Meier points out that the precise title "the Son of Man" is not found in the Old Testament or in intertestamental titles before Jesus. Yet Jesus refers to himself with this title in all four Gospels (though with some nuance of difference between the Synoptics and John). He does so in three contexts: his earthly ministry (Matt 11:19: "the Son of Man came eating and drinking, and they said, 'Behold, a glutton and a drunkard, a friend of tax collectors and sinners'"); himself in his passion (Luke 9:44: "The Son of Man is to be handed over to men"); and as a witness at the last judgment (Luke 9:26: "Whoever is ashamed of me and my words, the Son of Man will be ashamed of when he comes in his glory"). It is particularly this third reference to the Son of Man sitting in judgment that will figure prominently in Christian eschatology. Believers are familiar with the famous scene in Matthew

25:31–46, in which the Son of Man separates the sheep from the goats, according to the way in which they responded to his "least brothers and sisters."

THE DEATH AND RESURRECTION OF JESUS

It is clear, then, that Jesus's public ministry had eschatological overtones. In his words and actions, Jesus was revealing and incarnating the inbreaking of God in the world. God was drawing close to creation in a way that had definitive meaning and consequences. For the New Testament authors, the eschatological impact of Jesus's life and ministry culminated in his death and resurrection. They were convinced that the Jesus who had entered into the darkest realms of a horrific death had been raised to new life by the God whom he had addressed as "Abba."

New Testament scholars reflect deeply on the question of what can be said about Jesus's approach to his own death. The Gospels tell us that opposition to the teaching and some of the actions of Jesus arose early in his ministry. Mark situates this mounting hostility at the very beginning of his ministry in Galilee, after Jesus cures a man with a withered hand in a synagogue on the sabbath. The evangelist writes, "The Pharisees went out and immediately took counsel with the Herodians against him to put him to death" (Mark 3:6). It soon became apparent that Jesus's words and deeds provoked a negative reaction from some devout Jews and proved to be a threat to the religious and political establishment. John Meier highlights the two prophetic-symbolic actions of Jesus at the end of his life: his entry into Jerusalem on a donkey and his action in the temple of impeding the selling of sacrificial animals.[26] The entry into the city, even if in a more modest form than the way it is presented in the Gospels, would have meant that Jesus was making a symbolic claim to messianic status. "In his typically indirect fashion, Jesus claims to be that end time (no doubt, Davidic) king foretold by Zechariah."[27] And in his "cleansing" of the temple, Jesus "symbolically proclaims himself the master of the temple."[28] Meier concludes that these two actions led the high priest, Caiaphas, to respond to the threat that Jesus had become by conspiring with Pontius Pilate to do away with him.

While some New Testament scholars have asserted that we can know very little about Jesus's approach to his death because the Gospels reflect later interpretations of this death by the Christian community, other exegetes claim that we can draw at least some general conclusions about his attitude.[29] It seems clear that Jesus must have realized the danger that was mounting in his life. The death of John the Baptist would have compelled Jesus to reflect upon the lethal rejection of a contemporary prophet with whom Jesus had been associated. Near the end of his life, the prospect of a violent death must have become apparent. Raymond Brown argues that we should not undervalue the general agreement of the Gospel tradition that Jesus was convinced beforehand that, although his life would be taken from him violently, God would ultimately vindicate him. In addition to Jesus's consideration of the death of John the Baptist, his reflection on figures such as Jeremiah and the suffering servant of Second Isaiah may have inspired such a conviction.[30]

In treating the question of Jesus's approach to his death, Gerald O'Collins appeals to the conduct of his public ministry. The Gospel descriptions of Jesus's public ministry suggest that "he consistently behaved as one utterly subject to his Father's will and completely available for the service of those who needed mercy and healing."[31] We can be confident that this same commitment to service characterized Jesus's attitude to his death. "A straight line led from his serving ministry to his suffering death."[32] Jesus's message and behavior consisted of radical love for God and neighbor. His life was marked by humble service to and sacrifice for others. And this teaching and praxis were grounded in profound confidence in and surrender to the Father. It can be safely presumed that he approached his death in the same way in which he approached his life and ministry—in a spirit of self-giving, faithful service to others and reverent trust in his Father.

In his examination of the historical basis of the Last Supper traditions, Meier concludes that Jesus arranged to have this meal with his disciples on the Preparation Day for Passover, since he realized that he might not be able to celebrate the Passover meal with them. At this meal, he performed symbolic actions with the bread at the beginning of the meal and the cup near the end of the meal. His words over the bread and cup were most likely simpler in form than the gospel accounts of those words. Meier suggests that his words may have been "This is my flesh" and "This cup is the covenant [sealed] by my blood."[33] "With these final symbolic-prophetic actions Jesus interpreted his coming death as the total giving of himself to accomplish what his ministry had intended to accomplish but did not: the restoration of the covenant relationship of all Israel with God in the end-time."[34] He envisioned his death, then, "as some sort of covenant sacrifice."

Each of the evangelists paints his own portrait of the death of Jesus on the cross. Mark's rendition is "raw and stunning,"[35] with Jesus uttering the first line of Psalm 22 and expiring "with a loud cry" (15:37). Luke's portrait is of a more serene Jesus who in the words of Psalm 31 commends his spirit to the Father (23:46). John's portrayal is of a majestic Jesus who has accomplished his mission: "It is finished" (19:30). Like Mark, Matthew presents Jesus as uttering the opening words of Psalm 22, but he also describes apocalyptic happenings taking place at the moment of the death of Jesus:

> But Jesus cried out again in a loud voice, and gave up his spirit. And behold, the veil of the sanctuary was torn in two from top to bottom. The earth quaked, rocks were split, tombs were opened, and the bodies of many saints who had fallen asleep were raised. And coming forth from their tombs after his resurrection, they entered the holy city and appeared to many. The centurion and the men with him who were keeping watch over Jesus feared greatly when they saw the earthquake and all that was happening, and they said, "Truly, this was the Son of God!" (Matt 27:50–54)

Daniel Harrington explains that Matthew's inclusion of cosmic portents unleashed by the death of Jesus is based on Ezekiel 37:1–14, a biblical passage mentioned in the second chapter, wherein God raises the scattered, dry bones of his people to new life. "Matthew wanted to show that Jesus' death marks a turning point in human history because it makes possible the resurrection of other human beings (see 1 Cor 15:20–23)."[36] Matthew's comment that the coming forth of the saints happened "after his resurrection" appears to be Matthew's correction to an earlier tradition. The evangelist wants to portray the resurrection of the holy ones as dependent on the resurrection of Jesus. For Matthew, the resurrections of the saints "anticipate the fullness that accompanies the end-time."[37]

In his important work *Grammars of Resurrection*, Brian Robinette asserts that it is the resurrection of Jesus from the dead that constitutes the basic grammar for authentic Christian discourse and praxis. Robinette claims that what the exodus is to the Old Testament, the resurrection of Jesus is to the New Testament. The resurrection of Jesus "establishes the framework for all Christian discourse and imagination."[38] In a similar fashion, in his study of Christian eschatology Gerhard Lohfink observes that Christian knowledge of the eschaton is nothing other than an extrapolation of what happened in the resurrection of Jesus.[39] The authors of the New Testament reflected back on the life and ministry of Jesus of Nazareth through the lens of the resurrection. It was their conviction that Jesus had been raised from the dead by God that informed their proclamation of the gospel and their vision of Christian life.

The New Testament tradition about Jesus's resurrection is expressed in three main forms: confessional or creedal statements (e.g., 1 Thess 4:14; 1 Cor 15:3–8), stories about the empty tomb, and narratives about the appearances of the risen Jesus. The traditions about the finding of the empty tomb and the appearances of the risen Jesus vary considerably and cannot be conflated into a single, uniform account. The Gospel stories of the empty tomb are unanimous in reporting that women found Jesus's grave empty two days after his crucifixion. But they vary in a number of other details, including the message that the women receive and their reaction to it. Traditions about the appearances of the risen Jesus are attached to two distinct locales: Jerusalem and Galilee. Neither of these two traditions shows any awareness of a tradition of appearances in the other location.[40] There are other differences as well. Raymond Brown concluded that each tradition in the Gospels centers on an all-important appearance to the Twelve in which they are commissioned for their ministry. What was essential for the early Christian community was the testimony that a well-known apostolic witness had seen the risen Jesus.[41]

New Testament scholars highlight the enduring significance of the tradition about the resurrection cited by Paul in his First Letter to the Corinthians (1 Cor 15:3–8). Paul uses the technical terminology of "received" and "handed on" in this passage, thereby signifying a critical message of salvation. Whether this tradition was originally formulated in Aramaic or Greek is disputed among biblical scholars, but its antiquity is acknowledged.[42] It is somewhat fixed in its language and has a definite structure. Moreover, it is the direct expression of one who claims to have been an eyewitness of an appearance of the risen Jesus:

> For I handed on to you as of first importance what I also received: that Christ died for our sins in accordance with the scriptures; that he was buried; that he was raised on the third day in accordance with the scriptures; that he appeared to Cephas, then to the Twelve. After that, he appeared to more than five hundred brothers at once, most of whom are still living, though some have fallen asleep. After that he appeared to James, then to all the apostles. Last of all, as to one born abnormally, he appeared to me.

In this formula the title *Christ* functions like a proper name. The death of the Christ is understood to be "for our sins." His death is not simply a brute historical fact but is confessed as having salvific significance. The death and resurrection of Jesus are envisioned as "according to the scriptures." This is a general reference that views Scripture as a unity and confesses the destiny of Jesus to be integral to the revelation of God's saving will. Reference to the resurrection is stated in the passive voice: "he was raised" (*egēgertai*). This is a respectful divine passive indicating that Jesus's resurrection is an act of God, what N. T. Wright calls "a great act of the Creator himself."[43] The phrase "on the third day" is applied to the resurrection itself. This phrase may have a temporal reference, or it may have a theological meaning that denotes the moment of decisive action, as in Hosea 6:1–2. The term that is translated as "appeared" (*ōphthē*) is employed in the Greek translations of the Old Testament to speak of theophanies: manifestations of God (e.g., Gen 12:7; 26:24; Exod 6:3; 1 Kgs 3:5, 9:2). Raymond Collins observes that "the use of this verb form in the creedal formula indicates that the appearance of Jesus inaugurates a new era of salvation."[44] This word connotes an initiative from outside: the risen Jesus lets himself be seen by chosen witnesses. This experience establishes faith in Jesus's resurrection while also confirming the ecclesial status of the recipients. Commenting on this creedal formula, Wright observes, "In the tradition, then, firm, universal and early, we find unambiguous evidence that the earliest Christians believed both that Jesus had been bodily raised and that this event fulfilled the scriptural stories."[45]

After surveying the appearance narratives in the New Testament, Robinette concludes that these stories have four points in common: these experiences originate from the free initiative of the risen Christ; they are not expected by the witnesses; they involve historically and sensually mediating factors of embodied human experience; they occurred during a circumscribed period of time before the ascension.[46] Robinette draws on the work of the French philosopher Jean-Luc Marion in speaking of these experiences, especially Marion's categories of the "saturated phenomenon" and "bedazzlement." The saturated phenomenon is an object with a surplus of meaning, "which neither concept, signification, nor intention can foresee, organize or contain."[47] The encounter with such a reality entails bedazzlement. "Like the blindness that results when unadjusted eyes are flooded with intense light, the appearances of the risen Christ in his glorified corporeality 'bedazzle' witnesses."[48] Robinette also cites Walter Kasper in attempting to describe the Easter experiences: "We have before us a total state of being possessed by Jesus, a state of impact and absorption, the awakening of faith."[49]

Christian theologians as a whole offer diverse interpretations of the confession "Jesus is risen." There are, however, certain affirmations that are foundational for Christian belief in the resurrection. First, this confession refers to an event that affected Jesus personally. Jesus himself has been raised up by the Father; he now lives in a transformed state. The bodily reality of Jesus's resurrection implies the transformation of God's good creation. "His human life or total embodied history rose with him and was transfigured into a final mode of existence."[50] Second, the New Testament, through a variety of literary genres, speaks of something definite taking place after Jesus's death in and through which the presence of the risen Jesus was revealed to certain followers. There are elements of continuity and discontinuity in these accounts: it is truly Jesus of Nazareth who has been raised up, but now he exists in a transformed state. Third, the disciples' experience of the risen Jesus is spoken of using the language of sight, but this experience involves a distinctive kind of seeing that is different from ordinary empirical seeing. Kasper calls it a "believing seeing."[51] At the same time, it is an experience that leads to faith and generates a whole new perspective on reality.

Fourth, as John Galvin points out, the experience of the risen Jesus should be related to Jesus's entire life and ministry.[52] Just as one cannot understand the meaning and significance of Jesus's death apart from his life and message, neither can the meaning and significance of his resurrection be understood apart from his public ministry. Through his abiding trust in his Abba God, Jesus gave grounds for hope that he and his mission would be vindicated.

Gerald O'Collins elucidates the revelatory significance of Jesus's resurrection.[53] The experience of Jesus risen from the dead provided new insight into the person of Jesus, especially the uniqueness of his relationship with God. If Jesus has been raised up and exalted, then ultimately God has been revealed in Jesus. The resurrection revealed that in and through Jesus the kingdom of God had been inaugurated, even though its fulfillment was yet to come. It also showed that Jesus' death as an act of loving service had been accepted by the Father. Jesus and his mission had been vindicated by the living God. The raising of Jesus from the dead in anticipation of the universal resurrection manifested the universal significance of Jesus's person, message, and saving work. This conviction eventually led to the mission to the Gentiles. "In short, the resurrection fully and finally revealed the meaning and truth of Christ's life, person, work and death. It set a divine seal on Jesus and his ministry."[54]

The resurrection of the crucified Jesus also led believers to "a fresh understanding of God."[55] First, the vindication of Jesus in the resurrection discloses that God can be found in the suffering one, even in one who is undergoing a shameful and horrific death by crucifixion. "But with the resurrection the disclosive power of the cross comes into play, and shows that the weak, the despised, and the suffering—those who become fools for God's sake—can serve as special mediators of revelation (and salvation)."[56] The experience of the risen Jesus also suggests that the God of life proclaimed and made present in Jesus's ministry is the one who brings life out of death. This is God's signature activity. God is the resurrector, the one who raised the dead Jesus and who will raise all the dead. Finally, this experience proved to be the decisive manifestation of the character of God's love:

> In the story of Jesus' crucifixion and resurrection, Christians perceived the initiative of self-giving love which led God to be personally involved in our sinful history (Rom

> 8:3)—even to the extent of an appalling death on the cross: "God shows his love for us in that while we were yet sinners Christ died for us" (Rom 5:8).[57]

The crucified and risen Jesus became for Christians the love of God made flesh.

SHARING IN JESUS'S DEATH AND RESURRECTION

From the earliest days of the church, believers became convinced that the death and resurrection of Jesus was not an event that affected only him. It was a reality in which they were to share; disciples were called to envision their lives as a participation in the mystery of Jesus's death and resurrection. This belief was sacramentalized in the practice of baptism. Those who were baptized were immersed in the paschal mystery—the mysterious and transformative reality of Christ's life, death, and resurrection. Paul spells this out in a section of his Letter to the Romans, a passage that is proclaimed each year in the Catholic liturgy of the Easter Vigil:

> Are you unaware that we who were baptized into Christ Jesus were baptized into his death? We were indeed buried with him through baptism into death, so that, just as Christ was raised from the dead by the glory of the Father, we too might live in newness of life. For if we have grown into union with him through a death like his, we shall also be united with him in resurrection. We know that our old self was crucified with him, so that our sinful body might be done away with, that we might no longer be in slavery to sin. For a dead person has been absolved from sin. If then, we have died with Christ, we believe that we shall also live with him. We know that Christ, raised from the dead, dies no more; death no longer has power over him. As to his death, he died to sin once and for all; as to his life, he lives for God. Consequently, you too must think of yourselves as [being] dead to sin and living for God in Christ Jesus. (Rom 6:3–11)

In this passage Paul connects Christian participation in the death of Jesus with personal conversion—dying to sinful ways in one's life. This means liberation from "slavery to sin." New Testament authors also link sharing in Christ's suffering and death with a willingness to suffer because of one's witness to the gospel. Furthermore, this participation in Jesus's death and resurrection is also present and effective in the experience of death itself. For the Christian, death is not a dying alone; it is a dying with Christ. Jeannine Hill Fletcher observes, "With Christ's passion and death, death itself can now be seen as reunion and rebirth in God....To those who follow Christ, there is offered not merely death as the end of material, physical existence but 'death in the Lord' that is the fullness of God's promise for creation."[58]

A pertinent example of the call to share in Christ's sufferings and death through faithful witness to the gospel is found in the First Letter of Peter. The letter is addressed to Christians living in northern Asia Minor, who are called "exiles" (1:1) and "aliens" (2:11). It may be that the suffering they experienced was not systematic persecution by the Roman state but the ridicule that a dominant culture can inflict on a minority.[59] The author begins his letter by recalling the good news of the resurrection of Jesus and the experience of new life given to those baptized in Christ. He reminds the community that God in God's mercy gave them "a new birth to a living hope through the resurrection of Jesus Christ from the dead" (1:3–4). They can find meaning in the sufferings of Christ and in their own sufferings because of their belief in the resurrection. He exhorts these Christians to keep their eyes focused on the future, to look toward "a salvation that is ready to be revealed in the final time" (1:5). The author clearly believes that the end of history is imminent, and that injustice and suffering will soon be overcome.

The author of 1 Peter is particularly concerned about slaves and wives married to non-Christian husbands, two groups of people who may be especially vulnerable to abuse. He invites them to endure their sufferings in a way that will give testimony to their faith in Christ. Believers are called to witness to their faith by doing good, knowing that such a way of life may lead to unjust suffering, as it did for Jesus. Jesus is presented as the true exemplar of faith in adversity: "When he was insulted, he returned no insult; when he suffered, he did not threaten; instead, he handed himself over to the one who judges justly" (2:23). Believers can experience joy and hope in their sufferings by looking forward to the eschaton: "But rejoice to the extent that you share in the sufferings of Christ, so that when his glory is revealed you may also rejoice exultantly" (4:13). The notion of sharing in the sufferings of Christ represents an intensification of association with Christ that goes beyond imitation.[60] Through their suffering for the gospel, believers participate in the reality of Christ and share in his redemptive work of bringing the world to glorify God. They are united to Christ. Donald Senior comments on 1 Peter's focus on the mystery of death and resurrection: "The author lingers over Jesus' agonizing struggle from death to life because this is the decisive pattern of all Christian existence, indeed of all human existence."[61]

In the previous section of this chapter, we examined the ancient creedal formula about the resurrection that is quoted by Paul in 1 Corinthians 15. Paul proceeds in that chapter to mount an argument for belief in Jesus's resurrection, an argument directed to those in the Corinthian community who deny the resurrection of the dead (or at least those who deny their *bodily* resurrection). In an almost syllogistic way, Paul draws on the close connection between Christ's resurrection and the resurrection of members of the community: "If there is no resurrection of the dead, then neither has Christ been raised. And if Christ has not been raised, then empty [too] is our preaching; empty, too, your faith" (1 Cor 15:13–14). As Lohfink observes, Paul accentuates "the indissoluble bond between the resurrection of Jesus and that of all the dead."[62] Paul proceeds to declare, "But now Christ has been raised from the dead, the firstfruits of those who have fallen asleep" (15:20). By "firstfruits" (*aparchē*) Paul means a harbinger of things to come. Collins comments, "The idea of firstfruits implies that other fruits will be harvested at a later time. The notion implies not only temporal sequence but also some sort of relationship between the firstfruits and the later harvest; the harvest of firstfuits serves almost as a guarantee of the later harvest(s)."[63] Christ is not only the model of the resurrection of the dead; he is the agent of the resurrection of the dead.

In the latter part of this chapter, Paul addresses the "how" of the resurrection of the dead by discussing the nature of the resurrected body. New Testament scholars point out that the apostle has the creation stories of Genesis 1—3 in his mind as he makes his argument. This allusion is also evident in the comparison and contrast he makes between Adam and Christ, the new, or final, Adam.

Though he does not specifically employ the analogy of resurrection as a "new creation" by God, the idea seems to be present. Using analogies drawn from the agricultural (seeds and plants), zoological (the different kinds of flesh among species of animals), and astronomical (the different kinds of heavenly bodies) spheres, Paul distinguishes between the "natural body" (*sōma psychikon*) and the "spiritual body" (*sōma pneumatikon*). After contrasting Adam, who became "a living being," with the last Adam, who is "a life-giving spirit," Paul writes, "Just as we have borne the image of the earthly one, we shall also bear the image of the heavenly one" (15:49). Collins describes what Paul means by the spiritual body as "the human insofar as he or she is energized by the Spirit of the living God (*pneuma*)."[64]

In the Letters to the Colossians and the Ephesians, the Pauline author(s) (perhaps not Paul himself) speaks of the risen life as a present reality in the lives of believers. Reminding the Colossian community of the sovereign role of Christ in their lives, the author reflects on the effects of baptism: "You were buried with him in baptism, in which you were also raised with him through faith in the power of God, who raised him from the dead" (Col 2:12). The author of Ephesians extols the power of God's grace in bringing believers to new life in Christ: "But God, who is rich in mercy, because of the great love he had for us, even when we were dead in our transgression, brought us to life with Christ (by grace you have been saved), raised us up with him, and seated us with him in the heavens in Christ Jesus, that in the ages to come he might show the immeasurable riches of his grace in his kindness to us in Christ Jesus" (Eph 2:4–7). These letters affirm that believers already share in Christ's risen life through the Spirit who is given in baptism. Taking note of the ethical admonitions in these letters, Frank Matera points out that the author(s) of these two letters knows that the resurrection of the dead has not yet occurred. But the emphasis on the believer's close association with Christ's resurrection provides believers with a powerful motivation for living a morally good life.[65]

In the eighth chapter of his Letter to the Romans, Paul refers to a "groaning creation." This passage is sandwiched between two passages that speak of resurrection. Paul assures the community that the one who raised Christ from the dead will give life to their mortal bodies as well (8:11). Near the end of the chapter Paul poses a rhetorical question: "Who will condemn? It is Christ [Jesus] who died, rather, was raised, who also is at the right hand of God, who indeed intercedes for us" (8:34). In between these two affirmations of resurrection, Paul reflects on creation:

> I consider that the sufferings of this present time are as nothing compared with the glory to be revealed for us. For creation awaits with eager expectation the revelation of the children of God; for creation was made subject to futility not of its own accord but because of the one who subjected it, in hope that creation itself would be set free from slavery to corruption and share in the glorious freedom of the children of God. We know that all creation is groaning in labor pains even until now; and not only that, we ourselves, who have the firstfruits of the Spirit, we also groan within ourselves as we wait for adoption, the redemption of our bodies. (8:18–23)

Most biblical scholars interpret Paul's reference to "creation" here to mean nonhuman creation.[66] Paul's assertion that creation was made subject to futility has received a wide variety of interpretations in the history of Christian theology and among contemporary New Testament scholars.[67] For example, Matera interprets Paul to be saying that God subjected creation to futility because of Adam's transgression. When God's children attain their glory—the resurrection from the dead—creation will share in this resurrection glory.[68] On the other hand, Sheila McGinn reads Paul as saying that creation is not able to have meaning and purpose that is lasting. This is no fault of creation; instead, it is God who has placed that limit on creation for a time. McGinn suggests that Paul has in mind the fact that the experience of futility and death is one of the things that causes humans to ask the "ultimate questions."[69] The incomplete nature of creation would be a divine goad to prod humanity to recognize the Creator.

These diverse interpretations notwithstanding, what seems most important about this passage is Paul's affirmation of the inextricable link between the fulfillment of humanity in the resurrection and the fulfillment of all of creation. Matera observes that "Paul shows that the effects of Christ's resurrection are cosmic in scope; it is not just believers who will be saved but the whole of God's creation."[70] Similarly, in her commentary on this passage McGinn writes, "In Christ, nature is not destroyed but released from its bondage and renewed."[71] This implies that Paul's understanding of salvation is salvation *of* the world, not salvation *from* the world. This important Pauline text is often referred to by contemporary theologians who write about eschatology.

PAROUSIA AND JUDGMENT

In the discussion of Jesus's proclamation of the kingdom of God above, we saw that there is a tension between the present and future dimensions of the kingdom. In one sense, the reign of God has already arrived in and through the person and word of Jesus. Nevertheless, its fullness is yet to come; it is still a future reality. After Jesus's death and resurrection, yearning for the fullness of the kingdom came to be expressed in the hope for the return of the risen Christ. This became known as hope for the Parousia or second coming of Christ. The Greek term *Parousia* denotes "presence" or "the state of being present." It was a technical term used for the arrival or visit of a high government official. It could also be used as a cultic term for the coming of a deity to the place in which that deity was worshiped.[72] Other terms were sometimes used to denote the coming of Christ, but Parousia became the prominent word to refer to the return of Jesus Christ in the last days.

Mario Inzulza delineates certain general characteristics of the Parousia in the New Testament.[73] First, it will be visible: "The New Testament affirms that Jesus Christ's return is a visible, public manifestation of his lordship over all."[74] Second, the coming of Christ will be sudden. Images such as a thief in the night and the sudden labor pains of a pregnant woman convey the suddenness of the Parousia. Third, the Parousia of Christ will entail a coming publicly in glory. Glory (Greek: *doxa*) is a term that is attributed to God in the Bible. The Prologue to the Gospel of John affirms that when the Word became flesh in Jesus, "we saw his glory, the glory as of the Father's only Son, full of grace and truth" (John 1:14). At the Parousia the glory of the risen Christ will be evident to all. Fourth, the advent of the risen Christ will have cosmic significance for human beings and for the rest of creation. For human beings, it will mean the resurrection of the dead. For nonhuman creation, it will include catastrophic phenomena such as earthquakes (e.g., Matt 24:7). But it will also entail the fulfillment of creation, signified, for example, by the promise of a new heaven and a new earth (2 Pet 3:13; Rev 21:1). Inzulza observes, "Just as Christ's return entails hope in human beings' resurrection as the fulfillment of the whole person—including, therefore, the physical reality—his coming is also the basis for hope in the fulfillment of the whole of creation in all its aspects."[75]

The letters of Paul suggest that, at least early in his apostolic career, he thought that the return of Christ was imminent. When he writes his First Letter to the Thessalonians, he tries to reassure them that those in the community who have died will still share in the blessings associated with the return of Christ. In so doing he considers himself as among those who will still be alive at that moment:

> Indeed, we tell you this, on the word of the Lord, that we who are alive, who are left until the coming of the Lord, will surely not precede those who have fallen asleep. For the Lord himself, with a word of command, with the voice of an archangel and with the trumpet of God, will come down from heaven, and the dead in Christ will rise first. Then we who are alive, who are left, will be caught up together with them in the clouds to meet the Lord in the air. (1 Thess 4:15–17)

In a later letter to the Philippians, however, it is evident that Paul was reckoning with the prospect of dying before the Parousia: "For to me life is Christ and death is gain. If I go on living in the flesh, that means fruitful labor for me. And I do not know which I shall choose. I am caught between the two. I long to depart this life and be with Christ, [for] that is far better. Yet that I remain in the flesh is more necessary for your benefit" (Phil 1:21–24). Nonetheless, in his study of Paul's understanding of the economy of salvation, Brendan Byrne concludes that Paul was always convinced that God would soon intervene to pronounce judgment upon the world: "Within the apocalyptic perspective, Paul sees the entire world as heading toward an imminent great judgment."[76]

Each of the Synoptic Gospels includes an eschatological discourse given by Jesus as part of his final ministry in Jerusalem, immediately before his passion. Each discourse begins with a question about the Jerusalem temple and is marked by Jesus's prediction of the destruction of the temple. The scenario of the future coming of the Son of Man painted by Jesus is characterized by conflicts and eschatological woes. These include false messiahs, wars, famines, and earthquakes, as well as persecution of the disciples of Jesus. Jesus instructs his disciples to constant vigilance—"Be watchful! Be alert!" (Mark 13:33). There are dire warnings about being led astray. The hour of the coming of the Son of Man is unknown. In a remarkable christological statement in the Gospel of Mark, Jesus says, "But of that day or hour, no one knows, neither the angels in heaven, nor the Son, but only the Father" (Mark 13:32). As Christopher Rowland points out, the focus of attention in these Gospel discourses is not speculation about what will happen after the return of Christ; rather, the emphasis is on fidelity to Jesus in the present.[77] For example, in the well-known parable of the sheep and the goats found in Matthew 25, the focus is recognition of and attentiveness to the presence of the Son of Man in the persons of the poor and others in need.

The eschatological vision of the Gospel of John is distinct from that of the Synoptics. There are places in the Gospel that refer to final fulfillment in the future, to be brought about by Jesus the Son of God. In a discourse given after the cure of the man at the pool of Bethesda, Jesus promises those who believe in him that "the hour is coming in which all who are in the tombs will hear his voice and will come out, those who have done good deeds to the resurrection of life, but those who have done wicked deeds to the resurrection of condemnation" (5:28–29). And at the beginning of the Farewell Discourse, Jesus promises his disciples that he is going to prepare a dwelling place for them: "And if I go and prepare a place for you, I will come back and take you to myself, so that where I am you also may be" (14:3). Still, the overall focus of the Fourth Gospel is the present. The eschatology of the gospel is more vertical than horizontal. Rowland observes that "the focus is on the first coming as the critical moment when the eschatological decision is taken."[78] Judgment and eternal life are now. In the discourse that follows the cure of the crippled man, quoted above, Jesus also says, "Amen, Amen, I say to you, whoever hears my word and believes in the one who sent me has eternal life and will not come to condemnation, but has passed from death to life" (5:24). Jesus speaks of the indwelling of the Father and the Son in those who love him and keep his word (14:23). When Jesus departs to be with the Father he will send the Paraclete, who will guide them to truth and make his presence known to them (16:4–33).

The Book of Revelation is the only full-scale apocalypse in the New Testament. Noting that it begins with letters addressed to seven churches in Asia Minor, Adela Yarbro Collins asserts that Revelation "participates in both the genre apocalypse and that of a letter."[79] It was most likely composed near the end of the reign of the Emperor Domitian (81–96), who promoted worship of himself and of the goddess Roma (the goddess personifying the city of Rome). Yarbro Collins asserts that the main themes of the book "have to do with power, who holds it, how it is exercised and who recognizes its authority."[80] From this vantage point, the fundamental sin is idolatry—the sin that followers of Christ, who is the model of faithfulness, must resist. For Christians it is God and his Christ who have ultimate authority,

Through a narrative encoded in esoteric symbolism, John the Seer exhorts the seven churches to steadfast fidelity to Christ, and he offers a vision of hope in the ultimate victory of God. Christ is represented through the symbolism of the Lamb who was slain; he is the crucified and risen One who has already won the victory. Followers of Christ must resist the pressure to participate in the imperial cult, at the cost of their lives if necessary. The Parousia itself is symbolized by a rider on a white horse, who is called "Faithful and True," "the Word of God," and "King of kings and Lord of lords" (19:11–16). This is "an epiphany of the exalted Christ as judge of the world."[81] He is victorious over Satan and his minions not through a military triumph but through the sword of the word of God.[82] One dimension of this eschatological vision is the binding of Satan for a thousand years, during which time the souls of those who were martyred for their witness to Jesus come to life and reign with Christ for a thousand years. This notion of the saints reigning with Christ for a millennium has come to be known in the tradition as millenarianism (from the Latin term) or chiliasm (from the Greek term). We will see that this idea was discussed widely by early Christian theologians, appeared again in medieval theology, and is embraced by some modern Christians.

Revelation presents the culmination of God's victory as the coming down out of heaven of the holy city, the new Jerusalem, which is the bride of the Lamb. The seer hears a loud voice from God's throne declaring, "Behold, God's dwelling is with the human race. He will dwell with them and they will be his people and God himself will always be with them [as their God]. He will wipe every tear from their eyes, and there shall be no more death or mourning, wailing or pain, [for] the old order has passed away" (21:3–4). When the vision ends, John is told not to seal up its prophetic word, since Christ is coming soon. In response John cries out, "Amen! Come Lord Jesus!" (22:20).[83]

The problem of the delay of the second coming of Christ comes to the fore in the Second Letter of Peter (2 Pet 3:1–13). The author of this letter, thought by scholars to be among the latest of the works of the New Testament, speaks against people whom he calls "scoffers": "Know this first of all, that in the last days scoffers will come [to] scoff, living according to their own desires and saying, 'Where is the promise of his coming? From the time when our ancestors fell asleep, everything has remained as it was from the beginning of creation'" (3:3–4). These false teachers seem to want to justify an immoral way of living by arguing that the promised return of Christ has not happened, and the world is the same as it has always been. The author of Second Peter responds to these specious arguments by asserting that God's "time" is different from human time and that the Lord does not delay in keeping the promise. He contends that any delay in the Parousia is due to God's patience in giving people time for repentance. He proceeds to reassure the community that the promise will be fulfilled: "But the day of the Lord will come like a thief, and then the heavens will pass away with a mighty roar and the elements will be dissolved by fire, and the earth and everything done on it will be found out" (3:10). This final conflagration will be followed by the creation of new heavens and a new earth.

Christopher Rowland points out that other New Testament authors also had to face the issue of the nonappearance of the Parousia, though they did so in more implicit ways.[84] For example, Luke, by appending the Acts of the Apostles to his Gospel, inserted an extended period of time between the ascension of the risen Christ and his return. This is the time of the church. And the author of the Gospel of John, as we have seen, placed special emphasis on the fact that eternal life can be experienced in the present through a living relationship with Jesus, the Word made flesh. This issue of the delay of the Parousia will be a persistent one in the ongoing tradition of Christian eschatology.

Contemporary theologians also grapple with the question of how New Testament passages about eternal condemnation should be interpreted. For example, at the end of the passage about the sheep and the goats in Matthew 25, Jesus is presented as contrasting the destiny of the two groups of people: "And these [the "goats"] will go off to eternal punishment, but the righteous to eternal life" (Matt 25:46). Should this biblical text, and others like it, be interpreted as teaching the *fact* of eternal loss for some people? Or should it be interpreted as a *warning* against sin and godless ways but not necessarily as asserting that some people will suffer eternal punishment? This question is inextricably linked with that of universal salvation, or apocatastasis.[85] Should Christians hope that all will be saved? This issue will also be a persistent one for Christian eschatology up to the present day.

4

ESCHATOLOGY IN THE EARLY CHURCH AND MIDDLE AGES

In this chapter we explore the theologies of hope articulated by Christian thinkers from the second century CE up to the high Middle Ages. Addressing such a large span of time necessitates a selective approach to the themes and the authors that are treated. In the section of this chapter in which I explore the early church, I will discuss four themes: the resurrection of the body; prayer for the dead; millenarianism; and the scope of salvation. In looking at medieval eschatology I will address the thought of Joachim di Fiore; the birth of purgatory; and eschatological themes in the theology of Thomas Aquinas.

ESCHATOLOGY IN THE EARLY CHURCH

The Resurrection of the Body

In the exploration of the New Testament in chapter 3, we saw that belief in the resurrection of Jesus from the dead was the foundation of the hope of early Christians. The authors of the New Testament looked back on the life and death of Jesus through the lens of the resurrection. They were convinced that baptism grants believers a share in Christ's triumph over death. The aspect of this belief that becomes most significant—and at times most controverted—for early Christian theologians is the confession of a *bodily* resurrection. Christian authors connect this affirmation with belief in creation and the incarnation of the Word of God. Debates about how to conceive of bodily resurrection often center on the interpretation given by Paul in 1 Corinthians 15, which we explored in the last chapter.[1] What does Paul mean when he speaks of a "spiritual body" (*sōma pneumatikon*)? In what way is the risen body related to the body of the person who lived and died?

Writing at the end of the second century, Irenaeus of Lyons sought to counter the beliefs of certain Gnostic groups. *Gnosticism* is an umbrella term for a complex and varied movement that affected both Judaism and Christianity. Many Gnostics viewed salvation as entailing a release from the body and a restoration to a purely "spiritual" realm. Brian Daley explains that Gnostic theories "promised escape from matter and union with the transcendent source of being to the favored few who accepted the esoteric knowledge that the group possessed."[2]

Against such Gnostic theories, Irenaeus affirms the goodness of creation, both the spiritual and material dimensions of the world. Creation is one moment in God's great work of salvation, which is a continuous process leading to the incarnation and ultimately to final fulfillment in Christ. The goodness of the flesh was illumined in the incarnation of the Word. Irenaeus writes, "If the flesh were not in a position to be saved, the Word of God would in no wise have become flesh."[3] Irenaeus linked this belief in the resurrection of the flesh with the healing ministry of Jesus and with the effects of reception of the Eucharist. Reflecting on the Gospel testimony to Jesus's deeds of healing, Irenaeus asserts, "For life is effected through healing and incorruption through life. Whoever, therefore, confers healing, confers life; and whoever gives life, also works his handiwork in incorruption."[4] About the Eucharist Irenaeus argues, "For just as bread which is produced from the earth, receiving the invocation of God is no longer ordinary bread, but the Eucharist...so our bodies, receiving the Eucharist, are no longer corruptible, having the hope of resurrection."[5] In giving an apologia for the material reality of the resurrection Irenaeus further argues that it was humanity that perished through sin; since what perished (humanity) possessed flesh and blood, that which is saved by Christ must also possess flesh and blood.[6]

The North African theologian Tertullian (ca. 160–ca. 220) wrote *On the Resurrection of the Flesh.* In that treatise he asserts, "The resurrection of the dead is the Christian's confidence. By believing it we are what we claim to be."[7] Tertullian marshals a number of arguments in his defense of the resurrection of the flesh against Valentinian Gnostics. Like other writers he contends that because Christ was raised in the flesh, and his resurrection is the model of our own, so those who believe in him must also be resurrected in the flesh. He also appeals to the notion of justice in God's judgment of human beings: it must be the whole person who is judged because that is the state in which he or she has lived. So the resurrection of the dead must pertain to the whole person, spirit and flesh.[8] Finally, Tertullian appeals to the celebration of the sacraments, which involve the mediation of the flesh:

> To such a degree is the flesh the pivot of salvation, that since by it the soul becomes linked with God, it is the flesh which makes possible the soul's election by God. For example, the flesh is washed that the soul may be made spotless; the flesh is anointed that the soul may be consecrated; the flesh is signed [with the cross] that the soul may be protected; the flesh is overshadowed by the imposition of hands that the soul may be illumined by the Spirit; the flesh feeds on the Body and Blood of Christ so that the soul also may be replete with God.[9]

Origen of Alexandria (d. 253/254) was one of the most influential thinkers in early Christian eschatology. He was also one of the most controversial, and one area of controversy involved his understanding of the nature of the resurrected body. He emphasized Paul's teaching in 1 Corinthians 15 that the risen body will be a *spiritual* body, not a simple continuation of the earthly body. Joanne McWilliam Dewart points out that Origen had "a barely concealed contempt for those who taught the revivification of the material body."[10] In his *On First Principles*, Origen says that our bodies "rise again from the dead with corruption banished and mortality laid aside."[11] This is the body with which we will be "clothed" at the resurrection. The nature of the risen body will depend on the merit of the individual, "corresponding to the dignity of each one's life and soul."[12] There is continuity between the earthly and the risen body because the risen body will have the same form (*eidos*) as the earthly body: "So we must conceive for our present subject that the body that is to be will have the same form, though there will be the greatest possible change for the better."[13] It is fair to say, however, that the emphasis in Origen's writings is the *transformation* that is entailed in the resurrection—the greatest possible change for the better.

Some Christian thinkers concluded that Origen's reflections on the resurrected body obscured or even denied the continuity of eternal life with human life in this world. Among them was Methodius of Olympus (late third/early fourth century), one of Origen's harshest critics. Methodius emphasizes that the risen body will be in every sense the body we now possess.[14] Resurrection will entail the restoration to life of the corporeal body, though now gifted with incorruptibility. Both Dewart and Daley remark that Methodius often fails to understand Origen, especially the latter's appeal to the "form" of the body as Origen's way of expressing continuity between the earthly body and the resurrected body.

Augustine of Hippo (354–430) strongly defended Christian belief in the resurrection of the body. Against the Manicheans he affirmed the intrinsic goodness of the human body, which was created by an infinitely good God. He buttressed his arguments by referring to the mystery of the incarnation, whereby we see the goodness of the flesh in that the Word of God became flesh. Augustine counseled caution in speculations about the nature of the resurrected body. In a sermon on the topic, he declares that "one ought not to inquire with a perverse kind of subtlety what the form of the body will be after the resurrection."[15] Nevertheless, he did articulate his vision of the risen life in some of his writings. In *The City of God* he asserts that resurrected bodies will surpass even the bodies of our first parents before they sinned.[16] His interpretation of Paul's "spiritual body" is that the apostle meant that the body will no longer be an impediment to the vision of God. He says that the flesh "will be submissive to us in the resurrection and will cease to trouble us with the obstacles it puts in the way of us observing the law of God and the divine commandments."[17] The risen body "will have the perfect measure of its being, obeying and commanding, vivified and vivifying with such a wonderful ease that what was once its burden will be its glory."[18] It will have the vigor and age that Christ had before his death. Augustine says that "the time is coming when we shall enjoy one another's beauty without any lust."[19]

There was a provincial synod of seventeen bishops held at Toledo in 675 (the Eleventh Council of Toledo).[20] This synod issued a creed (symbol of faith) that, though never formally approved by a pope or general council, has been recognized as an authentic expression of the church's doctrine, especially in the Western (Latin) church. The creed includes a section about the fate of human persons after their death. It affirms that "there is a true resurrection of the body for all the dead." And it proceeds to declare that "we do not believe that we shall rise in an ethereal body or in any other body, but in this very body in which we live and are and move."[21] This synodal statement, then, emphasizes the continuity of the earthly and resurrected bodies. This teaching will be repeated in the profession of faith issued by the Fourth Lateran Council (1215), which states that all people "will rise again with their own bodies which they now bear."[22] What it means to say that we will rise "in this very body in which we live" invites interpretation by theologians, and it continues to be a subject of discussion today.

In his work *The Spirit of Early Christian Thought*, Robert Wilken notes the connection between eschatology and theological anthropology.[23] He emphasizes that early Christian belief in the resurrection of the body influenced Christian understandings of the human person: "The hope of resurrection led inevitably to the question of whether the body was part of the definition of the self." He claims that it took time for Christian theologians to answer this question, but they eventually "affirmed without qualification that in the absence of a body a soul is not a person."[24] Wilken points to Augustine's treatise *The Care to be Taken for the Dead* as a unique patristic affirmation of the dignity of the human body. Wilken concludes his observations in these words:

> The Christian doctrine of the Resurrection shaped Christian understanding of the human person and in turn formed the culture of the West. What Christian tradition bequeathed to our civilization was not, as some propose, gnosticism or shame over the body, but the psychosomatic unity of the human being. There is no self that is not embodied.[25]

PRAYER FOR THE DEAD

It is evident that Christians of the first centuries felt a close connection with those who had gone before them in faith. This bond pertained, first of all, to the martyrs, who were seen as heroes of the church and whose intercession was sought by the living. It also included other believers who had died and were thought to live in an interim state awaiting resurrection. Brian Daley observes that "early Christian theologians seem to share the general sense of their fellow believers that *the dead are still involved in the life of the Church*, both in praying for the living and experiencing the benefit of their prayers."[26] Augustine describes this bond with the deceased in *The City of God*: "For the souls of the pious dead are not separated from the Church, which even now is the kingdom of Christ; otherwise there would be no remembrances of them at the altar of God in the partaking of the body of Christ."[27]

Augustine's reference to the altar of God gives testimony to the memory of and intercession for the dead in the liturgical prayer of the church. One of the earliest references to intercessory prayer for the dead at the celebration of the Eucharist is found in Tertullian's *De Corona*: "Each year, on the day of their birthday [into heaven], we make offerings for the deceased."[28] Chapels found in the Roman catacombs show that the Eucharist was celebrated in them for the dead who were buried there.[29] John Baldovin points out that "from the late fourth century onward at the latest eucharistic prayers [also] include intercessions for the living and the dead."[30] For example, the Roman Canon, much of which probably dates from the fourth century, includes this intercessory prayer: "Remember also, Lord, your male and female servants who have gone before us with the sign of faith and sleep in the sleep of peace. We beseech you to grant to them and to all who rest in Christ a place of refreshment, light and peace."[31]

One of the most compelling testimonies to prayer for the dead is found in *The Passion of Perpetua and Felicitas*.[32] There was a persecution of Christians in North Africa in 203 in which Perpetua and Felicitas, along with three male Christians, were condemned to death. While in prison before her martyrdom Perpetua either wrote or dictated her memoirs to other Christians, one of whom edited the text and wrote an epilogue to it after the death of the five martyrs. Scholars affirm the authenticity of the text. In her memoirs Perpetua recounts a dream she had during her imprisonment, which featured her deceased brother, Dinocratus, who had died at the age of seven from the effects of a cancerous tumor that had disfigured his face. In the dream, Dinocratus appears clothed in rags, suffering from thirst, and bearing the cancerous tumor on his face. He attempts to take a drink of water from a basin filled with water, but the lip of the basin is too high for him to reach. She concludes that her brother was being tried in this postmortem ordeal. She says, "But I had no doubt that I could relieve him in his trial. I prayed for him every day until we were taken to prison in the Imperial Palace."[33]

Perpetua has another vision of Dinocratus a few days later. Dinocratus appears refreshed (*refrigerantem*), dressed properly, and now bears only the scar where the tumor had been. The lip of the water-filled basin has been lowered, and water flows out of it continuously. Dinocratus takes a drink from a golden cup and begins to play happily in the water. Perpetua says that she awoke and realized that his penalty had been lifted.

In his analysis of this text Jacques LeGoff highlights the word *refrigerantem*, which he says refers to the term *refrigerium*. LeGoff notes that this latter term was used in early Christian literature to refer to an interim refreshment "reserved for certain of the dead, singled out by God as worthy of special treatment between their death and the time of final judgment."[34] Sometimes this state of refreshment is identified with resting in the bosom of Abraham while awaiting resurrection. It is clear that Perpetua was convinced that her prayers for her younger brother had a positive effect in his transition to a state of refreshment.

Perhaps the most well-known example of prayer for the dead is found in book 9 of Augustine's *Confessions*, where he recounts the death of his mother, Monica. As Augustine and his brother are tending to Monica on their return from Italy to North Africa, Augustine's brother expresses his hope that his mother will be buried in her home country. Monica responds to her son by saying, "Bury me wherever you would like. Let no anxiety about that disturb you. I have only one request to make of you, that you remember me at the altar of the Lord, wherever you may be."[35] After his initial grief over the loss of his mother, Augustine realizes that he should pray for her. Though her life was replete with virtuous actions, Augustine petitions God for his mother's sins: "Now please forgive her her debts if she contracted any during the many years that have passed after she received the water of salvation."[36] In a touching ending to book 9, Augustine addresses his readers, asking them to remember Monica and her husband, Patrick, at the altar.[37]

Augustine advocates prayer for the dead in other works as well. For example, in his treatise *The Care to Be Taken for the Dead* he expresses his approval of a statement by his friend Paulinus of Nola about the practice of praying for the dead, and he says that "the authority of the universal church which clearly favors this practice is of great weight, where in the prayers of the priest which are poured forth to the Lord God at his altar the commemoration for the dead has its place."[38] Nevertheless, Augustine did not think this prayer of the church benefited all of the departed. In his *Enchiridion*, he wrote, "For there is a certain manner of living, neither good enough to dispense with the need for these acts after death, nor bad enough to preclude their being of advantage to it after death; and there is a manner of living which is so established in goodness as to dispense with the need for them, as again there is one so established in evil as to be incapable of benefiting even from these when it has passed on from this life."[39] Augustine thought that a person must have lived in such a way as to deserve that the prayer of the church would be of advantage to her or him.

As we will see further along in this chapter, the ancient practice of prayer for the dead will be appealed to as the idea of purgatory slowly develops through the centuries. There was no common view of the state of the deceased before the resurrection among the early fathers and mothers of the church. And there was no precisely developed understanding of the way in which prayer benefits the departed. Not all theologians envisioned a process of purification that the church's prayer could aid or expedite. This was a case in which "prayer for the dead predated any explicit theology elaborating its rationale."[40]

MILLENARIANISM

In the discussion of the Parousia and judgment, in chapter 3 I mentioned the passage from Revelation 20:1–6. In this text the author of Revelation envisions the binding of Satan and the Christian martyrs coming to life and reigning with Christ for a thousand years. This biblical text has been the foundation of millenarian thinking, dating back to the early centuries of the church. The details of these millenarian scenarios differ from author to author, but generally millenarianism "looks forward to a reign of Christ of a thousand years between his second coming and the final resolution of all things."[41] Part of the reward of the just is to share in the rule of Christ, which means that they must be embodied. Visionary passages of a renewed earth from the Old Testament like Isaiah 65:17–25 are appealed to in depicting the blessings of this reign.

Writing in the middle of the second century CE, the apologist Justin Martyr espoused millenarian views, especially in his *Dialogue with Trypho*. Though Justin's depiction of eschatological events is not precisely clear, Dewart concludes that he seems to have envisaged a resurrection of all to judgment, then the reign of the just with Christ for a thousand years, and the punishment of the unjust for as long as God sees fit.[42] This reign of Christ and the saints will take place in a renewed Jerusalem. Justin writes, "I and every other completely orthodox Christian feel certain that there will be a resurrection of the flesh, followed by a thousand years in the rebuilt, embellished, and enlarged Jerusalem, as was announced by the prophets Ezekiel, Isaiah and the others."[43]

We have already taken note of the importance of the eschatology of Irenaeus of Lyons, in which he emphasizes the resurrection of the flesh. His belief in an earthly kingdom to be established between Christ's second coming and the eschaton "is very much of a piece with his stress on the physical resurrection of the body."[44] In his depiction of this kingdom, Irenaeus draws on Old Testament passages that promise peace and prosperity to Israel. The promises of such a kingdom "signify the feasting of that creation in the kingdom of the just which God himself promised that he himself will minister."[45] At the end of this thousand-year reign, a new and eternal heaven and earth will come. Irenaeus envisions the millennial period as a time not only of joy and peace but one of preparation, in which a person "may be made capable of the glory of the Father," which will be made manifest when the reign with Christ will end.[46] The just must become gradually accustomed to "partaking of the divine nature."[47]

In *The City of God*, Augustine acknowledges that he once held literal millenarian views. His early writings contain allusions to the millennium, though his emphasis in those writings is not the physical delights of the kingdom but the future rest of the saints on earth.[48] In *The City of God*, however, Augustine moves to an ecclesiological interpretation of Revelation 20. He says, "Therefore, the Church even now is the kingdom of Christ, and the kingdom of heaven. Accordingly, even now his saints reign with him, though otherwise than as they shall reign hereafter."[49] Further along in this same work, he says, "The Church, then, begins its reign with Christ in the living and in the dead."[50] Commenting on Augustine's ecclesiological interpretation, Daley asserts, "Augustine undoubtedly laid the foundation for the widespread tendency of later Latin theology to identify the Kingdom of God, at least in its first stage of existence, with the institutional Catholic Church."[51]

THE SCOPE OF SALVATION[52]

The question of the scope of salvation received varying responses among early Christian theologians. Will all be saved, or just some? J. Patout Burns argues that there are two distinct accounts of the "economy" of salvation that are present in the theology of the early church.[53] Greek thought, expressed in the theologies of Clement of Alexandria (d. before 215), Origen of Alexandria, Gregory of Nazianzus (329/330–ca. 390), and Gregory of Nyssa (ca. 335–394), stresses the universal availability of salvation and a developmental continuity in holiness from birth to beatitude. This line of thinking envisions a universal operation of Christ, and it views the church as the fullness of Christ's effective presence in the world. These thinkers chart a lengthy path of spiritual growth leading to union with God. Latin theology, as represented by Tertullian, Cyprian of Carthage, and Augustine, tends to view salvation as available only through the Catholic church and to think of it in terms of a definitive divine intervention that raises the believer from death to new life. According to this perspective, "one must believe the teaching of Christ, receive baptism, and belong to the communion of the proper church in order to be freed from sin and raised to the glory of Christ."[54] Augustine gives the fullest expression of this account of the economy of salvation.

The Greek viewpoint inspired some theologians to propose universal salvation, or the universal restoration (*apokatastasis*) of all things. Clement of Alexandria speaks of a fire of divine punishment for sins in this life and after death, but he envisions this punishment as having a pedagogical, purifying, and healing function that will ultimately sanctify sinful souls.[55] This purification is not a matter of divine vengeance against the sinner. The goal of this divine purifying action is the perfect contemplation of God. Daley describes Clement as the first Christian writer to describe with caution the prospect of universal salvation for all intelligent creatures.[56]

The eschatology of Origen is complex and not always consistent, and it is marked by speculative theories such as the premundane existence of souls and their fall from a spiritual realm. Central to his thought, however, is his focus on the saving power of the divine Logos, "who is stronger than every sin and whose divine power will heal all, so that the final end of all things will include the destruction of evil."[57] Origen's reading of 1 Corinthians 15:23–28 leads him to conclude that the subjection of all things to Christ will entail the victory of God's saving love for all. He, too, usually views the "fire" spoken of in the Scriptures as having a pedagogical and purifying effect. For Origen, "God's judgment is at once an act of purifying, saving mercy, for God only punishes sinners in order to save them from their death-dealing entanglement with sin and to prepare them for the eternal happiness which God has prepared for them."[58] God's saving work in the life of the individual engages human freedom; God saves no one against his or her will. Nevertheless, as John R. Sachs points out, "Origen seems unwilling to view human freedom as a power equal to or commensurate with divine freedom and love."[59] He thinks that the persuasive power of God's love will ultimately save the sinner and lead her or him to eternal fulfillment in loving union with God.

Gregory of Nazianzus and Gregory of Nyssa were influenced by the thought of Origen, though each proceeds cautiously in his eschatology. Gregory of Nazianzus holds that there will be judgment and punishment for sins in this life and the next. He thinks that "it is our own sins that will condemn us before God."[60] But the overall emphasis of Nazianzus is the remedial or purifying character of divine punishment. Employing the image of divine fire (based on 1 Cor 3:12–15), he can identify this fire with Christ himself, who destroys what is evil. Though he sometimes speaks of eternal divine punishment, he often suggests the rehabilitation of the sinner through the mercy of God. Sachs argues that what makes Gregory hesitant about eternal punishment is his conviction that punitive punishment is unworthy of God.[61] He envisions God as leading all to divinizing union with

God, in which we attain to the perfect divine image. Significantly, this transformative process does not take place only for the individual person; it is one that involves the entire human race in the body of Christ. Christ is the new Adam—the "heavenly Adam"—in whom humanity finds salvation.[62] Daley concludes that on the issues of the purgative nature of divine punishment and the hope for universal salvation, "Gregory offers a cautious, undogmatic support of the Origenist position."[63]

Gregory of Nyssa rejects some of Origen's speculative theories, such as the premundane existence of disembodied souls. But his overall eschatological vision manifests the impact of Origen's thought. He envisions a process of purification from sin and of spiritual growth throughout earthly life and beyond, through which human beings will be restored to their original state as the image and likeness of God. Even in heaven, there will be continued growth through an ever-increasing desire for God. In the *Life of Moses*, Gregory says, "never to reach satiety in one's desire: one must look always through what it is possible to see towards the desire of seeing more, and be inflamed."[64] One dimension of his eschatology is his conviction that evil does not have a substance of its own but is a perversion of the good. As such, it can never be absolute and unlimited and so must eventually have an end.[65] Like Gregory of Nazianzus, he emphasizes the communal nature of salvation, arguing that the image of God will come to its full realization only in the human race as a whole.[66] In a text in which he develops his soteriological theory of ransom from the devil, Gregory of Nyssa speaks of the purifying nature of the action of God on behalf of humanity, removing the evil that is mingled with human nature: "When, over long periods of time, it [evil] has been removed and those now lying in sin have been restored to their original state, all creation will join in united thanksgiving, both those whose purification has involved punishment and those who never needed purification at all."[67] Daley observes that Gregory of Nyssa reaffirmed and refined Origen's eschatology, particularly the hope for universal salvation—"the restoration of intellectual creation to an 'original' unity with God in contemplative beatitude."[68]

For Augustine of Hippo, however, belief in universal salvation derives from a misguided sense of compassion. He taught that in order to receive the forgiveness of sins and the gift of the Holy Spirit one must be baptized into the death and resurrection of Christ and remain in communion with the Catholic church. Burns observes that for Augustine, "without the help available only from Christ through the Church, human persons cannot avoid sin and condemnation."[69] In *The City of God*, Augustine explicitly opposes the position of Origen on universal salvation, as well as the more modest views of "tender-hearted Christians" who think that condemned sinners "shall be delivered after a fixed term of punishment, longer or shorter according to the amount of each man's sin."[70] It is true that in some places he does speak of a purification after death for those whose sins are not grievous. As we saw above, those who are so purged from their sins are helped by the prayers of their fellow Christians. Nevertheless, he views the punishment of condemned sinners to be eternal. Appealing especially to the Matthean parable of the sheep and the goats (Matt 25:31–46), Augustine teaches that those who are condemned will be punished eternally, though the suffering of some will be mitigated, with that of unbaptized infants being the mildest. For Augustine, the sin of Adam, in which every human being shares, is such a heinous crime that if no one had been saved God's justice could not be questioned. The fact that any are saved—however few they may be—is a miracle of divine grace.[71] Augustine has to wrestle with the text from the First Letter to Timothy (2:3–4), which speaks of God willing that everyone be saved and come to knowledge of the truth. Since Augustine asserts the sovereignty of God's will, he argues that the passage must mean either that no one is saved unless God wills his or her salvation, or that "everyone" (*pantas anthropous*) in this text signifies that all varieties of human beings will be represented among those who are saved. It could not mean that God wills to save every human being.[72] If God did will the salvation of all then all would be saved, and Augustine seems convinced that relatively few will be saved.

Controversy about eschatology, especially about the idea of universal salvation, arose in the sixth century between rival groups of Palestinian monks.[73] One of these groups espoused a radicalized version of Origen's theology; it was sharply criticized by the "anti-Origenist" monks. Instigated by the Emperor Justinian (ruled 527–565), a provincial synod convoked at Constantinople in 543 condemned certain teachings associated with the Origenist monks. In 553, immediately before the opening of the Second Council of Constantinople, the assembled bishops issued fifteen anathemas condemning Origenist theology. Daley observes that the condemned theses included the proposition of the complete abolition of material reality in the world to come and "a doctrine of *apokatastasis* that went far beyond the hopes of Origen or Gregory of Nyssa."[74] Sachs asserts that the teachings that were condemned at this time represented exaggerations of Origen's thought, and he points out that the church did not condemn the ideas about apocatastasis taught by Clement or the two Gregorys, even though they argued in the same direction as Origen.[75] Sachs thinks that at the heart of this question about the scope of salvation is the thorny issue of the relationship between human freedom and divine grace. In the end, is human freedom powerful enough to defeat the saving grace of God in a definitive way?

In the epilogue to his in-depth study of the eschatology of the early church, Brian Daley concludes that the eschatological consensus of the early church was "far less well formed, far less consciously enunciated in the Patristic centuries, than was the orthodox Christian doctrine of God or of the person of Christ."[76] Daley enumerates areas of agreement about eschatology among theologians of the early church, as well as points of disagreement and ongoing controversy.[77] We have explored some of these areas in this chapter. Among the beliefs held in common was the insistence that the fulfillment of human history must include the resurrection of the body. There was also agreement about God's universal judgment and, from the end of the second century, about a judgment at the end of the life of each individual person. Daley also notes the general sense among early Christian theologians that the dead are still involved in the life of the church, as those who pray for the living and who benefit from the prayers of the living. Among the areas of disagreement was the controversy over the materiality and physicality of the resurrection. And as we have seen, there was also sharp disagreement over the idea of universal salvation. Finally, early Christian theologians also disagreed over the possibility of purification from sin after death.

MEDIEVAL THEMES

Joachim of Fiore

We have seen that some early Christian theologians, including Justin Martyr and Irenaeus of Lyons, adopted millenarian views of the future. Based on their reading of chapter 20 of the Book of Revelation, they envisioned a thousand-year reign of the saints with Christ, a time of peace and prosperity on earth. In his later writings, Augustine moved away from a literal millenarianism, adopting an ecclesiological interpretation of Revelation. Though millenarianism died down after Augustine, it has emerged in different forms in the history of the church, including the twelfth and thirteenth centuries. As Jacques LeGoff observes, there were individuals who "believed or hoped that, in keeping with the Book of Revelation, the end of the world would be preceded not only by the trials of the Antichrist but, before that, by an extended period of justice, the millennium."[78] Among these individuals was Joachim of Fiore (d. 1202).

Joachim was born in southern Italy around 1130.[79] As a young man he made a pilgrimage to the Holy Land and a retreat in Jerusalem. These experiences moved him to reorient his life. He returned to Sicily and entered a Cistercian monastery, though he did not take the habit. He dedicated himself to lay preaching. When church officials objected to his lay preaching, he entered another Cistercian monastery, took vows, and was ordained a priest. Later, in 1191, Joachim founded a more austere branch of the Cistercians at San Giovanni in Fiore. He was known by his contemporaries as ardent in his love for Christ, eloquent in his preaching, and strongly committed to the vow of poverty.

Joachim had two visionary experiences that inspired and shaped his thought. These took place most likely in 1183, when he was living at the Cistercian monastery of Casamari.[80] The first experience came on Easter, and it purportedly gave Joachim a deeper understanding of the Book of Revelation as well as new insight into the harmony of the Old and New Testaments. The second happened on Pentecost, and according to Joachim it illumined for him the mystery of the Holy Trinity. In this Pentecost vision Joachim said that a ten-stringed psaltery appeared in his mind. The psaltery is one of several symbolic images (*figurae*) with which Joachim illustrated his works and communicated his eschatological ideas.

The central focus of Joachim's thought is the presence and work of the Trinity within history. His theology is a theology of history. Bernard McGinn observes that he adopted a fundamentally apocalyptic stance that envisioned a divinely predetermined structure to world history.[81] He was convinced that the meaning of history had been revealed in the Bible, though many people failed to grasp it. His view of history was teleological, envisioning a progressive spiritualization of humanity under the action of the Trinity. Joachim proffered a tripartite division of history, with each age (*status*) related to one of the persons of the Trinity and assigned a definite *ordo*. The Old Testament was the Age of the Father. It was the age of the married and of the old, and it was characterized by fear and servile obedience to the law. The second age was the Age of the Son; it is the age of clergy and the young and is characterized by faith and filial obedience. According to Joachim's biblical calculations, this second age would end in about 1260 and be absorbed into the Age of the Holy Spirit. This third status had actually been inaugurated by Benedict (ca. 480–ca. 547), the founder of Western monasticism, though it had not yet emerged in its fullness. This would be the age of monks and infants and would be characterized by love and freedom. In this third age there would be "spiritual men" (*viri spirituales*) who would be "the most potent champions of the good at the time of the Antichrist" and would emerge triumphant.[82] The third status would be a time of the total renewal of the church in which monks would be preeminent, though there would still be a place for the laity and the clergy. It would be an age of contemplation in which Greeks and Latins would be reconciled, wars would cease, and Jews would become Christians. McGinn emphasizes that, despite the extreme opinions of some scholars, Joachim's vision of the age of the Holy Spirit did not see the end of the clerical order, the abolition of the sacraments, or the cessation of the papacy. McGinn concludes that Joachim's spiritualized church "is a higher level of what already exists, not its replacement."[83]

The Fourth Lateran Council (1215) rejected Joachim's trinitarian theology for its tritheistic tendencies, thus accusing Joachim of compromising the unity of God.[84] McGinn argues that Joachim did in fact adhere to the belief in the absolute unity of the divine nature, though the analogies he employed to speak of the Trinity were not always helpful in supporting that belief.[85] Thomas Aquinas sharply criticized Joachim both for his trinitarian theology and his proposal of a new age of the Holy Spirit.[86] In the debates among the Franciscans in the thirteenth and fourteenth centuries, the Spiritual Franciscans adopted and radicalized the teachings of Joachim. As Minister General of the Franciscans, Bonaventure rejected the extreme views of the radical Joachimites, though Joachim's influence on Bonaventure is evident in his *Collationes* on the six days of creation. Some of the Protestant Reformers, including Thomas Müntzer (1490–1525), were inspired by Joachim's utopian vision. In the twentieth century, the Marxist philosopher Ernst Bloch secularized the teaching of Joachim, arguing that Joachim constructed the most momentous social utopia of the medieval period because it abolishes both church and state.[87]

THE BIRTH OF PURGATORY

We have seen that the practice of prayer for the dead became widespread in the early church. Tertullian witnessed to intercessory prayer for deceased Christians at the celebration of the Eucharist on the anniversary of their deaths. The story of Perpetua's prayer for her deceased brother was a compelling testimony to the efficacy of intercession for the deceased. Augustine asked the readers of his *Confessions* to pray for his parents, Monica and Patrick. And he thought that the prayer of the church benefited those whose lives had been neither very good nor very bad.

We have also seen that early Christian theologians employed the image of fire for the process of the purification of the living and the dead. Clement of Alexandria spoke of a fire of divine punishment for sins in this life and after death, a punishment that has a healing and purifying effect. Origen of Alexandria also viewed the punishing fire spoken of in the Scriptures as having a purifying and pedagogical effect. Gregory of Nazianzus identified this purifying fire with Christ himself. The practice of prayer for the dead, along with theological reflection on that practice, coupled with the popular image of a divine fire that is purifying, healing, and instructive, eventually led to the teaching about purgatory as the place where the purification of the dead happens.

The biblical basis for the doctrine of purgatory is rather thin, but three passages were often referred to in support of it: 2 Maccabees 12:39–45; 1 Corinthians 3:10–15; and Matthew 12:32.[88] The text from Second Maccabees, already discussed in the second chapter, relates the story of the soldiers of Judas Maccabeus finding "amulets sacred to the idols of Jamnia, which the law forbids the Jews to wear" under the tunics of the slain comrades they are about to bury. The soldiers pray for these deceased comrades, and Judas takes up a collection and sends it to Jerusalem to provide an expiatory sacrifice. The biblical writer concludes the story by saying that Judas made atonement for the dead that they might be absolved from their sin.

The text from First Corinthians has been especially important in the history of doctrinal development. The original context is the tendency toward factionalism within the Corinthian community, with members aligning themselves with different preachers. Paul emphasizes that he and Apollos are simply ministers of the Lord, God's coworkers. Paul employs the metaphor of a builder to describe the work of these ministers. Some build with materials that will withstand a testing fire—gold, silver, and precious stones. Others build with materials that will be consumed by a testing fire—wood, hay, or straw. Paul asserts, "But if someone's work is burned up, that one will suffer loss; the person will be saved, but only as through fire." In the history of interpretation of this passage, the testing fire came to be understood as a purgative fire.[89]

The context of Matthew 12:32 is Jesus's healing of a man who is blind and mute, and the accusation by the Pharisees that he drives out demons by the power of Beelzebul, the prince of demons. Jesus responds to this accusation by affirming that he drives out demons by the Spirit of God. He goes on to teach that blasphemy against the Spirit is a sin that will not be forgiven.

The passage concludes with Jesus's words: "And whoever speaks a word against the Son of Man will be forgiven; but whoever speaks against the holy Spirit will not be forgiven, either in this age or the age to come." Early church and medieval commentators will interpret this Gospel passage as implying that other sins—those that are not against the Spirit—can be forgiven in the age to come.

A fourth passage—not as prominent in the doctrinal history—is Matthew 5:26. The context is Jesus's teaching against anger and his command to reconcile with one's brother or sister before offering a gift at the altar. A failure to reconcile may lead one's opponent to hand one over to the judge, with imprisonment as the result. Jesus says, "Amen, I say to you, you will not be released until you have paid the last penny." The notion of "paying the last penny" was sometimes applied to the suffering of purgatory to expiate one's sins or satisfy for the effects of sins already forgiven.

Brian Daley observes that it has long been debated whether Augustine presents "a doctrine of temporary, remedial suffering after death substantially corresponding to the later Latin doctrine of purgatory."[90] Daley argues that Augustine never presents this temporal punishment as happening in a particular place or as having a healing, cleansing effect on the sinner. Daley admits, however, that in some of Augustine's later works he speaks of some forms of punishment after death as expiatory and purgative. Augustine hesitantly speaks of a purgatorial fire (*ignis purgatorius*). In *The City of God* Augustine discusses a theory based on 1 Corinthians 3, which suggests that between death and the final judgment the bodies of the dead "shall be exposed to a fire of such a nature that it shall not affect those who have not in this life indulged in such pleasures and pursuits as shall be consumed like wood, hay, stubble, but it shall affect those others who have carried with them structures of that kind; if it be said that such worldliness, being venial, shall be consumed in the fire of tribulation either here only, or here and hereafter both, or here that it may not be hereafter—this I do not contradict, because it is possibly true."[91] So here Augustine admits the possibility of a purgative fire after death that purifies one of lesser sins. LeGoff argues, however, that Augustine's deeper instinct is to situate the experience of purgation in this world rather than the next.[92]

Gregory the Great (ca. 540–ca. 604) served as pope at a time when Rome was experiencing multiple calamities—a flood of the Tiber, invasions by the Lombards, an epidemic of the plague. These disasters led him to conclude that the world would soon end, and he exhorted Christians to be prepared for death. In his *Moral Reflections on the Book of Job*, he took an interest in the "geography of the hereafter."[93] And in his popular and influential *Dialogues*, he included anecdotal illustrations that dealt with life after death. In Book 4 of the *Dialogues*, Deacon Peter asks Gregory about the notion of a cleansing fire after death. He answers by saying that "one must hold that there is to be a cleansing fire before judgment, in regard to certain minor faults that remain to be purged away." Citing Matthew 12:32, he proceeds to say, "From this we learn that some sins can be forgiven in this world, and some in the world to come."[94] Gregory explains that this cleansing fire pertains to "slight transgressions" like idle talking and "immoderate laughter." Further along, however, Gregory suggests that the dread that grips a departing soul is sufficient to purify it of its minor faults.[95] Gregory was strong in his support of offering Masses for the souls of the deceased to bring about pardon for their sins. When in the *Dialogues*, Deacon Peter asks about ways to help the dead, Gregory responds that for sins that are not ineffaceable after death "the sacred offering of the Host" is generally of great help.[96]

His study of the development of the doctrine of purgatory leads LeGoff to conclude that the word *purgatory* as a noun (*purgatorium*) was not employed by Christian theologians until the twelfth century.[97] Before this, the adjectival use of the term was used, such as in references to "purgatorial fire" (*ignis purgatorius*). In the early twelfth century, a day for the commemoration of the dead on November 2 was introduced into the liturgy at Cluny. LeGoff notes that interest in what happens to the soul between death and resurrection is evident in theologians of the twelfth century, for example in the writings of Hugh of Saint Victor (d. 1141). This theological reflection developed with particular intensity at the chapter school of Notre-Dame in Paris and among the Cistercians at Citeaux. LeGoff pinpoints the theological beginnings of purgatory as a place between 1170 and 1180. He highlights the work of Peter the Chanter (d. 1197), a master of the school of Notre-Dame of Paris. He was "the man who first integrated Purgatory into theological teaching."[98] Peter asserts that venial sin causes a determinate penalty to be inflicted in purgatory. LeGoff notes Peter's multiple usage of the noun *purgatorium*, suggesting purgatory as a place, though he admits that in other writings he conceives of purgatory more as a state than a place.

The Scholastics of the thirteenth century incorporated purgatory into their theological systems. For example, the Franciscan Alexander of Hales, teaching at the University of Paris, held that purgatory purges venial sin and the penalties owed for mortal sins not yet sufficiently expiated. Teaching about purgatory attained doctrinal status at the Second Council of Lyons (1274), a council that unsuccessfully tried to reunite Greeks and Latins. Purgatory was one of the points of dispute between Greek and Latin Christians at the time. A profession of faith, which had been composed before the council, was read at the council, though it was neither discussed nor accepted by the Greeks as a basis for doctrinal agreement. In the section on eschatology, the profession described those who die in charity before having satisfied by penance for their sins as "cleansed after death by purgatorial and purifying penalties." It proceeds to affirm that to alleviate such penalties, acts of intercession (*suffragia*) by the living benefit the deceased. It specifies these suffrages as sacrifices of the Mass, prayers, alms, and other works of piety.[99]

LeGoff explains that medieval thinkers conceived of purgatory as an intermediate place, a place of passage, and a place of testing.[100] As an intermediate place, it could be situated closer to heaven or closer to hell. In his *Purgatorio* (completed in 1319), Dante envisioned purgatory as a huge mountain reaching from earth to the heavens. Those being purified must ascend the mountain by hard and dark roads. But the road becomes easier nearer the summit, which leads out to the terrestrial paradise, the last stage before mounting to the stars. While an intermediate place, purgatory is on side of light because those making the ascent are already the elect. Purgatory is also a place of passage—a transitory place. Those in purgatory are pilgrims, though they are being led rather than commanding the way. And purgatory is a place of tests, often depicted as testing by extreme heat or cold. There are many kinds of testing by fire, and here the scriptural foundation is once again 1 Corinthians 3. Other tests involve ordeals involving ice cold.

LeGoff points out that purgatory made more headway among the laity than it did with theologians and the clergy.[101] For one thing, purgatory provided "a definition of the bonds between the living and the dead and of the way these could be turned to account in suffrages."[102] Stories of apparitions were written, in which a soul in purgatory asks a person to whom they were related in life to offer suffrages for them. LeGoff also asserts that purgatory extended the possibility of pardon into the other world. On this last point John Thiel argues that in medieval Christianity there was a competitive spirituality within a hierarchy of discipleship. Laypeople were in competition with ascetics (mainly monks). Thiel thinks that purgatory "lengthened the layperson's temporal field of competition with the ascetic."[103] It allowed the laity to extend the time for judgment upon one's life into a temporal realm beyond death. Moreover, in stories depicting purgatory monks, priests and bishops were imagined as suffering the pains of purgatory (often more severe pains) alongside laypersons. Thiel comments, "The more rigorous the ascetical vows, the more intense the purgatorial punishment, an imaginative depiction of the 'third place' that strictly inverts the earthly hierarchy of discipleship and narrows the judgmental distance between ascetics and lay persons."[104]

THOMAS AQUINAS

I conclude this chapter with a brief discussion of the thought of one medieval theologian, Thomas Aquinas. This treatment will necessarily be very selective, as there is not space to address all the concepts and principles that pertain to eschatology in his vast work. Indeed, as Jeannine Hill Fletcher observes, Aquinas's vision of history (especially in his *Summa Theologiae*) perceives a procession of all creatures from God and the return of all to God. So in some sense his entire theology is eschatological in nature.[105] I will simply touch on some key ideas that influenced Christian eschatology in the centuries following Aquinas.[106]

As we saw in chapter 1, Aquinas treats the theological virtue of hope in his *Summa Theologiae*. He argues that the unlimited good for which we hope is life eternal, which is the possession of God's very self.[107] God is not only the ultimate end that is sought, God is also the primary source for attaining it; thus, the vision of God is made possible by God's grace. Aquinas insists that hope is entirely dependent on faith, since we could not hope if that for which we hope did not appear possible. Near the end of his discussion of hope in the *Summa Theologiae*, Aquinas observes that hope puts its trust in God's mercy and omnipotence. He is convinced that for anyone having faith, God's omnipotence and mercy are certainties.[108]

Aquinas, of course, strongly affirms the resurrection of Christ, and he thinks of it as both the model and the cause of our own resurrection.[109] Paul's description of Christ being raised from the dead as the firstfruits of those who have fallen asleep (1 Cor 15:20) reflects the notion of Christ's resurrection as the model or pattern of our own. Aquinas says, "We see in his exaltation, what is proposed to us to hope for through him."[110] The resurrection of Christ is also a true instrumental cause of both our spiritual and corporeal resurrections. Aquinas thinks that Christ's resurrection "was something under his own control and, as a consequence, something able to bring about for others what it constituted in reality itself."[111] Borrowing from John Damascene (ca. 675–ca. 749), Aquinas uses the category of *instrumental causality* to describe the way in which the humanity of Christ and his human actions have real effects because of the power of Christ's divinity working through them. As a living, active instrument of the Word/Son, Christ's humanity has a true salvific function. Thus, Jesus's resurrection from the dead is an instrumental cause of our bodily resurrection at the end of time and our spiritual resurrection in the here and now, that is, the justification and newness of life that are given us through Christ. Aquinas says, "Therefore, just as all the other things which Christ in his humanity accomplished or suffered for us are saving acts through the power of his divinity, so too is his resurrection the efficient cause of ours through the same divine power whose proper effect is to raise the dead to life."[112]Aquinas proceeds to argue that the presence of the risen humanity of Jesus in heaven has enduring salvific significance. About the risen Christ he says, "The presence of his human nature in heaven is itself an intercession for us, for God, who exalted the human nature of Christ, will also show mercy towards those for whose sake this nature was assumed."[113]

Aquinas conceives of the human person as a unity of soul and body. The soul is the substantial form of the body (*anima forma corporis*). As such, the soul is "the fundamental organizing principle of the body as well as its principle of life."[114] The soul for Thomas is the seat of human understanding and will. At death, the separation of the soul and body, the soul continues to exist as subsistent. It exists with God in the fullness of life, as being purified, or suffering from eternal loss. At the same time, Aquinas does not think that the soul separated from the body is the person. In his commentary on the First Letter to the Corinthians, he famously says that "my soul is not I."[115] In the *Summa Theologiae*, he argues that "the human soul, remaining in its existence after separation from the body, has a natural aptitude and a natural tendency to embodiment."[116] It is in this context that Aquinas turns to the Christian belief in the resurrection of the body. The reunion of the soul and the resurrected body will constitute the person. And for Aquinas, even for the soul blessed with the vision of God, happiness will grow when the body is reassumed. Aquinas argues, too, that there must be a material continuity between the earthly body and the resurrected body. He says that at the resurrection the soul "must be reunited to numerically the same matter."[117] He does not know how this will happen; he attributes its possibility to the knowledge and power of God.

Aquinas stopped work on the *Summa Theologiae* before he considered other eschatological topics. A group of his disciples, led by Reginald of Piperno, added a *Supplement* to the *Summa Theologiae* based mostly on his earlier writings, especially his commentary on Peter Lombard's *Sentences*. Topics in eschatology are addressed in the questions at the end of the *Supplement*. He also addresses eschatological matters in the final part of his *Summa Contra Gentiles*, thought to have been written between 1259 and 1265, before the *Summa Theologiae*. Aquinas maintains that at death the souls of the saints go immediately to heaven and the souls of the damned are immediately consigned to hell.[118] He acknowledges a limbo for children who die without remission of original sin, but he says that the only punishment they experience is the delay of glory.[119]

These questions also contain Aquinas's reflections on purgatory, though LeGoff asserts that he dealt with purgatory only because it was obligatory and not because the issue was for Aquinas a crucial one.[120] Aquinas appealed to divine justice in considering the rationale for purgatory, arguing that if the debt of punishment for sin is not paid after forgiveness in one's earthly life, or if venial sin remains, then justice demands that sin be set in order through punishment after this life. In the *Summa Contra Gentiles*, he asserts that "if the souls of the good have something capable of purgation in this world, they are held back from the achievement of their reward while they undergo cleansing punishments."[121] In his treatment of suffrages, Aquinas offers some compelling reflections on the union between the living and the dead: "Charity, which is the bond uniting the members of the church, extends not only to the living, but also to the dead who die in charity. For charity which is the life of the soul, even as the soul is the life of the body, has no end."[122]

Aquinas also takes up the question of the transformation of the world in the end time, a question addressed by many contemporary theologians.[123] He affirms that the world will be renewed. He supports his argument by saying that the dwelling should befit the dweller. Since human beings will be renewed in the resurrection it is fitting that the world be renewed as well.[124] This transformation of the world will mean that the heavenly bodies will shine more brightly, and the earth and its elements will also be endowed with brightness. Nevertheless, as Elizabeth Johnson points out, for Aquinas this transformation of the world does not include the *whole* world.[125] In the final article of this question, Aquinas asks whether plants and animals will be included in this renewal. He answers in the negative, supporting his argument in a couple of different ways. He asserts that the world was made for human beings. Plants and animals served human beings in two respects: for human sustenance and by helping humans to know God, since the Creator is known by his creatures. In the glorified world, these two services will not be needed. Human beings will be incorruptible and thus not need to eat, and God will be known directly through the beatific vision. As an additional argument for his position, Aquinas asserts that there is nothing incorruptible in plants and animals that makes them capable of eschatological transformation. For Aquinas, the heavenly bodies are incorruptible by their very nature, the elements as a whole are incorruptible, and human beings have a rational soul, which remains incorruptible after death. Plants and animals, however, have not been endowed with anything incorruptible as to their matter or their form.[126] Commenting on Aquinas's argument, Johnson says, "The relish with which Aquinas engaged the new science and natural philosophy of his day gives good reason to expect that he would shift his position on this question in light of the evolutionary knowledge of a later age."[127]

5

FROM THE HIGH MIDDLE AGES TO THE TWENTY-FIRST CENTURY

We now turn to explore selected themes and moments in the history of Christian eschatology from the fourteenth century to the present. We will see that many of the developments in the theology of the "last things" were occasioned by controversy—debates within the Catholic church and disputes between Catholics and the Protestant Reformers. The dialogue about Christian eschatology between Catholic and Protestant thinkers has continued in the twentieth and twenty-first centuries. From the Catholic side, the work of Karl Rahner has been particularly influential for those who build on his hermeneutical principles of eschatology as well as for those who criticize them. And the growth and development of liberation theology throughout the world has had significant implications for the ways in which Christian thinkers conceive of final fulfillment in God.

THE INTERMEDIATE STATE AND POPE JOHN XXII

Christian belief in the resurrection of the dead on the last day has given rise to questions about the condition of the departed between the time of death and the final fulfillment of all things. In the last chapter, we saw that Aquinas taught that the souls of the saints go immediately to heaven while the souls of the damned are immediately plunged into hell. We also took note, however, that for Aquinas the soul is the form of the body, so there is an incompleteness that marks the soul until it is reunited with the body. Thus, there is something provisional about the state of the dead before resurrection, that is, the intermediate state.

Jared Wicks gives a detailed account of the opinions about the intermediate state expressed by major theologians of the early church and Middle Ages.[1] These thinkers described the condition of souls in the intermediate state in a variety of ways. The fourth-century Syriac theologians Aphrahat and Ephrem "spoke of rewards and punishments beginning only with the resurrection, before which departed souls sleep in Sheol, where they sense only faintly the fate to be theirs after the resurrection and their judgment by Christ."[2] Augustine, in *The City of God*, taught that the separated souls of the saints are in peace, while those of the wicked are in pain and will be so until the resurrection of their bodies.[3] In his influential *Dialogues*, Gregory the Great affirmed that the souls of "the perfectly just" are received into the kingdom of heaven as soon as they leave the body.[4] In the twelfth century, Hugh of St. Victor and Peter Lombard taught that the souls of the dead, before the general resurrection, "exist in interim states of fiery punishment or heavenly reward."[5]

An exception to this general trend is found in the writings of the Cistercian abbot Bernard of Clairvaux (d. 1153). He cited the biblical passage from Revelation 6:9, in which the visionary sees the souls of the martyrs ("those who had been slaughtered because of the witness they bore to the word of God") underneath the altar. These souls cry out in longing for the avenging of their blood. Bernard claims that before Christ souls had no access to the heavenly kingdom. The saints were held in places of rest and consolation. At his death, Christ descended to lead the saints from their place of rest to an abode under God's altar until the full number of their sisters and brothers reach completion. Bernard interprets "God's altar" to refer to Christ's risen body, "in which the saints rest happily in union with the one whom, however, they know only in his servant form."[6] It is only at the resurrection of the dead and the final judgment that the holy ones will come to know the Lord in his divine form, as he leads them to encounter the triune God.

From his survey of twelfth- and thirteenth-century authors Wicks concludes that the leading university theologians "agreed in teaching that departed souls, before being reunited with their bodies, pass through the particular judgment into the final states."[7] These states are the punishment of hell for sinners and the happiness of heaven for the justified. At the same time, Wicks notes that the monastic tradition, as found especially in the sermons of Bernard, emphasized the corporate dimension of salvation, with souls resting until the number of the justified is complete. "Bernard's intermediate state would last until the communion of the saints reached completion and so pass to the vision of God and Christ in the communal definitive perfection of human beings."[8]

Beginning on All Saints Day in 1331, in Avignon, France (where the papacy was then located), Pope John XXII preached a series of sermons that elicited intense reaction and debate. Drawing on the sermons of Bernard and certain biblical texts, he asserted that, until the final judgment, the reward of the saints is to be "under the altar" (Rev 6:9) in a place of protection, rest, and consolation given by the humanity of Christ.[9] Only with the resurrection of their bodies on the last day, along with all who form the Body of Christ, will they contemplate the divinity of Christ, along with the Father and the Holy Spirit. John XXII thought that because the separated soul is imperfect until it informs the body, it cannot receive perfect joy in contemplating the divine. The pope said in these sermons that he was open to correction by anyone who might know the matter better. On December 3, 1334, the day before his death, John XXII made a notarized retraction of what he had said in his sermons about a delay in the vision of God until the final judgment.

Benedict XII, the successor to John XXII, convened a group of theologians to study this issue in the summer of 1335. In January 1336, he issued the constitution *Benedictus Deus*, an authoritative statement that was meant to put an end to the debates that had been stirred up by the teaching of John XXII. The constitution teaches that the souls of the blessed "immediately (*mox*) after death and, in the case of those in need of purification, after the purification mentioned above, since the ascension of our Lord and Savior Jesus Christ into heaven, already before they take up their bodies again and before the general judgment, have been, are and will be with Christ in heaven."[10] These souls "see the divine essence with an intuitive vision and even face to face."[11] The vision of God does away with the acts of faith and hope in these souls. The constitution proceeds to assert that those who die in actual mortal sin (it does not say that anyone has died in actual mortal sin) go down to hell immediately (*mox*) after death and there suffer the pain of hell. It teaches that on the day of judgment all will appear with their bodies before the judgment seat of Christ to give an account of their personal deeds.[12]

Commenting on *Benedictus Deus*, Joseph Ratzinger says that the ascension of Jesus "signifies that now, after Christ, there is no longer a closed heaven. Christ is in heaven: that is, God has opened himself to man [*sic*], and man, when he passes through the gate of death as one justified, as someone who belongs to Christ and has been received by him, enters into the openness of God."[13] At the same time, the constitution indicates that there is something provisional about the state of the separated soul inasmuch as reunification with the body and final judgment are still to come. Medard Kehl interprets this teaching of Benedict XII as "a dogmatically decisive moment."[14] But he criticizes the constitution for simply tacking on a reference to the resurrection at the end, without integrating it with its definition of beatitude or loss for souls before the last day.[15] In chapter 6 we will see that debate about the intermediate state continues in contemporary theology.

FLORENCE-FERRARA AND TRENT ON PURGATORY

Both the Council of Florence-Ferrara (1439) and the Council of Trent (1563) issued brief statements on purgatory.[16] The aim of Florence-Ferrara was to reunite the Orthodox and the Catholic Churches, though the reunion was short-lived. The Orthodox had the practice of offering alms, good works, and prayers (especially the Eucharist) for the dead. In comparison with the Western view of purgatory, their concept of purification after death was more mystical in nature, viewing it as a process of spiritual growth and maturation. "They had no teaching of purgatory as a place or a distinct state and were deeply suspicious of the image of purifying fire, which for them was associated with Origen's teaching of a fire that would ultimately purify and redeem all humanity and even the devil."[17]

They also held that the beatific vision would begin only after the general resurrection. The council sought to meet the concerns of the Orthodox in the section on Christian eschatology contained in its *Decree for the Greeks*. The decree omits references to fire and to purgatory as a place. It affirms that the souls of truly penitent people "are cleansed after death by purgatorial penalties (*poenis purgatoriis*)." These souls are helped by the acts of intercession (suffrages) of the living faithful—the sacrifice of the Mass, prayers, alms, and other works of piety.[18] It affirms that the souls of baptized dead that have no stain of sin and those that have been cleansed of sin "are received immediately (*mox*) into heaven, and see clearly God himself, one and three, as he is, though some more perfectly than others, according to the diversity of merits."[19] In this last phrase, the council added the notion of varying degrees of intensity of the vision of God, depending on the merits of the deceased.

At the Council of Trent, explicit discussion of purgatory was postponed until the council's last session, in 1563. Its teaching in the *Decree on Purgatory* is usually interpreted as more disciplinary than doctrinal in nature. The decree simply states that there is a purgatory (*purgatorium*) and that the souls detained there are helped by the acts of intercession (suffrages) of the faithful, "especially by the acceptable sacrifice of the altar."[20] It exhorts bishops to avoid the more subtle questions about purgatory in popular sermons and to forbid "those things that belong to the realm of curiosity or superstition, or smack of dishonorable gain."[21] The *Profession of Faith of the Council of Trent* includes the statement, "I steadfastly hold that a purgatory exists, and that the souls there detained are aided by the prayers of the faithful."[22] These two councils, then, issued quite limited statements about purgatory, affirming its existence (or, for Florence, affirming the existence of a purgatorial cleansing) and affirming the benefits for the deceased of acts of intercession by the living. The councils avoided allusion to imaginative representations of purgatory and speculations about the duration of the process for those undergoing it.

LUTHER AND CALVIN

When the Augustinian priest Martin Luther (1483–1546) posted his Ninety-Five Theses on the castle church door in Wittenberg in

1517, he was initially protesting church practices that he believed were abuses. These abuses particularly involved the selling of indulgences—promises of the remission of the temporal punishment due to sin (already forgiven) in this life and the next by applying to souls the abundance of the merits of Christ and the saints. The official title of the document popularly known as the Ninety-Five Theses was the Disputation on the Power and Efficacy of Indulgences. The practice of purchasing indulgences to free souls from purgatory had become widespread. In Thesis 27, Luther wrote, "There is no divine authority for preaching that the soul flies out of purgatory immediately the money clinks in the bottom of the chest.[23] While initially focused on abuses in this practice, the critiques advanced by Luther, John Calvin (1509–1564), and other Reformers soon addressed more fundamental practices and beliefs related to eschatology.

Luther did not have a clear teaching about the intermediate state between death and resurrection.[24] He sometimes employed the metaphor of "sleep"—the sleep of the soul until it is awakened by Christ on the Last Day. In one writing, he states, "We shall sleep until he comes and knocks on the tomb and says, 'Dr. Martin, get up'. Then in one moment, I will get up and I will rejoice with him in eternity."[25] But, as Schwarz points out, Luther admitted that we do not know very much about the state of the soul between death and resurrection. It may be that those who will be rejected will already suffer in this intermediate state, while the just will have the foretaste of the eternal joy for which they are waiting. But the Bible is not clear about this matter.[26] And the Lutheran confessional statements did not address this question of the way that the soul survives in the intermediate state.

Luther did not initially reject the doctrine of purgatory. His opponents correctly pointed out that for years after the controversy on indulgences, he did not deny its existence. But in 1530 Luther published his *Disavowal of Purgatory*.[27] And in the Smalcald Articles of 1537, which addressed the Mass as sacrifice, Luther wrote, "Consequently purgatory and all the pomp, services, and business transactions associated with it are to be regarded as nothing else than illusions of the devil, for purgatory, too, is contrary to the fundamental article that Christ alone, and not the work of a man [*sic*], can help souls. Besides, nothing has been commanded or enjoined upon us with reference to the dead."[28]

Luther and other Reformers found the reference to the biblical passages cited as the foundation of the doctrine of purgatory to be unconvincing. The passage from Second Maccabees 12 about the soldiers of Judas Maccabeus was not accepted as canonical Scripture by Luther. He also rejected the citation of Matthew 12 and 1 Corinthians 3 as biblical warrants for the teaching on purgatory. More fundamentally, Luther repudiated the notion of making satisfaction for sins already forgiven, as well as the practices associated with such satisfaction. Lutheran confessional statements asserted that the proclamation of free forgiveness in Christ is obscured by an emphasis on satisfactions still owed after forgiveness.[29] Lutherans believed that the idea of making satisfaction after death ran contrary to the foundational Reformation teaching about justification by grace through faith on account of Christ. It undercut belief in the sufficiency of the satisfaction made by Christ in his death and resurrection and thus obscured the Gospel. Luther and Lutheran confessional statements, especially the Apology for the *Augsburg Confession*, do acknowledge a process of transformation that follows the forgiveness of sin. This process is one conceived in the model of ongoing death and resurrection.[30] The Apology says that "regeneration itself occurs through a continuous mortification of our old nature."[31] These statements assume that the process of purgation of the old self is completed at the death of the body. "God works the transformation of the self into sinless heavenly glory through death as a moment in death-and-resurrection-in-Christ."[32] This transformation is effected by the gracious action of God, not through satisfaction made by human beings.

These foundational convictions influenced the way that Luther and his followers approached the practice of prayer for the dead. In his "Confession Concerning Christ's Supper," Luther said, "As for the dead, since Scripture gives us no information on the subject, I regard it as no sin to pray with free devotion in this or some similar fashion: 'Dear God, if this soul is in a condition accessible to mercy be thou gracious to it.' And when this has been done once or twice, let it suffice."[33] Luther immediately added, however, that "vigils and requiem Masses and yearly celebrations of requiems are useless and are merely the devil's annual fair."[34] In Article 24 of the Apology for the *Augsburg Confession*, there is a reference to the usefulness of such prayer without precisely defining the way in which such prayer aids the dead. This cautious approach to prayer for the dead was accompanied by rejection of the system of purgatory, Masses for the dead, and indulgences applied to the dead. "While prayer for the dead is not prohibited, the worry is evident that such prayers will be seen not as expressions of faithful dependence on God grace, but as meritorious works, the benefit from which can be applied, in an impersonal, juridical fashion, to the dead."[35] Moreover, Luther and his followers feared that extensive, repeated prayer for the dead might represent a lack of confidence in the sufficiency of Christ's saving work. In a letter to a man whose wife had died, Luther advises him to pray for his wife "once or twice," for extended prayer "is a sign that we do not believe in God and with our faithless prayers we only anger him more."[36] Luther also noted that if the existence of purgatory is denied and definitive judgment happens at death, there seems to be little reason to think that the deceased can be aided by the prayers of the living. These cautions and critiques eventually meant that "prayer for the dead mostly disappeared from Lutheran worship and piety."[37]

The most explicit doctrinal statement on eschatology of the Lutheran Reformers is found in Article 27 of the *Augsburg Confession*, composed by Philip Melanchthon, an associate of Luther. It affirms that Christ "will return on the last day for judgment and will raise up all the dead, to give eternal life and everlasting joy to believers and the elect but to condemn ungodly men [*sic*] and the devil to hell and eternal punishment."[38] The text proceeds to reject "the Anabaptists" who teach that the devil and condemned human beings will not suffer eternal pain and torment. Luther considered hell to be a real possibility for unrepentant sinners.[39] The Confession also rejects "certain Jewish opinions" which envision a worldly kingdom of the saints and godly people before the resurrection of the dead. This represents Luther's categorical rejection of millenarian scenarios.[40] It was a "condemnation focused on opposing groups that believed that the end of the world was at hand and that the true saints were now to take control of the world by force and eliminate all evil."[41]

John Calvin also strongly rejected the doctrine of purgatory. Writing from the Reformed tradition, Jürgen Moltmann observes that in the doctrine of purgatory Calvin and the other Protestant Reformers perceived a righteousness of works projected beyond death.[42] In the 1559 edition of his magisterial work, *Institutes of the Christian Religion*, Calvin gives a lengthy and spirited refutation of this doctrine:

> We are bound, therefore, to raise our voice to its highest pitch, and cry aloud that purgatory is a deadly device of

> Satan; that it makes void the cross of Christ; that it offers intolerable insult to the divine mercy; that it undermines and overthrows our faith. For what is purgatory but the satisfaction for sin paid after death by the souls of the dead? Hence when this idea of satisfaction is refuted, purgatory itself is forthwith overturned. But if it is perfectly clear, from what was lately said, that the blood of Christ is the only satisfaction, expiation, and cleansing for the sins of believers, what remains but to hold that purgatory is mere blasphemy, horrid blasphemy against Christ? I say nothing of the sacrilege by which it is daily defended, the offences which it begets in religion, and the other innumerable evils which we see teeming forth from that fountain of impiety.[43]

Though it is usually discussed in the theology of grace, the topic of predestination is also integral to eschatology. Calvin, influenced especially by the later writings of Augustine, developed a robust theology of predestination. Jaroslav Pelikan observes that in each subsequent edition of Calvin's *Institutes* (between 1536 and 1559), "the amount of space devoted to predestination increased, as did the consideration specifically addressed to the problem of the 'reprobate,' those whom God had predestined to damnation."[44] The foundational element in Calvin's theology of predestination is the sovereignty of God's will, which is the cause of all things that are. He argues that the will of God "is the supreme rule of righteousness, so that everything he wills must be held to be righteous by the mere fact of his willing it."[45] God, does not disclose to us the reasons for God's willing of things, and human beings should not inquire into them. Calvin maintains that if those who will be saved (the elect) are saved by the will of God, then those who will be eternally lost must be condemned by the will of God. He writes, "Those, therefore, whom God passes by he reprobates, and that for no other cause but because he is pleased to exclude them from the inheritance which he predestines to his children."[46] Pelikan points out that what set apart Calvin's teaching about predestination from that of other theologians was "the candid acknowledgment that 'reprobation' could not be merely the absence of a positive election to salvation, but must itself be a positive act of the divine will predestinating to damnation."[47] Neither election nor reprobation was based upon God's foreknowledge of human conduct; each was simply the result of the eternal will of God.

TWENTIETH-CENTURY DEVELOPMENTS IN PROTESTANT THEOLOGY

In the third chapter, we saw that Jesus made the kingdom (reign) of God the focus of his public ministry. He proclaimed the nearness of God's reign in word—especially through his parables—in his table fellowship, and through his deeds of healing and exorcism. We also noted the inherent tension between the present and the future dimensions of the kingdom as proclaimed by Jesus. Jesus taught his disciples to pray for the coming of the kingdom, yet the Gospels also depict him as making the kingdom present in the lives of people through his powerful words and deeds.

In the late nineteenth and early twentieth centuries, some prominent Protestant biblical scholars reclaimed the dominance of the gospel motif of the kingdom of God while also debating its meaning and relevance for modern believers.[48] Albrecht Ritschl (1822–1889), in his *Instruction in the Christian Religion*, asserted that the kingdom of God forms "the ethical ideal for whose attainment the members of the community bind themselves to each other through a definite type of reciprocal action."[49] As Hans Schwarz observes, Ritschl's emphasis was on human solidarity and human effort to live according to the ethical ideal of the kingdom.[50]

Johannes Weiss (1863–1914), Ritschl's son-in-law and former student, gave a quite different interpretation of Jesus's proclamation of the kingdom of God. In his *Jesus' Proclamation of the Kingdom of God*, Weiss argued that the kingdom of God was a thoroughly eschatological-apocalyptic idea through which Jesus proclaimed the imminent end of the world. The kingdom of God is otherworldly and only God can bring about its realization. "Humanity can only create the conditions for the kingdom demanded by God."[51] Thus the interpretation of the kingdom of God as an ethical ideal for the Christian community is mistaken. At the same time, Weiss conceded that, for modern believers, the kingdom of God is a concept that can awaken a committed life of discipleship. But when Christians conceive of the kingdom in such a way they need to admit that they are understanding it differently than the way that Jesus understood it. Weiss was convinced that modern Christians do not have the same eschatological worldview as did Jesus.

In his *The Quest of the Historical Jesus*, Albert Schweitzer also interpreted Jesus's proclamation of the kingdom of God as an eschatological-apocalyptic message. He was convinced that the ministry and the ethics of Jesus can be rightly understood only in view of his imminent expectation of the Parousia. His moral teaching is an interim ethics aimed at the preparation of the kingdom of God.[52] When Jesus sends out his disciples to proclaim the kingdom of God, "he does not expect to see them back in the present age."[53] The coming of the Son of Man will take place before they have finished their journey through the cities of Israel to announce it. But the Parousia does not happen and his disciples do return to Jesus. Jesus then becomes convinced that believers will be spared the tribulations of the messianic age because he will take them upon himself. "In the secret of his passion which Jesus reveals to the disciples at Caesarea Philippi the pre-messianic tribulation for others is set aside, abolished, concentrated upon himself alone, and that in the form that they are fulfilled in his own passion and death at Jerusalem."[54] However, the Parousia fails to materialize with the death of Jesus. Schweitzer thinks that, on the basis of the Easter experiences, the disciples developed a new expectation of the imminent end, but this, too, failed to happen. Christianity was then transformed into a religion that was ecclesiastical and sacramental. Schweitzer concludes that while modern Christians cannot adopt Jesus's eschatology, they can be inspired by his courage and his hope for the final moral perfecting of the world.[55]

The Catholic theologian Peter Phan observes that Weiss and Schweitzer compelled theologians to take into account the expectations in early Judaism and in the New Testament of "an imminent irruption of the old order and the establishment of God's reign in the world." Phan notes that the failure of nineteenth-century liberal theology's quest for the historical Jesus "produced one of the most momentous insights for contemporary theology, namely, that apocalypticism and eschatology stood at the center of Jesus' message and ministry and of early Christianity."[56]

The Protestant biblical scholar Rudolf Bultmann (1884–1976) applied his program of demythologizing to the eschatology of the New Testament. Bultmann concluded that Jesus and the New Testament writers believed that the end of history had come and that the end of the world was near.[57] But the Parousia did not happen as Jesus and the New Testament authors expected, and history continues to run its course. For Bultmann we cannot discern the meaning of history as a whole or have knowledge of any final end to history. We cannot repeat the eschatology of the New Testament because it is expressed in a mythical framework.[58] He does, however, see in the writings of Paul and John a move toward individualizing the eschaton and focusing on the present experience of salvation. While Paul did not abandon hope for a future coming of Christ, he did conceive of hope in terms of the individual who is given righteousness and true freedom in Christ. The author of the Gospel of John manifested an even more radical conception of the eschatological event as happening in the present for the individual. The believer has already passed judgment and has already been resurrected from death.[59] Bultmann cites these two New Testament authors in arguing for an existential interpretation of biblical eschatology. Jesus Christ is the eschatological event, the action of God by which God has set an end to the whole world. "In the preaching of the Christian church the eschatological event will ever again become present and does become present ever and again in faith."[60] Encountering Jesus in the word of preaching, one must decide for or against God. One must accept or reject the grace of freedom, by which he or she becomes free from self in order to gain self. The eschatological event is not a dramatic cosmic catastrophe but something that happens for the individual within history. Jesus Christ is the eschatological event as repeatedly present, addressing us in preaching and calling us to decide whether or not we will accept a new life grounded in the grace of God.

Jürgen Moltmann raises some important questions in response to Bultmann's interpretation of eschatology.[61] He notes that to replace world history by the historicity of individual existence does not make world history disappear. "To replace 'the Last Day' by my own death does not provide an answer to the question about the future of those who have died."[62] People ask not only about themselves but also about the future of the world of which they are a part. Moltmann avers, "Christian eschatology teaches hope not only for the soul...but also for the body; not only for the individual but also for the community; not only for the church but also for Israel; not only for human beings but also for the cosmos."[63]

KARL RAHNER ON THE HERMENEUTICS OF ESCHATOLOGICAL STATEMENTS

The German Jesuit theologian Karl Rahner wrote a significant essay on the hermeneutics of eschatological statements that was based on a lecture that he delivered in 1960.[64] He noted that treatment of the hermeneutics, or principles of interpretation, of eschatological statements had for the most part been omitted in Catholic dogmatic theology. Included in such a hermeneutics is consideration of the type of knowledge that is possible in such statements. Rahner proposed seven theses to guide the interpretation of eschatological assertions.

First, he argued that a Christian understanding of the faith must include an eschatology that bears on a future that is still to come. Rahner asserted this principle against the type of demythologizing of eschatology represented by Bultmann, whose interpretation of eschatology severed the link between *chronos*, time in the ordinary sense of a measure of duration, and *kairos*, the moment of critical decision. Rahner stated, "It cannot be doubted that the doctrinal preaching of the Church intends to make assertions about future events which are still to come in time."[65]

In his second thesis, Rahner affirmed that God knows future events and that human beings have the capacity to understand them if God chooses to reveal them. He argued that the positing of principles of interpretation did not entail a restriction on God's freedom to reveal to human beings truths about final fulfillment. He alluded to a "principle of open-mindedness" which means that "man [*sic*], as partner of the living God who can reveal himself, may not restrict beforehand the scope of God's possible word."[66]

Having affirmed that God can reveal truths about the eschaton to human beings, Rahner proceeds in his third thesis to acknowledge that God has not revealed the day of the end. This does not simply mean that we do not know the *date* of the end; it also points to the truth that the end has for us a character of hiddenness that is essential and proper to it. Here Rahner argues that if faith and hope are to exist, they demand that the future be essentially concealed. The revelation of the eschaton manifests that it is a mystery. In Rahner's words, "More than ever, revelation is not the bringing of what was once unknown into the region of what is known, perspicuous and manageable: it is the dawn and the approach of mystery as such."[67] This means for Rahner that whenever we encounter eschatological statements that present themselves as a report by a spectator of a future event, then what Rahner calls a "false apocalyptic" is at work. From the vantage point of Christian theology, such a "report" is different from a genuine eschatological statement. As a second element in his third thesis, Rahner affirms that the past and the future always bear on the present in human life. "Man [*sic*] possesses himself, disposes of himself, understands himself, in and by the anamnesis by which he retains his past and the prognosis by which he lays hold of what is to come."[68] With regard to eschatology, this means that knowledge of the future is an inner moment of a person's self-understanding in the present.

Following upon these observations, in his fourth thesis Rahner declares that what we know of the future, including the eschatological future, is knowledge of the futurity of the present. Thus, "eschatological knowledge is knowledge of the eschatological present."[69] This means that eschatological knowledge has the character of hiddenness. The mysterious character of the future relates to human freedom, which entails risk and abandoning oneself to the uncontrollable. What Christians know in faith about the eschaton is an extrapolation of the experience of the salvific self-communication of God that has been definitively given in Jesus Christ. Eschatology is a forward look from the experience of the grace of Christ. Rahner avers, "All that can really be said about the future is that it can and must be the fulfillment of the whole man [*sic*] by the incomprehensible God, in the salvation hidden in Christ which is already given us."[70]

The fifth thesis follows closely from the fourth. Rahner again states that Christians know of their future in as much as they know of themselves and their redemption in Christ through God's self-revelation. He contends that Christian eschatology must avoid the two extremes of a false apocalyptic, which entails reading eschatological texts as anticipatory reports of what will happen at the end of time, and a totally existential, demythologizing interpretation of statements about the eschaton, which denies the real, still-to-come events of the future.[71] Here he makes a sharp distinction between "eschatology" and "apocalyptic." In his words, "To extrapolate from the present into the future fulfillment of salvation is eschatology; to interpolate from the future into the present is apocalyptic." He argues that the former is true Christian eschatology; the latter—apocalyptic—is "either phantasy or gnosticism."[72]

Rahner's sixth thesis includes some implications of what he has expressed thus far. First, since eschatology is based on the experience of God's victorious grace in Christ, statements about salvation and statements about damnation are not on the same plane. Statements about salvation affirm a factual reality, while statements about damnation refer to a real possibility. Each individual must reckon with the possibility of eternal loss for himself or herself. Thus Christians cannot definitively declare that all will be saved , though they can hope for universal salvation. Neither can Christians hold that particular individuals have been damned. Second, Rahner affirms that there is an inherent duality in eschatological statements. They refer to the whole person, who is a unity of body (corporeality) and soul (spirit-person). And they entail statements about the fulfillment of the person as an individual and as a member of the human family. Third, if Christian eschatology involves an extrapolation of the present salvation into a future fulfillment that is hidden, there is no contradiction between an imminent and a distant expectation of the Parousia. Eschatological assertions must be actualized by the person in the present, but they must also be a distant expectation since they refer to the incalculable future. Fourth, the principle that eschatological statements are a forward look from the present experience of the salvific grace of Christ means that "*Christ* himself is the hermeneutic principle of all eschatological assertions."[73] Anything that cannot be understood as a christological statement cannot be understood as a genuine eschatological assertion. Fifth, Rahner argues that Christology determines not only the hermeneutics of eschatology but also the content of eschatology. He describes this content in these words:

> We can say that time will have an end, that towards the end the antagonism between Christ and the world grows fiercer, that history as a whole ends with the final victory of God in his grace, that the consummation of the world, in so far as it is the incalculable act of God's freedom, is called God's judgment, in so far as it is the fulfillment of salvation already real, victorious and definitive in Christ, is called the return and the judgment of Christ. In so far as it is the fulfillment of the individual, who cannot be wholly

> absorbed and lost in his function as moment of the world, it is called the particular judgment. In so far as the world is not just the sum of its individuals, it is called the general judgment. In so far as it is the fulfillment of the resurrection of Christ, it is called the resurrection of the flesh and the transfiguration of the world.[74]

In his seventh thesis, Rahner distinguishes between the form and content of statements about the eschaton. With Thomas Aquinas, he affirms that we always think and speak in images and that there is no concept without imagination. So there can be no hard and fast line drawn between content and image. But expressions of Christian belief in the eschaton can and should be given in images appropriate to each age. As he puts it, "The thing intended will be conceivable under a new form of expression, though formulated once more in a new type of imagery."[75]

Rahner's essay has been very influential for Catholic eschatology, but it has also been the object of some critique. His sharp distinction between eschatology and apocalyptic has been criticized for failing to recognize that (as we saw in our discussion of biblical eschatology) apocalyptic is one expression of eschatology.[76] In his later work *Foundations of Christian Faith*, it appears that Rahner moderates his assessment of apocalyptic, which he says "can be understood as a mode of expression in which man [*sic*] really takes the concreteness of his eschatological future seriously, and does not forget the fact that his final and definitive future really arises out of his present life, both individual and social, and that this future is the final and definitive validity of his free actions." He then proceeds to affirm that because we always speak in images and likenesses, "we cannot expect that there has to be a very sharp difference in their modes of expression between apocalyptic and the eschatology which Christianity really means."[77]

VATICAN II AND ESCHATOLOGY

In the neo-Scholastic manuals of theology that were used prior to the Second Vatican Council, treatment of the last things was reserved to the conclusion of dogmatic theology. Eschatology was not well integrated into the presentation of Catholic theology as a whole. About this approach to eschatology, Peter Phan observes, "An unintended but unfortunate result is that eschatology became a harmless appendix to the theological curriculum, as Karl Barth has wryly remarked, to satisfy human curiosity about the mysteries of the beyond, with little or no impact on how Christian faith is understood as a whole."[78] In addition, the focus of this eschatology was the destiny of the individual, with minimal attention given to the corporate and cosmic dimensions of Christian belief about the eschaton.

The Second Vatican Council took a different approach. It integrated eschatology into its teaching about the church, especially in its Dogmatic Constitution on the Church (*Lumen Gentium*). This eschatological vision is found in a focused way in chapter 7 of *Lumen Gentium*, which treats of the pilgrim church. It is also present in the Pastoral Constitution on the Church in the Modern World (*Gaudium et Spes*), where the themes of death and the eschatological consummation of the world are discussed. Tracing the history of the drafts of the conciliar documents, Carl Peter shows that the discussions of the texts eventually led the bishops "to put more stress on the collective, ecclesial, and cosmic dimensions of the future without omitting its individual, ascetical, and spiritual aspects."[79]

While Vatican II did not provide a systematic eschatology, it did succeed in locating it at the heart of Catholic theology. The chapter on the pilgrim church begins by acknowledging that the church will receive its true fulfillment only at the end of the ages:

> The Church, to which we are all called in Christ Jesus, and in which by the grace of God we acquire holiness, will receive its perfection only in the glory of heaven, when will come the time of the renewal of all things. At that time, together with the human race, the universe itself, which is so closely related to man [*sic*] and which attains its destiny through him, will be perfectly reestablished in Christ. (cf. Eph 1:10; Col. 1:20; 2 Pet 3:10–13) (LG 48)

Employing the "already/not yet" framework common in Christian eschatology, *Lumen Gentium* declares that this final renewal has already begun in Jesus Christ and continues through the Holy Spirit in the church:

> The promised and hoped for restoration, therefore, has already begun in Christ. It is carried forward in the sending of the Holy Spirit and through him continues in the church in which, through our faith, we learn the meaning of our earthly life, while we bring to term, with hope of future good, the task allotted to us in the world by the Father, and so work out our salvation (cf. Phil 2:12). (LG 48)

The church, then, is a church that is on its way to fulfillment; it is itself a pilgrim church that awaits the final revelation of God at the end of time. It is a "groaning" church:

> Already the final age of the world is with us (cf. 1 Cor 10:11) and the renewal of the world is irrevocably under way; it is even now anticipated in a certain real way, for the church on earth is endowed already with a sanctity that is real though imperfect. However, until there be realized new heavens and a new earth in which justice dwells (cf. 2 Pet 3:13) the pilgrim church, in its sacraments and institutions, which belong to this present age, carries the mark of this world which will pass, and she herself takes her place among the creatures which groan and travail yet and await the revelation of the sons [and daughters] of God (cf. Rom 8:19–23). (LG 48)

The constitution proceeds to accentuate the solidarity that exists among the living and the deceased members of the church. Here Vatican II offers a compelling account of the Christian belief in the communion of saints. The council points to the existence of three groups of disciples of the Lord: pilgrims on earth; those who have died and are being purified; and others who are "in glory," contemplating God, who is triune and one (LG 49). There is communion among the members of all these groups of believers:

> All of us, however, in varying degrees and in different ways share in the same charity towards God and our neighbors, and we all sing the one hymn of glory to our God. All, indeed, who are of Christ cleave together (Eph 4:16). So it is that the union of the wayfarers with the brethren who sleep in the peace of Christ is in no way

> interrupted, but on the contrary, this union is reinforced by an exchange of spiritual goods. (LG 49)

This chapter of *Lumen Gentium* reaffirms the practices of prayer for the dead and veneration of the saints. It quotes the text from the story of Judas Maccabeus and his soldiers, who prayed for their slain comrades who had been found with pagan amulets (2 Macc 12). Carl Peter points out that this biblical passage is not presented as a proof text for church's practice of offering suffrages for the dead. It was included to show the relation of the church to those in purgatory and to affirm that the prayers of the living help those who are being purified. At the same time, the council denied a request to state that those in purgatory aid the church on earth, because this idea was disputed among theologians.[80]

Lumen Gentium recalls that from the earliest days of the church the community of believers has cherished the memory of holy women and men. Beginning with the veneration of the apostles and martyrs, this devotion was eventually extended to those "whom the outstanding practice of the Christian virtues and the wonderful graces of God recommended to the pious devotion and imitation of the faithful" (LG 50). This veneration included asking for the help of their intercession. These holy ones are not only intercessors but are also our "companions" through whom God shows God's presence and face in a vivid way. Just as communion among living believers brings them closer to Christ, so our communion with Mary and the saints draws us nearer to Christ. Thus, our veneration of the saints does not distance us from Christ; rather it strengthens our relationship with him: "Every authentic witness of love, indeed, offered by us to those in heaven tends to and terminates in Christ, 'the crown of all the saints,' and through him in God, who is wonderful in his saints and glorified in them" (LG 50). The constitution warns against abuses in this devotion, teaching that authentic veneration of the saints "does not consist so much in a multiplicity of external acts, but rather in a more intense practice of our love" (LG 51).

The human experience of death is addressed in the council's most important pastoral document—the Pastoral Constitution on the Church in the Modern World (*Gaudium et Spes* 18). Death is the one reality that most places the human condition in doubt and evokes the dread of forever ceasing to be. The pastoral constitution cites Romans 5:21 in asserting that humanity would have been immune from death if human beings had not sinned—an idea that is disputed by contemporary theologians in view of scientific findings about the evolutionary development of life on earth. The council affirms that within ourselves we bear "the seed of eternity" and thus we rebel against death. While death is a mystery that exceeds human comprehension, Christians are convinced that God has created humanity in view of a destiny that transcends the limits of the human condition on earth. *Gaudium et Spes* then appeals to the victory over death that was won by Christ's death and resurrection. By his death Christ has freed humanity from death. Faith in Christ's overcoming of death offers an answer to our "anxious queries" about our future, and it inspires us to be united in Christ with our loved ones who have died.

Gaudium et Spes also treats the topic of the final consummation of the world (GS 39). The constitution begins by acknowledging the mysterious character of the final consummation of the earth and the entire universe: we know neither the moment of the consummation of the earth and humankind nor the way in which the universe will be transformed. Citing 2 Corinthians 5:2 and 2 Peter 3:13, it declares that God is preparing a new dwelling and a new earth in which righteousness will dwell and human happiness abound. What will endure will be charity and its works. Even though the distinction between earthly progress and increase of the kingdom of Christ must be acknowledged, the expectation of a new earth should not diminish our concern to develop this earth but rather inspire us to improve human society. This theme of the kingdom of God as both gift and demand, treated in *Gaudium et Spes* in a general way, has in recent years been addressed by many liberation theologians, for example, Gustavo Gutiérrez.[81] The council then affirms that in the eschaton all the worthwhile efforts of humanity on earth will be purified, illuminated, and transfigured.

The council also addressed the theme of the eschatological nature of the Eucharist in its Constitution on the Sacred Liturgy (*Sacrosanctum Concilium* 8). In the celebration of the Eucharist the living "take part in that heavenly liturgy which is celebrated in the Holy City of Jerusalem toward which we journey as pilgrims." We join those in heaven in singing a hymn of glory to the Lord, and we venerate the memory of the saints, hoping for some part with them. The celebration of the Eucharist also points us to the coming of Christ in glory, which we eagerly await.

The Second Vatican Council reaffirmed traditional teachings on eschatology such as heaven, hell, purgatory, the return of the risen Christ, the resurrection of all the dead, the particular and universal judgments, and the communion of saints. But it did so in a way that avoided undue speculation. Phan comments on the council's presentation of these themes:

> While rejecting nothing of the core eschatological doctrines, Vatican II avoids giving the impression of providing insider information on the afterlife but rather presents the teachings of the faith in a sober and restrained manner, by using mainly biblical language and images and eschewing graphic and detailed descriptions. More significantly, the council places eschatology in a new context, namely, that of a deep commitment to the transformation of the world and human history, thereby rebutting the Marxist charge that religion, especially Christianity, is the opiate for the masses.[82]

THE BIRTH OF LIBERATION THEOLOGY

The experience and teaching of the Second Vatican Council impelled the movement toward the inculturation of the gospel in Catholic theology and missionary outreach. As Rahner later observed, Vatican II marked the first steps of the church in slowly becoming a world church.[83] Catholic theologians and missionaries came to a deeper realization that in proclaiming the gospel the church had to move beyond "exporting" a Roman, or merely European, "product." It had to enable the gospel to take root in the rich variety of cultures of the world. Vatican II also catalyzed new thinking about the relationship between the church and the world. The documents of the council spoke of the church as the sacrament of salvation of the world (LG 48). As we saw in the discussion of *Gaudium et Spes*, the discussion of the mission of the church included the call to work for the transformation of the world. These and other impulses of the council paved the way for the development of liberation theology, beginning in Latin America and then expanding to many other regions of the world. The work of liberation theologians had implications for eschatology. Recognizing the diversity of liberationist thought, here I will briefly discuss the thought of the Peruvian theologian Gustavo Gutiérrez, whose book *A Theology of Liberation* became a seminal expression of this global stream of Christian theology.

Having studied in Europe, Gutiérrez was ordained a priest in 1959 and returned to teach in Lima at the Pontifical Catholic University. He attended the fourth session of Vatican II as a theological assistant to Bishop Manuel Larrain of Chile. He also became interested in popular movements that were taking place in Latin America in the church and among the poor. These movements included the growth of ecclesial base communities—small communities of Christians who met regularly to reflect together on the word of God and on their own lives of faith. Some of these communities also engaged in analysis of the social situation in which they lived, leading them to explore paths of liberation from oppression through social and political action. The thought of Gutiérrez was also deeply influenced by his participation in the meeting of Latin American bishops at Medellín Colombia in 1968. He served as an official theologian at the conference, drafting two major speeches for Cardinal Juan Landazuri Ricketts, archbishop of Lima.[84] These and other experiences led him to see the need for a distinctive approach to theology in the Latin American context, giving rise to *A Theology of Liberation* and a number of other significant writings.

Liberation theologians devote sustained attention to Jesus's proclamation of the kingdom of God. Gutiérrez's treatment of this eschatological theme is nuanced, reflecting careful consideration in the light of a variety of critiques of liberation theology. Arguing against an exclusively interiorized understanding of the kingdom, he describes it as "something planned by God that occurs at the heart of a history in which human beings live and die and welcome or reject the grace that changes them from within."[85] It is a reign of love and justice that is God's plan for human history. Gutiérrez develops a dialectical understanding of the kingdom: it is both gift and demand. The kingdom that Jesus proclaims is pure gift because it is the result of God's unmerited love for all human beings. It is not manufactured by human beings. At the same time, Jesus's proclamation of the kingdom includes a call to repentance, which means accepting the demands of the reign of God. Gutiérrez emphasizes that nothing makes more demands upon us than the experience of gracious, lavish love. This is precisely what happens in the lives of those who encounter Jesus. "Only when the gratuitousness of this love has been grasped is it possible to understand the imperious demands for works on behalf of the neighbor."[86] Acceptance of the kingdom requires believers to attend to the suffering of the poor. It means "refusing to accept a world that instigates or tolerates the premature and unjust deaths of the poor."[87]

Gutiérrez also insists that the kingdom of God is both universal and preferential. The kingdom of God is universal: no one is excluded from either the gift or the demand of the kingdom. Paul was the preeminent messenger of the universality of God's reign, grounding his proclamation of the gospel to all nations in the resurrection of Christ. The resurrection is "an affirmation and promise of life for all human beings without exception."[88] At the same time, Jesus's proclamation of the reign of God is characterized by preference for the least of this world. Gutiérrez argues that the gospel accounts of Jesus's ministry make it clear that the despised of the world are those whom God prefers. He often quotes the statement from the 1979 meeting of the Latin American bishops at Puebla: "The poor merit preferential treatment, whatever may be the moral or personal situation in which they find themselves."[89]

In a conversation at his doctoral defense in Lyons in 1985, Gutiérrez affirmed the profound importance of Christian belief in the resurrection of Jesus for liberation theology. He said that the theology of liberation "is, in a sense, a theology of life confronted with a reality full of death, physical and cultural death, but also death in the Pauline sense, since sin is also death."[90] Gutiérrez suggested that while the biblical theme of the exodus had been prominent in the early development of liberation theology, there had been an evolution in liberationist thought that was making it "increasingly a theology of life, of resurrection."[91] The resurrection of Jesus is both *confirmation* and *correction* in the theology of Gutiérrez. It is the confirmation of Jesus's mission, through which the Father confirms the gift of life that was offered in Jesus's proclamation of the reign of God. It is also correction, since it is the "death of death."[92] The resurrection of Jesus is the sign of God's liberation breaking into the world; it reveals that God is more powerful than the forces of sin and injustice. Gutiérrez emphasizes that Christians are called to bear witness to the resurrection through their commitment to their sisters and brothers, particularly by their preferential option for the poor. "The God in whom we believe is the God of life. Belief in the resurrection entails defending the life of the weakest members of society....To assert the resurrection of the Lord is to assert life in face of death."[93]

In the liberationist framework, soteriology (theology of salvation) is closely linked to eschatology. This has been a sensitive topic for liberation theology, one to which Gutiérrez has tried to be attentive. He does not want to present a view of the liberating work of Christ as a temporal or political messianism. But neither does he wish to espouse a spiritualized notion of salvation that limits it to an interior state of being or to the gift of eternal life. He insists that salvation history and human history are not two separate spheres of history. "Rather, there is only one human destiny, irreversibly assumed by Christ, the Lord of history."[94] Appealing to the Gospel testimony about the ways in which Jesus made the kingdom of God present in his ministry, Gutiérrez argues that to work to transform the world is a salvific work. To struggle against misery and exploitation and to work to build a more just society is already part of the salvific work of Christ that is moving toward its complete fulfillment. While the liberating work of Christ transcends anything that human beings can accomplish, actions on behalf of justice are integral to this liberation. He articulates his position on soteriology and eschatology in a nuanced way in a passage that discusses "the growth of the kingdom":

> The growth of the kingdom is a process which occurs historically in liberation, insofar as liberation means a greater fulfillment of man. Liberation is a precondition for the new society, but this is not all it is. While liberation is implemented in liberating historical events, it also denounces their limitations and ambiguities, proclaims their fulfillment, and impels them effectively towards total communion. This is not an identification. Without liberating historical events, there would be no growth of the kingdom. But the process of liberation will not have conquered the very roots of oppression and the exploitation of man by man without the coming of the kingdom, which is above all a gift. Moreover, we can say that the historical, political liberating event *is* the growth of the

> kingdom and *is* a salvific event, but it is not *the* coming of the kingdom, not *all* of salvation.[95]

The Vatican Congregation for the Doctrine of the Faith issued two Instructions on liberation theology, the first in 1984 and the second in 1986.[96] While reaffirming the church's commitment to the poor and recognizing the validity of the term *liberation*, these Instructions are sharply critical of the adoption of Marxist analysis by theologians, especially the notion that history is driven by class struggle. Related to this critique, the Instructions raise concerns about eschatology. The 1984 Instruction warns against the denial of a distinction between the history of salvation and "profane" history. It perceives in liberation theology "a tendency to identify the kingdom of God and its growth with the human liberation movement and to make history itself the subject of its own development, as a process of the self-redemption of man by means of the class struggle."[97] The 1986 Instruction echoes *Lumen Gentium* in describing the church as the seed and beginning of the kingdom of God (cf. LG 5), "which will receive its completion at the end of time with the resurrection of the dead and the renewal of the whole of creation."[98] It proceeds to underscore the need to make a careful distinction between earthly progress and the growth of the kingdom, "which do not belong to the same order."[99] At the same time, it acknowledges that this distinction is not a separation, "for man's vocation to eternal life does not suppress but confirms his task of using the energies and means which he has received from the Creator for developing his temporal life."[100] This Instruction asserts that the coming of the kingdom will entail justice for the living and the dead. Thus, "without the resurrection of the dead and the Lord's judgment, there is no justice in the full sense of the term. The promise of the resurrection is freely made to meet the desire for true justice dwelling in the human heart."[101]

The spread of liberation theology throughout the world has led to great diversity in a number of areas, including matters that pertain to eschatology. Thoughtful liberation theologians, especially Gutiérrez, while not agreeing with everything said about liberation theology in these Instructions, have given careful consideration to the concerns raised there. It seems to me that the discussion of Gutiérrez's very nuanced thought above shows that he does not equate temporal progress with the kingdom of God. He is not guilty of professing a "temporal messianism." He affirms that the coming of the kingdom is a gift from God, yet he also emphasizes that it makes demands upon those who accept the gift of the kingdom. Like the CDF, Gutiérrez upholds the distinction between earthly progress and the growth of the kingdom, while still insisting that this distinction should never become a separation.

RETRIEVING THE ESCHATOLOGICAL IMAGINATION

In recent years, some theologians have argued that in reacting against the detailed, concrete descriptions of the afterlife found in pre–Vatican II eschatology, modern discussions of the topic have become too abstract and limited in what they say about life after death. Some of these thinkers attribute the excessive modesty of Christian eschatology to the influence of the critiques of reason made by Immanuel Kant. They also question the assumptions of Karl Rahner in his influential work on the hermeneutics of eschatological statements, which was explicated above.

In his study of Christian belief in the resurrection, Brian Robinette speaks of retrieving the apocalyptic imagination.[102] Robinette is critical of Rahner's rather dismissive treatment of apocalyptic. Robinette thinks that by "de-apocalypticizing" eschatology, Rahner restricted the meaning of resurrection to the "grammar of fulfillment," which in Robinette's mind is only one of the grammars of resurrection. This means that Rahner "cannot adequately account for the prophetic and political magnitude of resurrection language."[103] Robinette thinks that Rahner's hermeneutics of eschatological assertions does not account for the grammar of reversal, which is an essential aspect of resurrection and an important dimension of the apocalyptic eschatology found in the Bible, including the Gospels and the letters of Paul. It envisions the action of God reversing the situation of oppression in which believers find themselves. "The present situation of dominated existence (the evil of 'this world,' of 'this age') demands a reversal so thoroughgoing (a 'new creation') that only a divine incursion into the present can ultimately bring it forth."[104]

Mario Inzulza crafts an extended argument in favor of retrieving the imagination and narrative in Catholic eschatology.[105] He refers to Kant's contention that, because we do not have sense experience of the last things, it is not possible to obtain knowledge about them. Inzulza also references the postmodernist critique of metanarratives given by Jean-Francois Lyotard, who maintained that "any narrative that claims universal validity immediately falls under a pall of suspicion because of its presumption of totalitarianism."[106] Inzulza thinks that the critiques given by Kant and Lyotard have influenced the work of theologians and preachers, with the result that "the Christian imaginary of the future shifted from being too concrete to being too abstract."[107] He contends that the hermeneutical principles given by Rahner furthered the process of losing the eschatological imaginary by stating epistemological limits to it.[108] A consequence of this trend is "the inability of the eschatological discourse to design and illustrate the hoped-for future, and, therefore, to effectively inspire the present time."[109] Inzulza perceives this sobriety of eschatological statements in the documents of Vatican II and the revised Catholic funeral liturgy that followed the council.

John Thiel argues in similar fashion. He thinks that the critiques given by Kant have often led modern theologians to "focus their efforts on the existential dimensions of Christian hoping" and to be "reluctant to speculate about the objects of hope professed in faith."[110] Thiel agrees with Rahner's hermeneutical principle that knowledge of the eschatological future is an extrapolation of the knowledge that arises from the present experience of grace. Nevertheless, Thiel parts ways with Rahner when the latter enfolds the eschata within the incomprehensible mystery of God's own being. This apophatic approach to eschatological realities leaves us with little to say about the life of the dead. "Even though eternity can be encountered within our personal histories, the eternal life of the dead, Rahner claims, eludes our conceptual and imaginative grasp."[111] Thiel argues that "the relationships between and among several basic Catholic doctrines encourage the theologian to say much more about eschatological events than Rahner is willing, while yet speaking about the eschata in and through the present historical moment, as Rahner insists is proper."[112] As we will see, Thiel will conceive of the blessed dead as busy about the ongoing and graceful work of reconciliation.

It may well be that theologians and preachers need to retrieve the eschatological imagination in order to inspire believers in the present time. The reduction of eschatological statements to affirmations that the deceased are "with God" or "in God" (or "alienated from God") lacks the qualities of consolation and challenge that eschatological statements are meant to have. Inzulza may be correct in his assertion that with regard to eschatology Catholic theologians have moved from being too concrete to being too abstract. At the same time, the history of theology and preaching manifests a tendency to present the "last things" in ways that forgot the metaphorical nature of the images that were employed, often leading to depictions that were intimidating and even vulgar. Visions of hell as a place of literal burning and of purgatory as a kind of torture chamber are just two examples of this tendency. In that respect, Rahner's respect for the mysterious nature of the eschata remains a salutary caution for both theologians and preachers. And, as explained above, Rahner was not entirely agnostic about the eschaton; he did enumerate fundamental Christian convictions about final fulfillment in God.

6
THE DESTINY OF THE INDIVIDUAL

We move now from consideration of the historical development of Christian eschatology to reflection on its meaning for contemporary believers. We focus in this chapter on the fulfillment of the individual; in the next chapter we will engage in theological reflection on collective and cosmic fulfillment. Nevertheless, these two chapters cannot be separated. The individual is inextricably connected to the entire human race and its history and is an integral part of the cosmos and its history. Thus, these two chapters must be held together.

FACING DEATH

In the introduction, I took note of the climate of secularization that pervades much of Western society and its effects on the ways in which people approach the reality of death and the possibility of eternal life. We saw that Jürgen Moltmann asserts that Western society tends to avoid death and to ignore the effects of loss on loved ones. Modern societies, at least in the West, have few rituals for dealing with dying, death, and mourning. Moreover, the positive images of life that are constantly set forth in the media are more often than not those of healthy and vigorous young people who are at the "prime" of their life. The cultures of the West appear to have great difficulty dealing with diminishment and decline as part of life.

For Christians, on the other hand, the paschal mystery offers the key to discerning the most profound meaning of life. We profess belief in the one who faced his death directly and courageously and in so doing was raised to eternal life. Christians claim that Jesus's death and resurrection was redemptive and life-giving. We affirm that the death of Jesus was the means of the transformation of death and the paradigmatic instance of right dying. It was in and through facing his death that the truth of Jesus's mission and purpose was revealed. For disciples of Jesus, then, following the crucified one calls forth an honest recognition of our mortality and inspires the effort to unite ourselves with Jesus in our own dying. Dermot Lane observes, "It is only when we have faced the question of death and accepted death in all its ambiguity that we have fully understood who God is and have come to grips fully with who we are."[1]

The modern Catholic theologian who addressed the question of death and dying in the most intensive way was Karl Rahner. In the aftermath of the definition of the dogma of the assumption of Mary (1950), Rahner wrote the monograph *On the Theology of Death*, and he further developed his thought on the topic in subsequent essays.[2] Rahner's thinking about death was influenced by the writings of his former philosophy teacher, Martin Heidegger. In his early work *Being and Time*, Heidegger undertakes his analysis of the human being (to whom he gives the name *Dasein*) as a being-unto-death.[3] For Heidegger, death is that impending reality that discloses the meaning of the being of *Dasein*. Our awareness of the possibility of death reveals the temporality, the finitude, of human existence. Because authentic existence can be actualized only by one who knows what it means to be, awareness of our temporality is the prerequisite for living in an authentic way. Heidegger discerned that we are always ahead of ourselves, moving toward a future that is coming toward us. If we are honest with ourselves, the most real aspect of our future is death. This death is an event in which we cannot be represented by another. Our future is made known to us in existential anxiety (*Angst*). The everyday, inauthentic self treats death in a fugitive manner, as something that belongs to another. For Heidegger, the authentic approach to death is the courageous act of allowing ourselves to experience anxiety in the face of death and adopting a posture of anticipatory resoluteness. This is an impassioned freedom toward death and a stance that answers the call of conscience to be a free self.

Rahner thought that the genius and enduring validity of Christianity, of the "idea of Christianity," lies precisely in the fact that it addresses the enigma of death, in a direct and forthright way. In his theology of death, Rahner often speaks of dying throughout one's life. He frequently cites the phrase of Gregory the Great, the *prolixitas mortis* (the long, drawn-out death). He asserts, "We must understand the *prolixitas mortis* in life itself as the permanent and inescapable even though unthematic confrontation of freedom with death in the whole course of one's history."[4] Among the experiences of impending death that Rahner enumerates are the mood of disappointment, the failure of one's efforts and plans, and physical illness. He thinks that sickness sharpens our awareness that we are not in total control of our lives, and it calls us to a patience rooted in faith. In sickness, and in other critical moments of life, we rehearse for death.[5]

Rahner argued that the traditional theological definition of death as the separation of body and soul was inadequate. He thought that this definition failed to address the fact that death is the event of finalization for the person. Rahner envisioned death as the act that sums up our existence in history and which, for that reason, can be an act of salvation or its opposite. It can be an act that culminates a life of entrusting oneself to God or of deciding against God. For Rahner, there is a dialectic that is inherent in death: it is at one and the same time "an active fulfillment from within, an act of self-completion, a life-synthesizing self-affirmation," as well as "destruction, a rupture, an accident which strikes man [*sic*] from without."[6] The dimension of death that is a destruction, a rupture, is emblematic of the death that should not be. This was Rahner's way of interpreting the church's traditional teaching that death is the result of sin.[7] He argued that the sinful provenance of death as we know it is discerned in death's obscurity and hiddenness. The suffering and darkness that characterize human dying veil the deepest meaning of death as the event of freedom's maturity. This is the aspect of death suffered as a passion.

But death can also be an active fulfillment from within, and this dimension of death is disclosed most luminously in the death of Jesus. His death was for Rahner both the means of the transformation of death and the paradigm of right dying. Jesus Christ is the one who took death upon himself, who made death his own, and in so doing changed its meaning. The dying of Jesus was a free surrender to the mystery of death in all its darkness. Jesus's confrontation with death was an encounter with the darkness, or as Rahner likes to say, the abyss, of death. In that encounter Jesus surrendered to the God whom he had addressed as "Abba": "As in this trackless dark there prevailed silently only the mystery that in itself and in its freedom has no name and to which he nevertheless calmly surrendered himself as to eternal love and not the hell of futility."[8] His death was the ultimate act of freedom—freedom understood as the capacity for definitive self-disposal before God. In his death Jesus freely entrusted himself and his life to the Father. It was the freedom of Jesus's act of dying that made this act timeless, that gave it an eternal validity. As such, for Rahner Jesus's death was a death into resurrection. The death of Jesus by its very nature was subsumed into resurrection.

Rahner observes that the Christian is one who is intimately linked with the death of the Redeemer. He thinks that the critical question that serves as a litmus test of the depth and intensity of a Christian's faith involves the willingness of the believer to acknowledge and accept the advent of death. This free acceptance does not happen only at the moment of clinical death. In fact, a person who is in the midst of dying may not be capable of such an act. The final act of dying is dependent on our response to the many manifestations of death throughout life. Throughout our lives, we forge the free response to death that will be ours and which will characterize the person we have become. For the Christian, dying itself—throughout life and in one's final moments—is a dying with Christ. This act of appropriating Christ's death is initiated and internalized in the sacramental life of the believer, especially in baptism and Eucharist. The Christian is called to trust that, with the death of Christ, what had been the manifestation of sin became in Christ an expression of grace and the advent of God's plenitude.

Rahner's theology of death has been criticized by a number of thinkers. In particular, some theologians feel that he presents death and dying in a far too positive light. Gisbert Greshake found fault with Rahner because he thought that Rahner's theology of death was not consonant with the clear focus on life that is found in the Bible. Rahner inverted the precedence of life over death, as recognized by human experience and affirmed in the Bible.[9] Greshake argues that the description of death as a dialectical unity of passive suffering and free action is not consistent with people's lived experience. Greshake's reading of the New Testament testimony about death indicates a view of death as a "nonsensical breaking off of life."[10] Other critics conclude that Rahner puts too much emphasis on the moment of death.

In response to these criticisms, it can be said that Rahner does not place all of the emphasis on the moment of dying. As we have seen, he speaks of the action of dying with Christ throughout one's life—in all the "rehearsals" of death that life gives us. And Rahner's theology of death can be read as supportive of a genuine commitment to life, rather than as an inversion of the biblical focus on life. A resolute anticipation of one's own death as a dying with Christ can engender a courage and freedom that empowers people to commit themselves wholeheartedly to the service of life. It can be argued that the selfishness that arises from an inordinate attachment to one's life and from a denial of death leads to many of the intrusions of death into life. In her classic work *On Death and Dying*, Elisabeth Kübler-Ross poses an intriguing question: Cannot the prevalence of war in human history be attributed to an ill-fated attempt to conquer and master death and to deny our own mortality?[11] She suggests that a more honest and accepting attitude toward death might greatly increase the chances of living in peace. While such a hypothesis is impossible to verify, it does elucidate the truth that many of our death-dealing attitudes and actions can be traced to a distorted kind of self-assertion that refuses to admit or to grapple with human limitations and mortality. Thus, one can conclude that the precedence of life over death is not inverted but strengthened in Rahner's theology of death.

THE RESURRECTION OF THE BODY

In our exploration of New Testament eschatology we saw that the eschatological hope of early Christians derived from their belief in the resurrection of Jesus from the dead. The authors of the New Testament, especially the four evangelists, reflected back on the life and ministry of Jesus through the lens of the resurrection. The apostolic experience of Christ risen, and the belief that was spawned by this apostolic testimony, had revelatory significance. It inspired the conviction that God had vindicated the person and ministry of Jesus and that God had been revealed in him in a definitive way. It disclosed that God had been personally present in the crucified one. This experience and belief also offered new insight into the character of God as the resurrector, the one who brings life out of death.

As we saw in the third chapter, the Easter experience also gave birth to the conviction that believers in Jesus are given a share in his death and resurrection. They are liberated from slavery to sin and participate in Christ's triumph over death. Paul speaks of Christ raised from the dead as "the firstfruits of those who have fallen asleep" (1 Cor 15:20). We saw that in the early church this hope of sharing in Jesus's resurrection led to debates about the bodily resurrection. Discussion of the way to conceive of the resurrection of the body revolved around the interpretation of Paul's notion of the "spiritual body" (1 Cor 15:44). In its important Symbol of Faith, the Eleventh Council of Toledo (675) taught that we will rise "in this very body in which we live and are and move."[12]

There is no proof of the resurrection of Jesus, if by "proof" one means a clinching logical demonstration. The closest thing to such a demonstration is found in reflection on the behavior of Jesus' disciples. Once frightened and locked-away disciples, who had deserted their teacher in his passion, came back together and began to boldly proclaim him as risen from the dead, risking their personal freedom and their very lives in doing so. Jürgen Moltmann asserts, "The about-turn from disappointment to certainty and from deadly fear to a faith which is not afraid of death is the real proof of the reality of Christ's resurrection."[13] This radical change in behavior reflects an experience that transformed their thinking about Jesus and about what God had accomplished in and through Jesus. It gave them a completely new perspective on history and the future. Brian Robinette argues that approaching the resurrection is more like being approached. It is more like receiving a gift—a gift that reveals "what 'history' really *is*, what it *can be*, what it *will be*."[11] Hospitality is required to receive this gift of the resurrection.

The teaching of the church and the work of modern theologians continue to affirm the foundational significance of belief in the resurrection of the dead, which is grounded, of course, in belief in the resurrection of Jesus. Gerhard Lohfink observes, "Christian knowledge of the *eschata*, the 'last things,' is nothing but an extrapolation of what happened in the resurrection of Jesus."[15] A statement on eschatology published in 1992 by the International Theological Commission begins, "Without the affirmation of Christ's resurrection Christian faith is in vain (cf. 1 Cor 15:14). Since there is indeed an intimate relationship between the fact of Christ's resurrection and our hope for our own future resurrection (cf. 1 Cor 15:12), the Risen Christ also constitutes the foundation of our hope, which opens itself up to horizons far beyond the limits of this earthly life."[16]

The Christian tradition recognizes the resurrection of Jesus as both the *model* and the *cause* of our own resurrection. Paul's use of the metaphor of "firstfruits" bespeaks the notion that our resurrection will be modeled on that of Jesus: there is more fruit still hanging on the vine. And Paul also speaks of the agency of Jesus in the resurrection of the dead when he claims that "death came through a man; hence the resurrection of the dead comes through a man also" (1 Cor 15:21). Thomas Aquinas, drawing on the metaphysics of Aristotle, argues that in every genus that which is first is the cause of those who come after it. He concludes that in Christ our resurrection has begun, and his resurrection is the cause of ours.[17] Elizabeth Johnson observes, "In view of the solidarity of the human race, his [Christ's] destiny means that our hope does not merely clutch at a possibility but stands on an irrevocable ground of what has already transpired in him."[18]

Christian belief in the resurrection of the dead entails a radical affirmation of the intrinsic goodness of the human, the body, and matter itself. Karl Rahner has accentuated this foundational conviction in compelling ways. He asserts that because the Lord is risen, Christians are "the most sublime of materialists."[19] Rahner avers, "We neither can nor should conceive of any ultimate fullness of the spirit and of reality without thinking too of matter enduring as well in a state of final perfection."[20] Christians believe that matter will last forever and be glorified forever. In an essay titled "A Faith That Loves the Earth," Rahner states that Jesus allowed himself to be conquered by death so as to be swallowed up by it and thereby reach earth's very center, where he could infuse the earth forever with his divine life.[21] In his resurrection, Jesus has been born anew as a child of the earth. Rahner can depict Jesus's resurrection as like the first erupting of a volcano, which shows that the fire of God is already erupting in the world. The new forces of a transfigured world are already at work.[22]

The transfiguration of Jesus's humanity in the resurrection also means that his humanity has abiding salvific significance.[23] Rahner emphasizes an insight that he often repeats, namely, that the nearer one comes to God the more real one becomes. What has been created by the God who is pure love "is the valid, eternal, living reality, that which truly is."[24] This means that the incarnation "is both the unique summit and the ultimate basis of God's relationship to his creation, in which he and his creation grow in direct (and not in converse) proportion."[25] Precisely because of its union with divinity, the humanity of Jesus must be the most really real of all realities. From here Rahner draws the conclusion that the created human nature of Jesus is the gateway through which every creature must pass if it is to receive its perfection in God. Even in the direct vision of God in heaven, the risen Christ remains the mediator between God and humanity. He "is *now* and for all eternity the *permanent openness* of our finite being to the living God of infinite, eternal life."[26]

THE INTERMEDIATE STATE

In post–Vatican II Catholic theology, there has been extended discussion about when the resurrection of the dead takes place. The traditional teaching of the church has been that at death the soul is separated from the body and meets God in "particular" judgment. The soul lives on with the gift of the vision of God, experiences purification, or suffers eternal loss. On the last day, at the Parousia, the soul will be reunited with its body. The *Catechism of the Catholic Church* states, "God, in his almighty power, will definitively grant incorruptible life to our bodies by reuniting them with our souls, through the power of Jesus' Resurrection."[27]

Some theologians have questioned the notion of a "separated soul" (*anima separata*) and the view that this soul must "wait" for the bodily resurrection until the last day. The German theologian Gisbert Greshake has been a leading critic of this traditional conception.[28] He argued that the idea of the soul that was developed in Catholic theology was too dependent on the Greek philosophical tradition and not faithful to biblical anthropology. Greshake contended that the original tension between a postmortal fulfillment of the individual and an end-time fulfillment of all became distorted into a tension between the fulfillment of the soul and the fulfillment of the body for the individual human being.[29] He thinks of the body as an essential element of our being itself, through which we experience connection to fellow creatures and communicate with them. Thus, human fulfillment cannot be thought of only as the fulfillment of the soul; it must also be the fulfillment of the body. Greshake asserts, then, that resurrection of the body happens in death. This resurrection entails a transfigured corporeality, which is more than just the prolongation of an empirical anthropology. Thus the presence of the corpse (or the cremains) in the grave is not a problem. There is an intermediate state in the sense that ultimate human fulfillment is possible only with the fulfillment of all. In this sense, speaking of the resurrection on the last day is meaningful and necessary. Mary, through her bodily assumption into heaven, is the "Realsymbol" of the church. The difference between Mary and the rest of us is that her humanity was not darkened by sin and guilt, and thus her corporeality did not need any purification. Her corporeality, therefore, is transfigured in a higher measure than is ours.

Gerhard Lohfink has also advocated the notion of resurrection in death. He considers the idea of a delayed resurrection of the body to be a devaluation of the body. If the soul already lives in the full vision of God, the later addition of the body becomes unnecessary.[30] He also criticizes the traditional conception of fulfillment for its assumption that time goes on beyond death just as it did before death. He insists that the process of purification "after" death should not be thought of in terms of earthly time. He posits that individual judgment in death and general judgment at the end of the world come together as one. The encounter with God in death is an event that cannot be separated from the resurrection of all the dead. He concludes that "the deceased is no longer subject to earthly time but in death has 'already arrived' at the resurrection of all the dead."[31]

Karl Rahner also suggested the possibility of resurrection in death, though his position was cautious and nuanced. In his earlier writings on death, he speculated about a "pancosmic" relation of the separated soul, through which the soul would maintain a connection with the matter of the cosmos. In a later essay on the intermediate state, he admitted that this connection might be better maintained by affirming the "enduring 'informedness' of the glorified body by the perfected spiritual soul"—that is, resurrection in death.[32] He argued that the idea of an intermediate state and the corresponding notion of a disembodied soul was not a defined doctrine of the church and could be given up. In his later *Foundations of Christian Faith*, he simply says that, since the human being is an absolute unity that cannot be split up into body and soul, the fulfillment of the soul and the fulfillment of the body are not such that they could be completely separated from each other and assigned to different realities. They are two dialectical statements that cannot be subsumed into a higher synthesis. In our eschatological statements, we must speak both spiritually and corporeally.[33] In his discussion of purgatory in the same work, he does speak of an "interval," saying, "If then, we can hardly deny an interval in a person's destiny between death and the corporeal fulfillment of this person as a whole, then neither can anything be said against a personal maturation in this interval...."[34] Rahner's final position on this debate is, then, not precisely clear, though it is evident that he did insist on maintaining the unity of body and spirit (soul) in his theological anthropology.

The well-known dogmatic theologian Michael Schmaus also affirmed the possibility of resurrection in death.[35] He argued that there is no binding teaching of the church that defines death in terms of the separation of body and soul. The church's teachings on this matter are meant only to affirm the continued life of the person beyond death. Schmaus concludes that "the theory that immediately upon his death man [*sic*] attains a new physical existence, while his earthly body lies in the grave and decomposes or is destroyed by cremation, is not opposed to any revealed truth."[36] Schmaus adduces evidence in favor of such a theory, especially the biblical emphasis on the unity of the human person.

Joseph Ratzinger vigorously opposed the idea of resurrection in death. Ratzinger argued that the Christian notion of a separated soul was not Platonic (as many of its critics have contended) because the understanding of the soul that developed in Catholic theology was distinctive; it was neither purely Aristotelian nor Platonic. Attaining its culmination in the work of Thomas Aquinas, this theology envisioned the soul as both personal and the form (animating principle) of the body. Aquinas took over Aristotle's stress on the unity of body and soul without binding the soul to matter in a way that would disallow the soul's continued existence when the matter perished.[37] This conception of the soul-body relationship entails a duality that is not dualistic. Ratzinger claims that this notion of soul "is a product of Christian faith, and of the exigencies of faith for human thought."[38] Ratzinger proceeds to argue that the idea of resurrection in death, with its concomitant notion of a transfigured corporeality, dematerializes the resurrection. The resurrected body has no relation to the corpse in the grave. The theory of resurrection in death "entails that real matter has no part in the event of the consummation."[39] Ratzinger contends, too, that resurrection in death would constitute a personal fulfillment that removed the deceased from ongoing history. It would individualize eschatological fulfillment. He states that while we step beyond history in death, "this does not mean that we lose our relation to history; the network of human relationality belongs to human nature itself. History would be deprived of its seriousness if resurrection occurred at the moment of death."[40]

In 1979 the Congregation for the Doctrine of the Faith issued a brief document addressed to the bishops of the church that was titled "Letter on Certain Questions Concerning Eschatology."[41] We briefly adverted to this document in the first chapter. The letter enumerated central church teachings on eschatology, including belief in the resurrection of the dead, which it described as the extension to human beings of the resurrection of Christ itself. On the intermediate state, it affirmed that "a spiritual element survives and subsists after death, an element endowed with consciousness and will, so that the 'human self' subsists." It said that the term *soul* has been used to designate this spiritual element. The congregation admitted that this term has diverse meanings in the Bible, but it taught that there is no valid reason for rejecting it. The congregation adds that this soul that survives is deprived for the present of the complement of its body. The letter went on to affirm that the church looks for the glorious manifestation of Christ, "believing it to be distinct and deferred with regard to the situation of people immediately after death." It envisioned the bodily glorification of the Blessed Virgin Mary as "an anticipation of the glorification that is the destiny of all the other elect." The congregation conceded that "[n]either Scripture nor theology provides sufficient light for a proper picture of life after death." In eschatological matters, believers must uphold the twin principles of (1) the fundamental continuity between our present life in Christ and the future life and (2) the radical break between the present life and the future one, "due to the fact that the economy of faith will be replaced by the economy of fullness of life."

In 1992 the International Theological Commission issued a lengthy document on eschatology.[42] It was sharply critical of the idea of resurrection in death. The commission asserted that this notion "appears to pose a grave threat to the realism of the resurrection, since the resurrection is affirmed without any relationship to the body that once lived and is now dead."[43] It refers to older formulas of the faith that spoke forcefully about the raising up of the same body that is now alive. The commission emphasizes that the idea of resurrection in death is not found in the New Testament; the New Testament always speaks of the resurrection at the Parousia of the Lord, not at the time of a person's death. It proceeds to examine the notion of the separated soul, which it acknowledges is an ontologically incomplete reality, though it is still conscious and capable of enjoying the full beatitude of the intuitive vision of God.[44]

Dermot Lane attempts to take a mediating position in this debate. Lane is critical of the traditional conception of individual eschatology involving a separated soul, saying that it is based on a dualistic anthropology. At the same time, Lane wants to affirm that the total perfection of the individual involves the perfection of humanity and the cosmos. He accentuates the radical relationality of all individuals to each other within creation.[45] He develops a kind of processive account of a person's sharing in Christ's death and resurrection. He builds on certain Pauline texts (e.g., Rom 6:3–4; 8:11) that depict believers as participating in the death and resurrection of Christ in this life. Lane proposes that resurrection "is something that begins in this life through our paschal relationship with the risen Christ, that this relationship with Christ comes to a point of fruition in death through individual resurrection, and that this personal resurrection is taken up into the general resurrection at the end of time with the second coming of Christ."[46] In this view, the person who undergoes resurrection in death continues to have a relationship with those still journeying on earth and with creation itself.

Lane's proposal is attractive especially because it attempts to integrate the principles of continuity and discontinuity that were set forth by the Congregation of the Faith. On the one hand, it is essential to preserve the relationship of the deceased to ongoing history and to affirm the significance of the final consummation of history that will take place in the eschaton of Christ. With that in view, we need to think of some sense of duration in the life of the deceased—a duration that is analogous (having similarity but even greater dissimilarity) to earthly time. Even the activities of knowing and loving God that the blessed dead enjoy imply some sense of duration. And the deceased continue to live in relationship with those whom they have left behind and with the rest of human history. The deceased also look forward to a consummation of human history and the cosmos that is still future to them.

At the same time, the language of "separated soul" does seem to be problematic. In chapter 1, we explored the understanding of the person as an embodied self and the notion of the soul as the foothold for relationship with God. When we remember and pray for our deceased loved ones, we don't think of or imagine them as bodiless souls. We think of them as we remember them—embodied selves who were created and loved by God. Imagination has a role to play in prayer and in eschatology. And as a number of theologians have pointed out, modern neuroscience has made it quite difficult to conceive of the activity of the human mind in a being without a brain. The notion of a thinking, willing, loving human self seems to assume some form of corporeality, even if we are unable to comprehend the precise nature of that corporeality.

Those who advocate the traditional view of a separated soul awaiting reunion with its body argue that the idea of resurrection in death entails a "second" body that is unrelated to the body that once lived and that now lies in the grave. But is the gift of a transfigured corporeality at the death of the individual really more unrelated to the person who lived than the reunion of the soul with a body that had decomposed millennia ago? A strict interpretation of the traditional teaching might answer that question in the affirmative. But I wonder if that answer is really compelling. It may be wise to admit that we find ourselves in the realm of mystery here and that neither of these theological approaches resolves all of the questions. As the Congregation for the Doctrine of the Faith said, "Neither Scripture nor theology provides sufficient light for a proper picture of life after death."

Would the gift of a transfigured corporeality after death negate the significance of the Gospel testimony that two days after Jesus's crucifixion disciples found his tomb empty? I do not think so. The resurrection of Jesus was an absolutely unique event; it was the model and cause of our own resurrection. Many New Testament scholars conclude that if the tomb of Jesus had not been empty, the disciples of Jesus could never have proclaimed his resurrection in Jerusalem and its environs. It seems to me that it is possible to affirm the Gospel witness to the empty tomb of Jesus and still conceive of some form of transfigured corporeality for the deceased.

PARTICULAR JUDGMENT

The biblical testimony and the Christian theological tradition make it clear that human beings are held accountable for their lives before God. This conviction is rooted in the belief that God is just as well as merciful. In this regard, there is a distinction made between particular judgment (the individual's encounter with God [or with Christ] at the end of her life) and the general judgment (the encounter of all humanity and all creation with God at the end of time). The *Catechism of the Catholic Church* states that each person receives eternal retribution at the very moment of death, "in a particular judgment that refers his life to Christ: either entrance into the blessedness of heaven—through a purification or immediately—or immediate and everlasting damnation."[47]

This notion of particular judgment does not receive much explicit reference in the Hebrew and Christian Bible, though the conviction that God judges the actions and lives of humanity is found throughout. The New Testament speaks primarily of general judgment at the second coming of Christ, for example, in the famous passage in Matthew 25:31–46 about the judgment rendered by the Son of Man. New Testament passages where the judgment of an individual in or after death may be implied include the parable of Lazarus and the rich man (Luke 16:19–31); Jesus's words to the penitent thief (Luke 23:43); the words of Paul written to the Philippians in which he expresses his longing to depart this life and to be with Christ (Phil 1:23); and the passage in Paul's Second Letter to the Corinthians that says, "For we must all appear before the judgment seat of Christ, so that each one may receive recompense, according to what he did in the body, whether good or evil" (2 Cor 5:10). Michael Schmaus points out that there was a lack of clarity with regard to the particular judgment among early Christian authors, though from the fourth century on it was accepted as a fact. This conviction is expressed in an explicit way by John Chrysostom and Augustine of Hippo.[48]

Thomas O'Meara comments about the way in which images and descriptions of judgment that became prominent in the Middle Ages provoked great fear in believers.[49] The *Dies Irae* hymn in the Christian funeral liturgy from the fourteenth century included lyrics about the "day of wrath, that dreadful day" and a "just judge," and these words inspired deep eschatological anxiety in ordinary believers. O'Meara observes, "The poem's place in the texts of the ancient Requiem Mass, for long the Roman Catholic funeral liturgy, brought dread to those dying and anxiety to mourners. The poem's theology surrounds death with fear, and often its lines are not Christian."[50]

Many modern theologians conceive of particular judgment as the coming to light of the deepest truth of a person's life. Judgment is not an extrinsic evaluation rendered by God. Rather, it is the clear vision of the character of one's life and of the person one has become. In this sense, judgment becomes more akin to self-judgment rather than judgment by God. Zachary Hayes articulates this conception of particular judgment:

> Instead of thinking of judgment as something that happens to the human person from the outside, this theology is inclined to see it as the full personal realization of the individual's own decisions. The encounter with God has as its intrinsic effect the full illumination of the person's life-history with all the personal decisions that have made the person to be precisely what he or she brings into the encounter with God. In the presence of God, my true reality becomes fully clear to me. The divine judge needs to do nothing. Judgment is the experience of the reality I have made of myself as seen in the presence of God.[51]

Other writers express their understanding of particular judgment in similar ways. In his book on eschatology, Joseph Ratzinger asserted, "In death, a human being emerges into the light of full reality and truth....Judgment consists in this removal of the mask in death."[52] Gerhard Lohfink remarks, "When we encounter God in death we will for the first time recognize with full clarity who we really are....We ourselves will judge and condemn the evil in ourselves."[53] Nevertheless, Jürgen Moltmann poses some questions about this popular theological construal of particular judgment.

Moltmann critiques the notion of God as merely the "executor or accomplice of the human being's free choice."[54] As we will see further along in this chapter, Moltmann wants to speak of God's creative justice, which brings healing to both the victims and the perpetrators of human history. God is active in the moment of judgment. In his encyclical *Spe Salvi*, Pope Benedict XVI (formerly Joseph Ratzinger) makes an analogous comment about the encounter with Christ at the end of our lives: "At the moment of judgment we experience and we absorb the overwhelming power of his love over all the evil in the world and in ourselves."[55] These theologians suggest that it is the God of grace who will have the final word in our lives.

PURIFICATION IN/AFTER DEATH

The historical narrative in the previous two chapters has shown that the idea of purgatory as a place seems to have arisen in the early Middle Ages (the twelfth century, according to LeGoff). However, the notion of the purification of the soul in or after death was proposed by some theologians of the early church, for example, Clement of Alexandria, Origen of Alexandria, Gregory of Nazianzus, and Augustine. Some patristic theologians employed the image of fire in their depiction of this purification. The existence of purgatory was officially taught at the Second Council of Lyons (1274), the Council of Florence-Ferrara (1439), and the Council of Trent (1563). These conciliar statements were couched in modest terms, avoiding excessive speculation about the purification that was envisioned and cautioning against pastoral practices that smack of commercial exchange. Orthodox Christians developed an understanding of purification after death that was more mystical in nature, seeing it as a process of spiritual growth and maturation rather than as expiatory suffering. We saw, too, that Martin Luther eventually came to reject purgatory, viewing the idea of making satisfaction for sins already forgiven as contradictory to the proclamation of the free forgiveness of sins in Christ. And John Calvin strongly rejected the doctrine of purgatory, interpreting the idea as the work of Satan.

Statements about purgatory in recent magisterial documents are relatively brief and general. The 1979 letter of the Congregation for the Doctrine of the Faith simply affirms that the church "believes in the possibility of a purification for the elect before they see God, a purification altogether different from the punishment of the damned."[56] The *Catechism of the Catholic Church* states, "All who die in God's grace and friendship, but still imperfectly purified, are indeed assured of their eternal salvation; but after death they undergo purification, so as to achieve the holiness necessary to enter the joy of heaven."[57] It proceeds to affirm that from the beginning the church has honored the memory of the dead and offered prayers in suffrage for them.[58] The treatment of purgatory given in the 1992 statement of the International Theological Commission is more fulsome, though also questionable in part. It speaks of "stains" that darken our friendship with God and require a prior purification, noting that "any stain is an impediment when it comes to our intimate meeting with God and Christ."[59] These stains involve venial sins and the remains of sin that may persist when guilt has been remitted and its attendant eternal punishment. While the view that purification from sin and the effects of sin in our final meeting with God is standard, the assertion that any stain is an impediment to our meeting with God and Christ is a bit jarring, given the Gospel testimony to Jesus's meetings with many people who were far from "stainless."

Modern Catholic theologians generally support the possibility of some form of purification in or after death in the process of the person's final journey to God. Like the idea of judgment, they often relate this purification to the encounter with God. They also connect it with the ongoing relationship between the living and the dead. Jeannine Hill Fletcher cites the church's teaching that personhood continues after death, and she proposes that "the relationships with God and others aimed at in this life might find their fullness in a process that continues after death."[60] She draws on the writings of John Thiel and Joseph Ratzinger in suggesting that, because our relationality continues after death, the work of the blessed dead might include ongoing reconciliation and forgiveness (see below on Thiel).

Karl Rahner observes that human beings are complex creatures consisting of many levels. Drawing on the notion of fundamental option, Rahner asserts that a person's fundamental choice in life may be for God, but that does not mean that this basic disposition has permeated her or his entire being. There are inconsistencies in the life of each person as well as tensions that can draw one away from a fundamental choice for God. The process of purification would be "a process in which his [her] basic decision permeates the whole length and breadth of his [her] reality."[61] Purgatory would then be a process of maturation involving the integration of one's free self-disposition for God into one's entire being. Rahner is cautious about employing temporal categories in describing this process, since he insists that eternity and time are distinct. In an essay on the topic, he does concede that this process might be seen as analogous to present time.[62] He also mentions the possibility that this purification could take place in death itself, with the depth and intensity of pain that one experiences in the process of dying. Rahner also suggests that the doctrine of purgatory might speak to the problem of the final condition of those who have never experienced real freedom in their earthly lives. It might be an opportunity for a postmortal history of freedom in which one has the opportunity to choose for God.[63] True to his insistence on the hiddenness of eschatological realities, Rahner maintains a certain ignorance about purgatory, giving space for diverse possibilities with regard to it.

In his encyclical *Spe Salvi*, Benedict XVI connected purgatory with a person's encounter with God in death. Like Rahner, he suggested that there can be a difference between one's basic decision for God and the complete permeation of that choice in a person's life. Benedict speaks of "an ultimate interior openness to truth, to love, to God" that "is covered over by ever new compromises with evil."[64] He uses the image of purity covered over by filth. The pope draws on Paul's words in 1 Corinthians 3:11–15 about being saved but only as through fire to affirm that "in order to be saved we personally have to pass through 'fire' so as to become fully open to receiving God and able to take our place at the table of the eternal marriage-feast."[65] Benedict adverts to the work of other theologians who think that the fire which burns and saves is Christ himself, the judge and savior. He speaks of a painful encounter but calls this pain "a blessed pain in which the holy power of his [Christ's] love sears through us like a flame, enabling us to become totally ourselves and thus totally of God."[66] This process cannot be specified in terms of earthly time. It is, in Benedict's words, "the heart's time, it is the time of 'passage' to communion with God in the Body of Christ."[67]

Dermot Lane also reflects on the inner tensions and contradictions between a positive response to God's offer of self and the ambiguous ways in which people use their freedom. In his retrieval of the teaching about purgatory, he emphasizes the need for ongoing conversion to Christ—a transformation that is not always completed in one's earthly life:

> The unconditional love of God offered to humanity in Christ calls forth in this life and in death a personal response that involves a purging conversion and transformation. That response is ultimately one of being configured to the crucified and risen Christ both in this life and in death. Anyone who is in touch with the ambiguous dispositions of the human self and who has at the same time some sense of the gracious forgiving love of God will hardly find it difficult to accept that eternal life with God will require a radical transformation and adjustment in the life of the individual; it is this transformation and adjustment that is at issue in the doctrine of Purgatory.[68]

It is worth noting, too, that the U.S. Lutheran-Catholic dialogue that addressed eschatological issues was able to forge some common affirmations with respect to purification in or after death. Participants agreed that "the effects of sin in the justified are fully removed only as they die, undergo judgment, and encounter the purifying love of Christ....All, even martyrs and saints of the highest order, will find their encounter with the Risen Christ transformative in ways beyond human comprehension."[69]

Purgatory has had a troubled history of interpretation, especially in popular preaching and imagination. The picture that has often been painted is that of a celestial torture chamber wherein people undergo punishment to expiate their sins and to counteract the effects of sins. Preachers expounding the doctrine of purgatory have often turned metaphorical fire into literal fire. Coupled with that troubling image has been the commercial notion of obtaining indulgences in order that others or oneself may be released from a quantifiable time of confinement in purgatory. This practice has often led to abuses. Still, it does make some theological sense to envision a process or moment of transformation in one's final journey to God. Those who explicitly or implicitly desire to respond positively to the offer of God's love and grace grapple with their innate tendencies to selfishness. We can resonate with Paul when he says, "What I do, I do not understand. For I do not do what I want, but I do what I hate" (Rom 7:15). We long for that complete integration of virtue in our relationships and activities, but it escapes us. So we need the transforming power of God's grace to make our choice for God whole and complete. If we wish to speak of the transformation that a person undergoes in their journey home to God, it seems preferable to conceive of it as encompassing both purification and healing. Yes, most of us need to be purified of those ways of thinking and acting that distance us from God and others. This process of purification may be painful, in the sense that Benedict XVI speaks of a "blessed pain." But even more, we can think of this transformation as a process of healing. Sinners inflict wounds on those they sin against. But in so doing sinners also wound themselves. So we need to be healed of the wounds we have inflicted on ourselves through our own wrongdoing. A relevant image for this transformation may be that of rehabilitation, as when the life of an addict is transformed through a process of rehabilitation. That process includes purification of the addict by withdrawal of the harmful substance from her or his system. But it is also entails healing of the harmful effects of active addiction.[70] Such a comprehensive healing can come only from the God who creates and re-creates God's beloved sons and daughters.

PRAYER FOR THE DEAD

Discussion of purgatory leads us to consider the practice of prayer for the dead in the liturgy of the church and in personal piety. We saw that praying for the deceased became a practice early in the history of the church, making its way into the Eucharistic liturgy fairly soon. The practice of praying for the dead predated the theology undergirding it. Augustine envisioned it as a dimension of Christians' care for the dead. In the Middle Ages, Thomas Aquinas observed that charity extends not only to the living but to the dead as well. As belief in purgatory developed and expanded, prayer for the dead became more widespread and was even seen as an urgent necessity for believers. This gave rise to the popular appeal of obtaining indulgences, which, as we have seen, degenerated into a commercial practice of dubious value. We saw, too, that the Second Vatican Council, in its Dogmatic Constitution on the Church, affirmed the communion that exists between the living and the dead and the practice of offering suffrages for the dead (LG 50).

In the years since Vatican II, the value and importance of praying for the dead has been reasserted in official church teaching and in the writings of Catholic theologians. In its 1979 letter to bishops on eschatology, the Congregation for the Doctrine of the Faith said, "The church excludes every way of thinking or speaking that would render meaningless or unintelligible her prayers, her funeral rites and the religious acts offered for the dead. All these are, in their substance, *loci theologici*." Thus, these liturgical and pious practices are envisioned as sources of the church's theology. As the traditional adage goes, the law of praying is the law of believing (*lex orandi, lex credendi*). Catholics have become accustomed to praying for the dead at liturgical celebrations, not only at funerals but also in every celebration of the Eucharist. We pray for those who have gone before us in the general intercessions (Universal Prayer), as well as in every Eucharistic Prayer. For example, even the briefest of the major eucharistic prayers of the church (Eucharistic Prayer II) contains this petition: "Remember also our brothers and sisters who have fallen asleep in the hope of the resurrection, and all who have died in your mercy: welcome them into the light of your face."

Gerhard Lohfink and Pope Benedict XVI offer insightful reflections on prayer for the dead. Lohfink connects it with the process of purification undergone by the deceased as they face the consequences of what they have done wrong in their lives.[71] Our harmful words and actions, even when they have been forgiven, have consequences that affect others and ourselves in ways of which we may not even be aware. Lohfink asserts that our prayer for the dead, especially in the celebration of the Eucharist, is meant to mitigate the consequences of the wrongs committed by our beloved dead. In his words, "Hence care for the dead means above all limiting or even eliminating the consequences of what they have done wrong because these consequences beset the dead and make the process of their purification more difficult, since it is also part of that purification that they are made free from all the negatives they have left behind in the world."[72] We offer this prayer in the community of the church. This practice, Lohfink argues, is what is meant by the term *indulgence*, though he thinks that the word is so freighted with negative connotations that it should no longer be employed. When the granting of indulgences is seen as a way of lessening the "temporal punishment due to sin," what is really meant is "acting against the 'consequences' of sin, by the grace of Christ, in the communion of the church."[73]

In his encyclical *Spe Salvi*, Benedict XVI offers some compelling insights into the practice of prayer for the dead.[74] He understands it as a way in which love reaches into the afterlife. He asserts that it has been a fundamental conviction of Christianity through the ages that reciprocal giving and receiving is possible beyond the limits of death. Benedict argues that even if purification is envisioned as taking place in our encounter with the Lord, prayer for the dead can be meaningful and efficacious. Here he reminds us of our identity in relation with others: "No one lives alone. No one sins alone. No one is saved alone."[75] Our prayer for another can play a small part in her or his purification. We do not need to try to calculate its effects in terms of earthly time. Benedict observes, "Our hope is always essentially also hope for others; only thus is it truly hope for me too. As Christians we should never limit ourselves to asking: how can I save myself? We should also ask: what can I do in order that others may be saved and that for them too the star of hope may rise? Then I will have done my utmost for my own personal salvation as well."[76]

In the previous chapter, we noted that Martin Luther did not reject prayer for the dead. Though he found no scriptural basis for such a practice, he regarded it as permissible. He did reject the popular practices of celebrating vigils and requiem Masses. The U.S. ecumenical dialogue between Lutherans and Catholics has revealed a growing convergence in thinking and practice with respect to prayer for the dead.[77] The Lutheran and Catholic parties to the dialogue observe that the funeral liturgies of both churches emphasize the abiding communion of the living and the dead. Lutheran participants acknowledged that many Lutheran funeral liturgies now include commendations of the dead that are clearly a form of prayer for the dead. In a common statement, the parties affirmed, "While this convergence in practice does not extend to a common practice of prayer for the dead beyond funerals, it does indicate a growing unity in our practices in relation to those who have died in Christ."[78] Lutherans do object if such prayer is seen as making "satisfaction," though this language has not been prominent in recent Catholic presentations on prayer for the dead. The parties concluded, "Thus we agree that prayer for the dead, considered within the framework of the communion of saints, need not be a church-dividing or communion-hindering issue for Lutherans and Catholics."[79]

Commenting on Eastern Orthodox eschatology, Andrew Louth also emphasizes the importance and efficacy of prayer for the dead.[80] Louth explains that in Orthodox eschatology the period of forty days after death is seen as a passage from death to a period of waiting for the last judgment. In popular belief and liturgical practice, the departed soul is viewed as passing through certain toll houses, in which the soul is examined with regard to its conduct on earth. During this passage, the soul is assisted by its guardian angel, the prayers of the saints, and the prayers of those living on earth.[81] On the fortieth day the soul undergoes its particular judgment and then is assigned to its intermediate state, a place of waiting in paradise or Hades. Louth points out that this process of passage through forty days has never been formally defined as dogma. However, what can be claimed as formal Orthodox dogma is "that the departed are supported by the prayers of Christians, that the communion of living and departed has not been severed by death, and that there is hope for 'a place of light, a place of refreshment, a place of repose, whence pain, sorrow and sighing have fled away' for the departed."[82]

THE LIFE OF THE BLESSED DEAD

In the previous chapter, we explored the controversy that arose in the fourteenth century in the wake of Advent sermons given by Pope John XXII. The pope, speaking as a private theologian, suggested that after death the blessed enjoy only the vision of Christ's glorified humanity. Access to the vision of the Trinity will be given only after the resurrection of all the dead, on the last day. This led to intense debates before and after the death of the pope and was settled by his successor, Benedict XII, with the constitution *Benedictus Deus*. This constitution stated that the souls of the blessed immediately after death (or after purification for those in need of it) "see the divine essence with an intuitive vision and even face to face, without the mediation of any creature by way of object of vision; rather the divine essence immediately manifests itself to them, plainly, clearly and openly, and in this vision they enjoy the divine essence."[83] The constitution proceeds to affirm that this vision of the divine essence "will continue without any interruption and without end until the last Judgment and from then on forever."[84] The use of the language of vision, a vision that brings unending happiness, both reflected theological descriptions of heaven that antedated the constitution and strongly influenced those that came after it. Thus, the notion of beatific vision has become standard in the tradition.

Almost two centuries earlier, Thomas Aquinas had written about the knowledge of God's essence enjoyed by the blessed, made possible through the gift of what he called the "light of glory." In his description of the ultimate fulfillment of the human person, Aquinas used the language of "vision" and "seeing." As we saw in chapter 4, he argued that what makes us human is our ability to understand. Final fulfillment, then, can consist of nothing else than the vision of the divine essence, which is the fulfillment of all understanding. In the *Summa Contra Gentiles*, Aquinas puts it simply when he says that "in the felicity that comes from the divine vision, every human desire is fulfilled."[85] He teaches that no created mind can see the essence of God unless God by his grace joins Godself to that mind as something intelligible to it. Drawing on Aristotelian epistemology, he asserts that when a created intellect sees the essence of God the divine essence becomes the form through which the intellect understands.[86] For this vision, God gives the person a light that illumines the mind. Through this light the person is made Godlike (deiform). This light of glory perfects and strengthens the mind so that it may see God. Aquinas thinks that a person may have a greater or lesser share in this light of glory. Those who share more in the light are those who have more charity.[87] The knowledge of God given in this fulfilling vision is not comprehensive, if by "comprehensive" is meant comprehending the being of God. The Infinite cannot be contained in the finite. However, it is comprehensive in the sense that the blessed see God and possess God, holding God forever in their sight and enjoying God as their ultimate goal fulfilling all their desires.[88]

Aquinas's account of the life of the blessed, then, is one that focuses on contemplation. The goal of human life is found in contemplating God, who is infinite truth and infinite goodness. He appeals to the story of Mary and Martha in the Gospel of Luke, in which Jesus says that Mary has chosen the better part (Luke 10:38–42). Aquinas thinks that in the resurrection the active life will come to an end; only the contemplative life will persist: "In fact, the contemplation of truth begins in this life, but reaches its climax in the future; whereas the active and civic life does not go beyond the limits of this life."[89]

Neil Ormerod and John Thiel read Aquinas's interpretation of the life of the blessed with appreciation as well as with some criticism. Ormerod notes that Aquinas and *Benedictus Deus* focus on the vision of the divine essence, rather than the vision of the Trinity.[90] Ormerod proposes a trinitarian understanding of the beatific vision. He presents it as a supernatural participation in the life of the triune God. In particular, he conceives of the life of the blessed in terms of created participation in the four trinitarian relations: paternity, filiation, active spiration, and passive spiration. He interprets the meaning of these relations in terms of speaking a word and giving a gift. In the beatific state, we imitate the Father (and thus participate in filiation) by speaking our own word of love, a word of praise and adoration before God. In imitation of the Son (participation in paternity), the word spoken is ourselves. In imitation of the Father and the Son (participation in passive spiration) we give the gift of our love to God without limit. And in imitation of the Holy Spirit (participation in active spiration) we are that very gift of love, we give our very selves to God.[91] The blessed speak this word and give this gift to God and to the other blessed in heaven. Ormerod argues that this approach to the beatific vision avoids the danger of an overly individualized view of ultimate fulfillment, since it views the life of the blessed in interpersonal terms. He likens it to the exchange of vows between a couple in marriage, wherein each spouse "gives the gift of love to the other, and each spouse is that very gift given to the other."[92] In this account, therefore, the life of the blessed is a dynamic sharing in the mutual giving and receiving that is the life of the Trinity.

John Thiel takes issue with Aquinas's position that the blessed are not engaged in the active life.[93] Thiel draws on the resurrection appearance accounts in the Gospels of Luke and John. In these stories, the risen Jesus keeps the promises he had made to his disciples, bears the pain of his life without reproach, reconciles the failures of his disciples, and shows himself to be who he is.[94] Thiel points to the narrative in John 21 wherein Jesus reconciles the failure of Peter, allowing Peter to mend their broken relationship. Thiel then proposes that the blessed dead imitate the activity of the resurrected Christ, particularly by engaging in the ongoing work of reconciliation. He envisions forgiveness as "an ongoing moral endeavor of the blessed dead, an endeavor that completes the salvation of the saints in heaven into eternity."[95] While there is no sinning in heaven, the effects of sin linger in the resurrected life. Thiel imagines the blessed dead as "presently engaged in the same graceful activity of reconciliation, both among themselves and toward those in earthly life where the actuality of sin ever threatens the solidarity of the saintly community."[96] For Thiel, the blessed dead are busily engaged in the activity of forgiveness and reconciliation.

The constitution *Benedictus Deus* says that the blessed see the divine essence without the mediation of any creature by way of object of vision. As we noted above, Karl Rahner contends that this teaching does not exclude the mediation of the risen Christ. He argues that the resurrected humanity of Jesus has eternal significance for our relationship with God.[97] His argument is based on the fundamental principle that the nearer one comes to God the more real one becomes. This principle pertains to God's relationship with the entirety of creation, especially to God's relationship with humanity. When God draws close, the human is not nullified, absorbed, or abbreviated; it is brought to perfection. If in Jesus we have the closest possible union between the human and the divine, then the humanity of Jesus must be the most real of all. And it continues to be the most real in the risen Christ. Thus "it must simply be the case that the humanity of Jesus is the medium through which our immediate relationship with God is achieved."[98] Rahner observes, "One always sees the Father only through Jesus. Just as immediately as this, for the directness of the vision of God is not a denial of the mediatorship of Christ as man."[99]

Many theologians conceive of the life of the blessed dead in terms of the dynamics of love. And this construal means that heaven is a social reality. Gerald O'Collins enumerates eight characteristics of love and then applies his analysis to eschatology.[100] For example, he observes that love has a redemptive quality; real love sets people free and heals the hurts of life. He proceeds to note that "the activity of God's redeeming love will reach its climax in the eschaton."[101] In his encyclical *Spe Salvi* Benedict XVI likens eternal life with God as "like plunging into the ocean of infinite love, a moment in which time—the before and after—no longer exists."[102] Writing before he was pope, he emphasized that if heaven is a christological reality, then it is an experience of life with others:

> If heaven depends on being with Christ, then it must involve a co-being with all those who, together, constitute

> the body of Christ. Heaven is a stranger to isolation. It is the open society of the communion of saints, and in this way the fulfillment of all human communion.[103]

In the first chapter of the Dogmatic Constitution on the Church (*Lumen Gentium*), the Second Vatican Council described the church as "in the nature of a sacrament—a sign and instrument, that is, of communion with God and of unity among all [human beings]" (LG 1). This same constitution acknowledged that the church has been established by Christ as "a communion of life, love and truth" (LG 9). If the nature and mission of the church, the Body of Christ in the world, is to be an efficacious sign of communion with God and among people then it seems appropriate to imagine the life of the blessed dead in terms of communion. As Ratzinger phrased it, heaven is the fulfillment of all human communion. Thus, it is a graced experience of sharing in the dynamic personal communion of life and love that the Trinity is; it is participation in the mutual giving and receiving of love among the three divine persons. The life of the dead is a social (not an individualized) experience because it is communion with others in heaven and with those who are still living their earthly lives. It entails the vision (contemplation) of the infinite, boundlessly loving triune God. But it also includes activity, the activity of promoting solidarity and communion with the other blessed dead and with believers and others on earth. This activity would be especially directed toward those with whom one has experienced (and perhaps contributed to) painful alienation and division. Heaven is also communion with the entire reality of the cosmos and the vivid perception of this cosmos as the loving gift of the Creator God. Paraphrasing Aquinas, one can affirm that the happiness that comes from the experience of communion in heaven fulfills every human desire.

THE POSSIBILITY OF ETERNAL LOSS

In the fourth chapter, we explored the patristic discussion around the scope of salvation. We saw that the teaching about universal salvation (apocatastasis) by some Palestinian monks who saw themselves as followers of Origen was rejected by the church in the sixth century. The affirmation of eternal loss for those in serious sin was echoed in several later councils, including Lateran IV (1215), Lyons II (1274), and Florence (1439). The constitution *Benedictus Deus* declared that "those who die in actual mortal sin go down into hell immediately (*mox*) after death and there suffer the pain of hell."[104] The main focus of this constitution was the immediacy of retribution, but this entailed a reaffirmation of eternal loss for those who die in a state of grave sin.

The official teaching of the contemporary Catholic Church continues to state that believers must acknowledge the possibility of eternal separation from God because of a sinful life. The 1979 letter from the Congregation for the Doctrine of the Faith stated, "She [the church] believes that there will be eternal punishment for the sinner, who will be deprived of the sight of God, and that this punishment will have a repercussion on the whole being of the sinner." The *Catechism of the Catholic Church* declares, "To die in mortal sin without repenting and accepting God's merciful love means remaining separated from him for ever by our own free choice. This state of definitive self-exclusion from communion with God and the blessed is called 'hell'" (*CCC* 1033). The *Catechism* proceeds to state that the teaching of the church affirms the existence of hell and its eternity (*CCC* 1035). The 1992 statement on eschatology by the International Theological Commission reaffirms this teaching, highlighting God's respect for human freedom, through which we can accept or reject God's grace. This statement contends that "we should avoid attempts to grasp in concrete detail how to reconcile God's infinite goodness and human liberty."[105]

In the past century, there has been sustained theological debate about how to understand and interpret this teaching about eternal loss. Much of this debate has centered on how to conceive of the relationship between God's redemptive grace and human freedom. In a very lucid essay, John R. Sachs enumerates five propositions that most Catholic theologians hold with reference to the theme of eternal loss.[106] First, because human beings are free, they are able to reject God. Hell is a real possibility. Salvation cannot be forced on anyone. Second, hell is viewed as a self-chosen state of alienation from God and not an additional punishment inflicted by God upon the sinner. Ratzinger argues that Christ himself is sheer salvation; he inflicts perdition on no one. Perdition comes to be where a person distances himself or herself from Christ.[107] Third, though final damnation remains a possibility with which every individual must reckon, neither Scripture nor church teaching claims that anyone in fact has been or will be finally lost. Fourth, Sachs says that for most Catholic theologians the real possibility of hell must be understood in terms of the gospel of God's universal saving will, which is revealed and effected in Jesus Christ. Heaven and hell, then, should not be considered equally possible outcomes, either for humanity as a whole or for individuals. As his fifth and final proposition, Sachs states that while certain knowledge about the final outcome of judgment for individuals is impossible, because of Christ's victory over sin and death, we may and must hope that all people will in fact be saved.

The writings of Karl Rahner and Hans Urs von Balthasar on eschatology reflect the propositions expounded by Sachs. In an essay on guilt and punishment, Rahner proposes that the idea of "punishment by God" should not be construed as an extrinsic, additional punishment inflicted on the sinner by God. Rather, it should be seen as the consequence or inner moment of the definitive decision a person makes about her or his life through the exercise of freedom. God can be called the punisher of sin only insofar as God has created the objective structures of humanity and the world that include the fact that sinful actions have consequences which affect the whole reality of the person.[108] With this acknowledgement of the reality of human freedom, Rahner says that "a person cannot say that absolute loss as the conclusion and outcome of his [her] free guilt is not a possibility with which he [she] has to reckon."[109] At the same time, Rahner emphasizes that the eschatological doctrine of Christianity is not a teaching about two parallel ways, as found, for example, in Deuteronomy 30. Christians proclaim the victory of God's saving grace for humanity as a whole. They profess that "the world and the human race as a whole will find a blessed and positive fulfillment in Jesus Christ by the power of God's grace."[110] Thus, while Christians affirm the *possibility* of eternal loss, they proclaim the *fact* that the world as a whole will enter into eternal life with God.

Balthasar addressed the issues surrounding the teaching about hell in a number of significant writings, including his book *Dare We Hope "That All Men Be Saved?"*[111] Balthasar stresses that to hope for one's own salvation and not for the salvation of all is un-Christian, since Christ died for all people. Deeply influenced by the mystical visions of Adrienne von Speyr, Balthasar engages in extensive theological reflection on the mystery of Holy Saturday. The self-emptying of Jesus on the cross attains its ultimate end in his descent to the dead. Rather than envisioning Christ's descent as the triumphant entry of the victor to break open the gates of hell and liberate the just, Balthasar views it as the crucified Christ's being with the dead. Christ is in the closest possible solidarity with those who have lost their way from God. For Balthasar, who employs the notion of substitution in his soteriology, Christ's solidarity with the lost in hell completes his standing for sinful humanity before God. In order to pay the entire penalty imposed on sinners, Christ willed not only to die but also to go down, in his soul, *ad infernum*.[112] Stripped by the cross of every power and initiative of his own, the dead Christ serves as a sermon for the dead. He is dead together with them. "And exactly in that way, he disturbs the absolute loneliness striven for by the sinner; the sinner who wants to be 'damned' apart from God, finds God again in his loneliness, but God in the absolute weakness of love who unfathomably in the period of nontime enters into solidarity with those damning themselves."[113] Thus, even hell is a christological place. Perhaps the vision of the love of the crucified one will be capable of melting the heart of even the most hardened sinner. Von Balthasar repeatedly stated that he did not wish to espouse a theory of universal salvations, but, as Sachs notes, he pushed a theology of Christian hope to its very limits, a hope that is universal.[114]

Other Christian theologians take a position that moves them a bit beyond Rahner and von Balthasar. Hans Küng, like Rahner and Balthasar, interprets the New Testament statements about hell as exhortation—a warning to take one's life choices with the utmost seriousness. The biblical notion of judgment, which in his view has a "judicial-purifying character"—must be upheld.[115] No one can exclude the "absolutely final possibility of distance from God."[116] Still, Küng seems to inch closer to proposing that universal salvation is the more likely scenario. He says that "the 'eternity' of the punishment of hell may never be regarded as absolute. It remains subject to God, to his will and his grace."[117] He adds that individual New Testament texts (he points especially to Rom 11:32) suggest a reconciliation of all, an act of universal mercy.

Eschatology has been an abiding concern for the Protestant theologian Jürgen Moltmann from the beginning of his career. Detained in a prisoner of war camp for three years after the end of World War II and tempted to despair, Moltmann has written extensively about the nature of Christian hope. In his work *In the End—the Beginning*, he offers a sustained reflection on the last judgment. he asserts that the approach to the last judgment in Christian preaching has been a threatening message that "poisoned the idea of God in the soul."[118] Not unlike Balthasar, Moltmann argued that Jesus suffered real abandonment from the Father on the cross; this happened so that human beings would never have to suffer such abandonment. Jesus, then, became the brother of the dead and their redeeming ancestor. Thus, he has opened the world of the dead for the future of resurrection and eternal life. Moltmann insists that the judgment that Christ will bring is not retributive justice but God's creative justice.[119] Divine justice heals and saves both the victims and the perpetrators of oppression. It brings justice to the victims and enables the perpetrators to die to their evil actions and the burden of their guilt and to discover new life together with their victims.[120] Moltmann says of Christ's judgment, "The purpose of his judgment is not reward or punishment, but the victory of the divine creative righteousness and justice, and this victory does not lead to heaven or hell but to God's great day of reconciliation on this earth."[121] In the meantime, all the dead are kept sheltered in God, awaiting the day of resurrection.

There is another approach to the possibility of eternal loss, which has sometimes been called the "annihilationist" view. Proposed by various writers in the history of the Christian tradition, it has been suggested more recently by Edward Schillebeeckx.[122] Like Rahner and Balthasar and many others, Schillebeeckx observes that heaven and hell are asymmetrical affirmations of faith. Christian belief in eternal life with God is based on the experience of living communion with God in grace. This gift of grace is made possible by God's overcoming of death in the resurrection of the crucified Jesus. Christian belief in heaven has a definitive quality about it that is not true of the possibility of eternal loss. Schillebecckx rejects the notion of hell as a state of eternal torment, existing alongside heaven. Such a view is based on vengeance. Nevertheless, he argues, the seriousness of the human drama should not be trivialized by a cheap view of divine mercy. Schillebeeckx proposes that those who do evil—the oppressors in human history—may punish themselves "thoroughly for ever."[123] It may be that such evildoers simply no longer exist at death. They cease to exist and will not be remembered in heaven. There is no ground for their eternal existence because they have failed to love. "The evil do not have eternal life; their death is in fact the end of everything: they have excluded themselves from God and the community of the good, nor does any new heaven await them on earth."[124] This exclusion is not the result of a punitive act of God. Rather it is something that people who definitively choose evil do to themselves. As Schillebeeckx puts it, "God does not take vengeance; he leaves evil to its own, limited logic."[125] Schillebeeckx's proposal is intriguing, but one is compelled to ask how Adolf Hitler would not be remembered by the victims of the Shoah.

In his analysis of Catholic approaches to the possibility of eternal loss, Sachs raises questions about the power of human freedom in relation to the power of divine grace.[126] In particular, he questions the ability of human freedom to reject God finally and irrevocably. Drawing on Rahner's theology of grace and freedom, Sachs argues that human freedom essentially means the capacity for God, not the capacity for God or something else. He asserts, "Therefore, it would seem that human freedom can attain real finality only when it reaches the definitiveness for which it is specifically created."[127] So long as human freedom rejects God, it cannot attain finality. Sachs is willing to speak of the *indefinite* persistence of a free no to God, but not of its finality or eternity.[128] Sachs proceeds to argue his case by reflecting on divine judgment. Because human freedom is created and dependent on God, no human being is capable of making a final judgment about herself or himself. That judgment belongs to God alone. In this respect, Sachs appeals to Rahner's theology of the fundamental option and Rahner's admission that no one can make an absolute judgment about her or his stance before God. Sachs rejects the notion of divine judgment as a mere illumination and acknowledgement of the truth of the person's life. He claims that "if the process of Christian dying were nothing more than a 'freezing' of what we have already accomplished (or failed to accomplish!), then the gospel would hardly be good news and we should approach death and judgment with horror."[129] Sachs concludes that divine judgment "is a *life-giving* judgment which forgives, heals, purifies, and bestows fullness and, *therefore*, finality upon human life, that final identity for which it was created and toward which it is directed."[130]

Theological discussion about the possibility of eternal loss is intricately nuanced and replete with "both/and" statements. In particular, one is challenged to affirm both the power of divine grace and the reality of human freedom. We utter our yes or no to God in and through all the daily as well as the more momentous choices and actions in our lives. Sachs is right, however, in reminding us that human freedom is a gift from God and is dependent upon God, and thus it is made for God. In Rahnerian terms it is the capacity for definitive self-disposal before God. Thus, the misuse of human freedom—a choice for evil—is intrinsically self-contradictory. Freedom discovers its true finality only in God.

In my view, if Christian discourse about life after death involves a projection forward of the present experience of the grace of God in Christ, then it is hard to conceive of God allowing anyone to suffer eternal perdition. Once again, imagination has a role to play in eschatology. The idea that the God who revealed Godself most definitively in the crucified and risen Christ would consign or even allow a person to suffer exclusion from God's presence for eternity is difficult to imagine. I prefer the perspective of Gregory of Nyssa, whose eschatology was never repudiated by the church.[131] We saw that he envisioned a process of purification from sin and spiritual growth throughout earthly life and beyond. The purifying action of God removes the evil that is mingled with human nature. It enables the image of God to come to its full realization in the human race as a whole. From this perspective, sin and its baneful effects are taken seriously. Presumably, the process of purification from sin will be of much greater intensity and duration for some than for others. Evildoers will come face to face with the evil they have perpetrated and the suffering that it has caused. This is not a superficial or "cheap" understanding of divine mercy. This approach does, however, leave the final word to God's grace—to the self-communication of God, which purifies, heals, and gives life. The revelation of the boundless mercy and love of God experienced in the life of grace gives reason to have a firm hope that the God of steadfast love and mercy will eventually embrace every person whom God has created.

LIMBO

What is the destiny of babies who die without having been baptized? This question has challenged the thinking of theologians from the early church to modern times. The International Theological Commission published a lengthy study of this question in 2007.[132] In chapter 4, we saw that Augustine was convinced that in order to be saved, one must be baptized and remain in communion with the Catholic church. He included unbaptized infants among the condemned, though he said that they would suffer the mildest punishment. Some medieval theologians strove to develop alternative approaches to this question. Pope Innocent III taught that unbaptized infants who die, because they have not been freed from original sin, lack the beatific vision.[133] Peter Abelard, Peter Lombard, and some other medieval theologians argued that unbaptized infants suffer no other penalty except the privation of the vision of God. Thomas Aquinas "thought that unbaptized children feel no pain at all or even that they enjoy a full natural happiness through their union with God in all natural goods."[134] The term *limbo* (from the Latin word *limbus*, meaning "border") was brought into the theological discussion at the end of the twelfth and beginning of the thirteenth centuries, and it continued to be used into the twentieth century. Limbo came to be understood as "a state which includes the souls of infants who die subject to original sin and without baptism and who therefore neither merit the beatific vision nor yet are subjected to any punishment because they are not guilty of any personal sin."[135] The International Theological Commission pointed out that the theory of limbo never entered into the dogmatic definitions of the magisterium.

The ITC accepts the teaching of Innocent III that original sin deprives a person of the beatific vision, but it argues that there are ways other than sacramental baptism through which God can act to remove original sin. This argument is grounded in the biblical affirmation of the universal salvific will of God (1 Tim 2:4). In this regard, the commission refers to an important passage in Vatican II's *Gaudium et Spes*: "Since Christ died for all, and since all are in fact called to one and the same destiny, which is divine, we must hold that the Holy Spirit offers to all the possibility of being made partners, in a way known to God, in the paschal mystery" (GS 22). The commission also appeals to the doctrine of the immaculate conception, which affirms God's unmerited gift to Mary "by which God simply acted to give her in advance the grace of salvation in Christ."[136]

The ITC document notes that at the time of the Second Vatican Council there was a request made for the council to state that unbaptized infants who die are definitely deprived of the vision of God. The council did not accept this request in part because bishops testified that this was not the faith of their people; it did not correspond to the *sensus fidelium*.[137] The *Catechism of the Catholic Church* makes no mention of limbo; it simply says of children who have died without baptism that the church entrusts them to the mercy of God. The universal salvific will of God and the Gospel witness to Jesus's tenderness toward children give hope that there is a way of salvation for children who have died without baptism.[138] These same sentiments are found in the funeral liturgy of the church. At the vigil for a deceased child, the opening prayer that is used in the case of a child who died before baptism reads, "God of all consolation, searcher of mind and heart, the faith of these parents [N. and N.] is known to you. Comfort them with the knowledge that the child for whom they grieve is entrusted now to your loving care. We ask this through Christ our Lord."[139]

The International Theological Commission concludes its study of this question with these observations:

> Our conclusion is that the many factors that we have considered above give serious theological and liturgical grounds for hope that unbaptized infants who die will be saved and enjoy the beatific vision. We emphasize that these are reasons for prayerful hope rather than grounds for sure knowledge. There is much that simply has not been revealed to us (cf. John 16:12). We live by faith and hope in the God of mercy and love who has been revealed to us in Christ, and the Spirit moves us to pray in constant thankfulness and joy (cf. 1 Thess 5:18).

7

CORPORATE AND COSMIC FULFILLMENT

The Christian tradition speaks of final fulfillment not only for individuals but for humanity as a whole and for the entire cosmos. In this chapter we explore themes related to corporate and cosmic fulfillment: the communion of saints, the Parousia, the general judgment, and the dialogue between scientific cosmology and Christian eschatology on the future of the cosmos.

THE COMMUNION OF SAINTS

In our survey of Christian eschatology, we have seen that believers found hope and encouragement in the bonds of faith and charity that they had established with their fellow Christians. They came to perceive these bonds as enduring even through death and beyond. This conviction is especially evident in the practice of prayer for the dead, which began in the early church. We took note of Brian Daley's observation that early Christian theologians and believers affirmed that the dead are still involved in the life of the church, both in praying for the living and in benefiting from the prayers of the living. The witness of the martyr Perpetua, who prayed for her deceased brother Dinocratus, is particularly redolent of this conviction. Augustine advocated prayer for the dead in his treatise *The Care to Be Taken for the Dead*. In Aquinas's discussion of suffrages, he affirmed that charity, which is the bond uniting the members of the church, extends not only to the living but also to the dead who die in charity. Charity has no end.

These convictions and practices impel us to consider Christian belief in the communion of saints. The Latin term *communio sanctorum* is grammatically ambiguous. The word *sanctorum* can be read as the genitive plural of the masculine word *sancti* or of the neuter word *sancta*. If it refers to the former, it designates a communion among holy persons. If the latter, it refers to a communion in holy things, that is, communion in the sacraments, especially the Eucharist. Susan Wood points out that in the Apostles' Creed this ambiguity serves the text, for it means both. The sacramental meaning is causative of the personal meaning. Participation in Christ through the sacraments creates the unity of the church, leading to a community of persons in Christ.[1] "The sacramental participation in Christ creates with all others in union with him an interrelationship so close and interdependent that it is best described as the communion of a 'body.'"[2]

As we saw in chapter 5, Vatican II's Dogmatic Constitution on the Church highlighted the enduring bonds among the living and between the living and the dead. It distinguished three groups of disciples of Jesus: those who are pilgrims on the earth, others who have died and are being purified, and others who are in glory, contemplating the triune God. The constitution said, "All, indeed, who are of Christ and who have his Spirit form one Church and in Christ cleave together (Eph 4:16). So it is that the union of the wayfarers with the brethren who sleep in the peace of Christ is in no way interrupted, but on the contrary, according to the constant faith of the Church, this union is reinforced by an exchange of spiritual goods" (*Lumen Gentium* 49).

The communion of saints is experienced, first of all, among living Christians. The "saints" are not only those who have been officially canonized by the church. The biblical testimony speaks of the holiness of all who are partners in the covenant with the God of Abraham and Sarah and in the case of Christians with the God of Jesus Christ. In the Old Testament, the people of Israel are named as a "holy" people: "Since I, the Lord, am the one who brought you up from the land of Egypt that I might be your God, you shall be holy, because I am holy" (Lev 11:45). The people of Israel are holy not because they are morally perfect but because they belong to the holy God. They have been consecrated to God. Holiness is about belongingness. As Elizabeth Johnson describes it, holiness in the Jewish tradition "is a gift freely bestowed by God in view of the inscrutable divine choice to forge a covenant relationship with this small, powerless, enslaved people."[3] This same biblical view of holiness carries over into the writings of the New Testament, especially in the letters of Paul. Writing to the Christian community at Rome, Paul says, "Through [Christ] we have received the grace of apostleship, to bring about the obedience of faith, for the sake of his name, among all the Gentiles, among whom are you also, who are called to belong to Jesus Christ; to all the beloved of God in Rome, called to be holy" (Rom 1:5–7). Paul addresses the Christians at Philippi as "all the holy ones in Christ Jesus who are in Philippi" (Phil 1:1). These Christians are "saints" (holy ones; *hagioi* in Greek) because they are "in Christ Jesus;" through the life, death, and resurrection of Jesus they have been given a share in the life of the holy God. This participation in the divine life is expressed and brought about in the sacraments of baptism and the Eucharist.

The Second Vatican Council retrieved this biblical understanding of holiness, articulating it in the fifth chapter of *Lumen Gentium*. The constitution affirms that the church is "unfailingly holy" because Christ "loved the church as his bride, giving himself up for her so as to sanctify her" (LG 39). Therefore, all in the church are called to holiness. Holiness is described in the constitution as "the perfection of love" (LG 39). The council proceeds to teach that disciples of Jesus, who are called by God not in virtue of their own works but by his design and grace, "have been made sons and daughters of God in the baptism of faith and partakers of the divine nature, and so are truly sanctified" (LG 40). It then exhorts believers to hold on to and perfect in their lives the sanctification they have received from God. In this teaching, Vatican II echoes the indicative/imperative structure of Paul's teaching about Christian holiness. The members of the church *are* holy because of God's gracious gift; they are then called to *act* as God's holy people by growing in faith and charity.

Pope Francis continues this practice of affirming the holiness of "ordinary" Christians. In his apostolic exhortation *Gaudete et Exsultate* (Rejoice and Be Glad), he includes a section that is titled "The Saints Next Door."[4] Francis teaches that the Holy Spirit bestows holiness in abundance among God's holy and faithful people. Eschewing a purely individualistic conception of the Christian life, the pope declares, "In salvation history, the Lord saved one people. We are never completely ourselves unless we belong to a people. That is why no one is saved alone, as an isolated individual."[5] Christians are challenged to view themselves as belonging to a people made holy by the grace of God. Francis proceeds in this exhortation to offer examples of the holiness that is present in the everyday lives of people. He invites his readers to take notice of the holiness that is present in their very midst: "Very often it is a holiness found in our next-door neighbors, those who, living in our midst, reflect God's presence. We might call them 'the middle class of holiness.'"[6] In sum, the symbol of the communion of saints refers, first of all, to the solidarity that followers of Jesus have with their fellow Christians around the world. Every believer belongs to a people who have been sanctified, and she or he is called to reflect the presence and holiness of God in everyday life. And, since God's grace is offered to every person, Christians are also summoned to recognize the workings of divine grace in the lives of people of other faith traditions as well as of those who do not profess any religious faith.

The symbol of the communion of saints expands to include the enduring connection between the living and those who have gone before us in faith. This is evident in the practices of prayer for the dead and the veneration of the saints, mentioned above. In *Lumen Gentium* the council declared that it "accepts loyally the venerable faith of our ancestors in the living communion which exists between us and our brothers [and sisters] who are in the glory of heaven or who are yet being purified" (LG 51). On the Solemnity of All Saints, the church celebrates the countless ranks of those who are "in the glory of heaven"—both the saints who have been canonized and those who have not received such official recognition by the church. Karl Rahner observes that on the Solemnity of All Saints, the church celebrates the fact that women and men have attained to their ultimate and definitive goal. Rahner observes, "That in itself constitutes something that is wonderful."[7] Rahner asserts that the message of this annual festival is "that God can make all into saints, into miracles and masterpieces so full of unexpected blessedness that one's heart can be transfixed with delight at them a whole eternity through."[8] He argues that the celebration of All Saints should be a source of encouragement and hope for all Christians. "We should realize that in the course of the world's history an innumerable multitude has already been drawn into the eternity of God before us, so that we are the late-comers. And the realization of this should generate hope and consolation in us, courage and trust."[9]

The doctrine of the communion of saints does shine light on our relation to those saints who have been officially recognized by the church. Elizabeth Johnson describes these men and women as "paradigmatic figures." They "focus the energies of the Spirit for a local community with its own needs and dreams."[10] The author of the Letter to the Hebrews tries to encourage the disheartened Christians to whom he is writing by chronicling the fidelity of the "ancients," beginning with Abel and Noah, moving on to Abraham and Sarah, Jacob and Moses, and finally admitting that he does not have the time to tell of others like David and the prophets (11:1–40). He goes on to encourage these believers to recall this "great cloud of witnesses" (12:1) and to persevere in running the race that lies ahead of them. The image is one of a stadium in which the runners are preparing for a race. In the stands are the "veterans" who have run the race before and now are encouraging those who are still in the contest. The message is one of hope and empowerment—the living memory of those who have been exemplary in their discipleship both consoles and emboldens believers who are facing opposition or other difficulties in living their faith.

Veneration of the saints emerged slowly in the early church. The lives of the apostles and martyrs were remembered and celebrated during the era of persecution of the church by the Romans. Christians displayed special affection for the martyrs, whose graves became places of pilgrimage and prayer. On the anniversaries of their deaths, vigil was kept culminating in the celebration of the Eucharist early in the morning. Commenting on this early development Johnson says, "In this era, the communion of saints was practiced as a disciplined way of remembering across the generations that empowered Christian life."[11] When the era of persecution ceased, other figures of sanctity began to be remembered and honored: confessors, who had suffered for the faith but not been killed; Christians revered for their ascetical lifestyles, like the mothers and fathers of the desert; and teachers and leaders known for their wisdom and courage. Among these were Mary the mother of Jesus, whose veneration slowly emerged in the first centuries of the church, reaching a high point in 431, when the Council of Ephesus named her as *Theotokos*, Mother of God (God-bearer). During the first millennium the naming of holy women and men happened "more or less spontaneously by the people and their bishops in different locales."[12] But by the thirteenth century, naming new saints (inscribing them in the church's official canon of holy people) was restricted to the papacy alone.

What is the theological rationale for the church officially recognizing the holiness of certain people through the process of canonization? Rahner addresses this question in his reflections on the Solemnity of All Saints. He acknowledges that for the church to make such a judgment about the holiness of an individual is a bold step, given the biblical injunction against judging our brothers and sisters. Nevertheless, Rahner argues that the church is the "incarnation of the divine compassion" and as such she is holy in a visible sense.[13] He says, "Rather [the church] is the compassion of God as eschatologically victorious. She is the victory of that grace which has not merely *sought* to save men [and women], but actually *has* saved them."[14] The church canonizes certain individuals as a witness to the fact that the grace of God is present in the world as eschatologically victorious. This act should serve as a source of hope for the living.

Speaking of the saints who have been officially recognized by the church, *Lumen Gentium* says, "God shows to men [and women], in a vivid way, his presence and his face in the lives of those companions of ours in the human condition who are more perfectly transformed into the image of Christ (cf. 2 Cor 3:18)" (LG 50). Here Vatican II depicts our relationship with the saints in terms of companionship. Johnson argues that the use of the language of companionship by Vatican II represents a shift in models from the approach that preceded the council.[15] She observes that in late antiquity there was a change from a companionship model of relationship to a spiritual patronage system, modeled on the Roman system of civic patronage. With this shift, the saints (including Mary) became heavenly patrons of individuals or communities. This patronage paradigm became even more intense in the years after the Council of Trent, with the saints being perceived as mediators between believers and Christ, obtaining favors for petitioners. Johnson envisions the approach taken at Vatican II as a return to the ancient model focused on companionship and solidarity. Mary and other holy people are not depicted as standing between Christ and believers but alongside their fellow believers, offering their support and encouragement. The emphasis here is that "in the light of salvation by God in Jesus Christ, the relationship between all of the redeemed is fundamentally mutual and collegial."[16] At the same time, as Johnson acknowledges, sometimes companionship does entail intercession for the person whom I am companioning. So perhaps there is the need to integrate the values of both of these models of relationship between the saints and pilgrims on the earth.

Johnson's study of the symbol of the communion of saints is also important for its critique of the tradition of the saints, expressed from the perspective of feminist theology.[17] Feminist scholars point out that the official list of saints contains a majority of men, most of whom are celibate. Married women saints are few in number. Canonized women are mostly virgins and martyrs, "described with stereotypical feminine virtues."[18] In this tradition Mary is often depicted as "the silent embodiment of the so-called feminine ideal of sweetness and nurture."[19] The vital agency of these holy women is muted in the tradition. As a partial exception to this mindset, Johnson cites the apostolic letter of Pope Paul VI, *Marialis Cultus*. In that letter, the pope emphasizes that modern presentations of Mary must take into account the emergence of women as equal to men in fields of public endeavor. He describes Mary as "a woman of strength, who experienced poverty, flight and exile." She is the disciple who works for that justice that sets free the oppressed and that charity which assists the needy.[20]

Some scholars who focus on contextual theology perceive a connection between the Christian symbol of the communion of saints and the tradition of ancestor veneration, especially in cultures in Asia and Africa. In a study of this possible connection from the perspective of the African churches, Edward Fasholé-Luke contends that "if Christian theologians in Africa give the doctrine of the communion of saints the centrality which it deserves, it could provide a possible framework for incorporating African ideas about ancestors into Christian theology."[21] He admits that this must be a critical incorporation. For example, the idea that no death can take place except by the will of the ancestors must be rejected in light of the Christian belief that life and death are in the hands of God and that Christ is the Lord of the dead and the living. Still, he concludes by suggesting that "the veneration of ancestors in Africa and our passionate desire to be linked with our dead in a real and genuine way can be satisfied by the development of a sound doctrine of the communion of saints."[22]

The doctrine of the communion of saints has profound pastoral and spiritual significance. Among pilgrims on earth, the symbol connotes deep connections between believers and, indeed, among all "men and women of good will in whose hearts grace is active invisibly" (*Gaudium et Spes* 22). In and through Christ God has forged a solidarity of believers with one another that lies deeper than all of our differences. And, as Johnson suggests, at a time in which we are more aware of our ecological responsibilities, this communion of "holy things" can be extended "to include the gifts of air, water, land, and the myriad creatures that share the planet with human beings in interwoven ecosystems."[23] For those who have lost a loved one in death, the symbol of the communion of saints can engender hope and serve as a deep source of consolation. The bereaved often feel an aching sense of emptiness—a void that has been created by the death of someone they loved. They are struck by the apparent finality of death and the feeling that all communication with the deceased has been terminated forever. While not a magical "cure" for grief, belief in the communion of saints can awaken the hope that the bonds of faith and love that we have forged with our loved one have not been severed by death. Death is powerful, no doubt; but Christians believe that it is not as strong as the redeeming, life-giving love of God. Therefore, we can continue to relate to our beloved dead who are present to us in a distinct but real way. Nowhere is this presence more real than at the celebration of the Eucharist. There are always more people gathered around the Eucharistic table than those we can perceive with our physical eyes. Those who have gone before us in faith are present with us, offering praise and thanksgiving to God and praying for us, as we also pray for them.

THE PAROUSIA

In chapter 3 we saw that the hope for the full realization of the kingdom of God preached by Jesus became referred to in the theological tradition as the Parousia of Christ. While other terms are also used in the New Testament to denote this culminating event, the Greek term *Parousia* became the prominent word to refer to the return of Jesus Christ in the last days. Drawing on the analysis given by Mario Inzulza, we noted certain general characteristics of the

New Testament witness to the Parousia. It will be visible; it will be sudden; it will entail a coming publicly in glory; and it will have ultimate significance for human beings and the rest of creation. We also recognized that the "timing" of this culminating event is viewed in diverse ways in the New Testament. In his early letters, Paul seems to have thought that the return of Christ was imminent. His later epistles, however, show that he was reckoning with the prospect of dying before the Parousia. The eschatological vision of the Gospel of John includes references to final fulfillment taking place in the future, but its overall emphasis seems to be that judgment and eternal life are experienced in the present. We saw that the problem of the delay of the coming of Christ is addressed in the Second Letter of Peter, as the author attempts to refute "scoffers" who want to justify an immoral way of life by pointing out that the promised return of Christ has not happened. Luke addresses the nonappearance of the Parousia in a more implicit way by inserting the time of the church as the period between the ascension of the risen Christ and his return.

Belief in the Parousia found its way into the symbols of faith (creeds) that were promulgated by the church and in the prayers of the liturgy, both of which remain an integral part of Christian life and practice today. When reciting the Apostles' Creed, which developed in the West from the third century on and is rooted in the baptismal practice of the church of Rome, contemporary believers profess, "He [Jesus Christ] ascended into heaven, and is seated at the right hand of God the Father almighty; from there he will come to judge the living and the dead."[24] In the Nicene-Constantinopolitan Creed (381), we say, "He ascended into heaven and is seated at the right hand of the Father. He will come again in glory to judge the living and the dead and his kingdom will have no end."[25] In 1215, the Fourth Lateran Council issued a symbol of faith to counter the heresies of the Albigensians and the Cathars. It says of Christ,

> He shall come at the end of time to judge the living and the dead and to render to each one according to his works, to the reprobate as well as to the elect. All of them will rise with their own bodies which they now bear, to receive according to their works, whether these have been good or evil, the ones perpetual punishment with the devil and the others everlasting glory with Christ.[26]

The prayers of the Eucharist also include references to the coming of Christ. Immediately after the institution narrative in Eucharistic Prayer III, the priest prays, "Therefore, O Lord, as we celebrate the memorial of the saving passion of your Son, his wonderous resurrection and ascension into heaven, and as we look forward to his second coming, we offer you in thanksgiving this holy and living sacrifice." In Eucharistic Prayer IV, we hear,

> Therefore, O Lord, as we now celebrate the memorial of our redemption, we remember Christ's death and his descent to the realm of the dead, we proclaim his resurrection and his ascension to your right hand, and, as we await his coming in glory, we offer you his body and blood, the sacrifice acceptable to you which brings salvation to the whole world.

The eucharistic assembly also proclaims the Christ who will come again in the Memorial Acclamation, for example: "We proclaim your death, O Lord, and profess your resurrection, until you come again." And in the prayer that follows the recitation of the Lord's Prayer, we pray that we may be free from sin and safe from all distress, "as we await the blessed hope and the coming of our Savior, Jesus Christ."

What is it that Christians are looking forward to as they await Christ's coming in glory? How should we conceive of the Parousia today? A brief survey of the interpretations by some recent theologians on this doctrine can shed some light, though differences among them remain.

Karl Rahner reflects on the theme of the coming of Christ and the end of the world in various writings throughout his career. In an early essay on the resurrection of the body, he asserts that the end of the world will mean the perfection of what has already gained its decisive victory in Jesus Christ and his resurrection. The victory of Christ will be manifest to all; it will break through into experience. This transformation will affect not only human beings but the world as a whole: "The world as a whole flows into his resurrection and into the transfiguration of his body."[27]

In a reflection titled "He Will Come Again," Rahner focuses on the message given to the community of believers after the ascension of Jesus: "This Jesus who was taken up from you into heaven will come in the same way as you saw him go into heaven" (Acts 1:11).[28]

Rahner emphasizes the promise that the risen Jesus will come "in the same way." The one who will come again is the same person who walked the roads of Galilee and appeared to followers after the resurrection. Rahner says, "There is no need for us to fear that because he has gone away he may return as someone else who, in the meantime, has undergone a transformation, so that he is no longer the person whom we knew, and of whom we have experience."[29] The Jesus who will come again will return as the person he was then, "as the man who went to his death, as the man who has already experienced everything that we have to bear in the way of joy and pain, life and death, victory and defeat."[30] This belief is a source of profound hope for all Christians.

In his lengthy prayer, "God Who Is to Come," Rahner articulates a kind of "progressive" conception of the one, single coming of Christ.[31] The incarnation was the beginning of Christ's coming. And Christ is still coming:

> It is said that You will come again, and this is true. But the word *again* is misleading. It won't really be "another" coming because You have never really gone away. In the human existence which You made Your own for all eternity, You never left us. But still You will come again, because the fact that You have already come must continue to be revealed ever more clearly. It will become progressively more manifest to the world that the heart of all things is already transformed, because You have taken them all to Your Heart.

In his magisterial work *Foundations of Christian Faith*, Rahner does not directly discuss the return of Christ, though he does address the final fulfillment of human history and of the world as a whole. He argues that we must develop a "collective eschatology," which complements individual eschatology. Rahner asserts that Christian eschatology says that "as a whole the history of the world, the history of spirit, and the history of salvation and its opposite is a one-directional history moving towards its final and definitive validity, and hence that it is not a history continuing on into infinity."[32] In this discussion, Rahner entertains the possibility of the existence of subjects with unlimited transcendentality and freedom in other places in the cosmos. With that possibility in mind, he speaks of moving toward the idea "that the material cosmos as a whole, whose meaning and goal is the fulfillment of freedom, will one day be subsumed into the fullness of God's self-communication to this material and spiritual cosmos, and this will happen through many histories which do not only take place on our earth."[33]

Michael Schmaus conceives of the Parousia in terms of manifestation.[34] He points out that the New Testament Pastoral Letters use the term *epiphany* (*epiphaneia*) instead of Parousia to depict the coming of Christ (1 Tim 6:14; 2 Tim 1:10). Schmaus asserts that the second coming of Christ is not a spatial event but a personal experience. He argues that because of his resurrection his life was cut off from historical existence and thus not perceptible from within history. "The return of Christ will mean an actualizing of his glorified mode of existence whose effect will be that it can no longer be veiled: his presence will be immediately visible, so that no one can fail to see him."[35] This experience presumes a transformation of humanity that will enable all to recognize the glorified Christ. No one will be able to avert his or her gaze.

In his major work on eschatology Joseph Ratzinger links the Parousia with the liturgy. He argues that in talking about the return of Christ early Christians were influenced by the Roman cult of the emperor and by the Jewish liturgy (especially the celebration of Rosh Hashanah). For Christians, the day of the LORD referred to in the Old Testament became the day of Jesus Christ. In adopting the cosmic symbolism that was characteristic of these civil and religious liturgical events they depicted Christ as the one who overturns the powers of this world.[36] It is Christ who is the true cosmocrator, not the emperor. Ratzinger emphasizes that the cosmic imagery of the New Testament is not a prediction of a future chain of cosmic events. Rather, "these texts form part of a description of the mystery of the parousia in the language of liturgical tradition."[37] He describes the Parousia as "the highest intensification and fulfillment of the liturgy" and the liturgy as "a parousia-like event taking place in our midst."[38] In the liturgy Christians experience the tension between the present and the future of fulfillment in Christ: "Every Eucharist is parousia, the Lord's coming, and yet the Eucharist is even more truly the tensed yearning that he would reveal his hidden Glory."[39]

Consistent with his theory of resurrection in death, Gerhard Lohfink proposes that the Parousia takes place for every person in death.[40] He argues that the Parousia is "comprehensible and plausible" if we do not transfer earthly understandings of time to time in the presence of God.[41] We should, rather, think of Christ appearing before all people in their death. All people encounter the risen Christ in their deaths "together" and "simultaneously." Lohfink asserts,

> This book, then, says good-bye to the idea that the soul must wait with God in an "*earthly*-temporal sense" until the end of the world, until the judgment of the world, until the resurrection of all the dead, when it will finally receive its glorified body. The "in-between" that is rightly called for cannot be defined in *earthly*-temporal terms. Therefore the end of the world is present to the dying "with" death; the return of Christ takes place "in" death; the resurrection happens "in" death; and so does the judgment of the world.[42]

Lohfink is convinced that this conception of the end-time events enables Christians to live in the same eschatological awareness as the early Christians.

I have already pointed out that the theology of Jürgen Moltmann prioritizes the future.[43] In his work *The Coming of God*, he speaks of God as "the Coming One." He says that "God now already sets present and past in the light of his eschatological arrival, an arrival which means the establishment of his eternal kingdom, and his indwelling in the creation renewed for that indwelling."[44] This coming of God out of the future reveals to men and women "new, open horizons, which entice them to set forth into the unknown and invite them to the beginning of the new."[45] This orientation to the future leads to Moltmann's emphasis on the doctrine of the Parousia. Rather than treating the Parousia as an afterthought in Christology, as has sometimes been the case in Christian theology, he thinks of it as the keystone in the Christian understanding of the person and work of Jesus. Though Jesus inaugurated the kingdom of God through his ministry, death, and resurrection, he is still the Messiah who is on his way to establishing the fullness of the reign of God. Jesus's person and mission will be seen in their complete truth and significance only when the new creation is established. He conceives of the appearances of the risen Jesus to his followers as experiences in which they saw him as he will be in the future, in the coming glory of God.[46] The future is already present in the risen Christ. At the same time, Christ is still at work in history, still completing his mission as the Messiah. He is still the suffering servant who heals through his wounds and endures the birth pangs of the new creation. Moltmann even suggests that Jesus "grows into" his messiahship, "since he is molded by the events of the messianic time which he experiences."[47] The risen Christ "is not yet the Christ of the parousia who comes in the glory of God and redeems the world, so that it becomes the kingdom."[48] Christians must keep in mind that, while the love of God has become manifest in Jesus, "the glory of God has not yet broken forth out of its hiddenness."[49] Moltmann envisions the Parousia of Christ as the completion of the way of Jesus: "'Christ on the way' arrives at his goal. His saving work is completed."[50] He asserts that the dead are not yet risen, but they are with Christ on his way to his future. "When he appears in glory, they will be beside him and will live eternally with him."[51] Christian praxis in the present should consist of action inspired by the vision of the kingdom given by Jesus; it must be shaped by the coming reign of God, which invites us to new possibilities in the present.

This brief survey of the ways in which prominent theologians interpret the teaching about the Parousia shows that this anticipated "event" is shrouded in mystery. The imagery for the return of Christ found in the New Testament and in some theological accounts cannot be taken as a literal description of Christ's coming. The biblical and theological tradition does envision the Parousia as a collective event that will disclose to all people the ultimate meaning of human history. In my judgment, Lohfink's proposal of the Parousia as taking place in the death of every individual does not do full justice to the Parousia as a symbol of the consummation of history in God. As we have seen, he speaks of this encounter of all with the risen Christ as taking place in death "together" and "simultaneously," and he draws a sharp distinction between earthly time and "time" with God. His description seems to fragmentize the Parousia and, in so doing, to fail to attend to the corporate nature of this encounter with the risen Christ that discloses the meaning of history.

I find the treatment of the Parousia given by Zachary Hayes helpful in approaching this mystery: "The Parousia is not a return of the Lord who has been absent from the world since the resurrection, but the final breaking through of the victorious presence of divine grace that has been present continuously throughout history and in a special way since the death and resurrection of Christ."[52] This description bears resemblance to the statements by Rahner quoted above. Hayes proceeds to say that the Parousia "symbolizes the saving presence of Christ to history and the completion on a cosmic scale of the process begun in his life, death and resurrection."[53] Thus the "coming back" of Christ will really be the self-manifestation of the risen Christ who has been present to every moment of human history; this history will find its consummation in him. The question of the way in which this encounter with Christ entails the completion of the cosmos will be discussed in the final section of this chapter.

GENERAL JUDGMENT

The "coming" of Christ that we have just explored is affirmed in the creeds of the early church as a coming with a purpose—to judge the living and the dead. We have already addressed the theme of particular—individual—judgment. We saw that many contemporary theologians imagine it as a manifestation of the truth of a person's life and character in the presence of ultimate Truth. Some theologians simply address the theme of judgment without distinguishing between particular and general judgment. It is often pointed out that the eschatological hope of the early church focused mainly on the collective judgment that would be rendered at the Parousia. This belief was a symbol of hope, especially during times when Christians were persecuted. However, there was a shift in the early Middle Ages that resulted in a preoccupation with the judgment of the individual. As I noted above, descriptions of judgment became ever more ominous and frightening. One may think here of the monumental depiction of the last judgment painted by Michelangelo in the Sistine Chapel.

Luke Timothy Johnson observes that there are a variety of scenarios related to Christ's coming in judgment in the New Testament.[54] Paul can reflect on the end of history without alluding to the coming of Jesus or to judgment (see 1 Cor 15:24–28). In First Thessalonians, Paul speaks of rescue from the wrath that is coming, but he does not explicitly mention judgment or punishment (1 Thess 1:10). The apocalyptic scenario presented in Mark 13 depicts the coming of the Son of Man to save the elect from tribulation, but it does not explicitly refer to judgment or punishment. Luke portrays the coming of the Son of Man in a cloud with power, but he does not offer a scene of judgment. Matthew, however, "massively expanded the scenario of the end-time and connected it to the final judgment by the Son of Man."[55] The theme of judgment is found throughout chapters 24 and 25 of Matthew: in Jesus's comparing of that time to the days of Noah; his telling the parables of the wicked household manager, the wise and foolish virgins, and the talents; and especially in Jesus's depiction of the Son of Man separating the sheep from the goats, according to the criterion of whether they have welcomed the little ones (Matt 25:31–46). Matthew's portrayal of the judgment exercised a powerful influence on the tradition of Christian eschatology. In the Book of Revelation, the author portrays all the dead gathered before the throne of God. The book of life is opened, and the dead are judged according to their deeds. Those whose names are not written in the book of life are thrown into a pool of fire, along with Death and Hades (Rev 20:11–12).

The particular judgment and the general judgment are not separable; they are more accurately seen as intrinsically related. Zachary Hayes describes individual and collective judgment as "two interrelated dimensions of one, unified mystery: the manifestation of the truth of history, individual and collective, in the light of the truth of God."[56] The doctrine of the general judgment is expressive of the inherently social nature of the human person. It illumines the fact that our lives are interconnected and that our deeds—for good or ill—have a profound impact on others. For Christians, the notion of being a member of the Body of Christ sheds light on this reality. Joseph Ratzinger says, "Even though the definitive truth of an individual is fixed at the moment of death, something new is contributed when the world's guilt has been suffered through to the bitter end. It is at this point that one's final place in the whole is exhaustively determined."[57] As noted in chapter 6, Jürgen Moltmann envisions the perpetrators of history as standing alongside their victims at the final judgment. Moltmann emphasizes that the judgment of Christ is always a social judgment. "The accused do not stand solitary and alone before their judge, as they do in human criminal courts, and in the solitary torments of conscience. The victims stand together with their perpetrators, and the perpetrators with the victims, Cain with Abel, Israel with the nations, the rich with the poor, the violent with the helpless, the martyrs with their murderers. The history of human suffering is indissolubly bound up with its history of guilt."[58] The doctrine of the general, or last, judgment situates the life of each individual within the context of the history of humanity and the cosmos as a whole.

John Thiel expands on this idea of the social nature of final judgment.[59] He emphasizes that judgment for the individual will be historically complete only when history comes to an end. The doctrine of the last judgment is expressive of "an appreciation for the myriad ways that all of our lives are bound together across time and space that elude individual perception."[60] This judgment will reveal all the virtue that has been exercised across the ages. As we have already seen, Thiel thinks that the blessed dead will continue to grow in virtue by engaging in the work of reconciliation and forgiveness throughout eternity. But final judgment will also bring to light the tragedy of sin and its devastating effects throughout human history. This judgment "will also reveal the complex ways in which personal acts, consciously and unconsciously, so readily enter into partnership with evil in order to thwart God's graceful purposes, and so all the peculiar ways in which individuals are responsible for the horrors of history that, in history, would seem disconnected from their agency."[61] The last judgment is, then, the completion of particular judgment through the revelation of the history of virtue and of sin. Thiel asserts that there is an appropriate suspense about the last judgment that the saints should share, but it is a suspense born of hope—"a suspense generated by God's infinite love alone and the hope that God's grace and mercy will extend to all."[62] Gesturing toward the possibility of universal salvation, Thiel describes this eschatological hope as "at once an ardent act of faith in a God who is believed to be so gracious toward creation and so intent on the subversion of evil that this God would not allow any creature to be lost when eternal life offers an infinite horizon for one's redemptive response to the judgment to be enacted."[63]

The symbol of the last judgment signifies the definitive establishment of divine justice. The final coming of Christ will result in right relations throughout the cosmos. In his encyclical *Spe Salvi*, Benedict XVI says, "Faith in Christ has never looked merely backwards or merely upwards, but always also forward to the hour of Justice that the Lord repeatedly proclaimed."[64] Human efforts within history on behalf of justice always fall short of creating perfect justice. While Christians are summoned to commit themselves to living the values of the reign of God, we know that we cannot manufacture the kingdom. It must be given by God. Nor can we vindicate the lives of the countless victims of human injustice whose lives have been consigned to oblivion. Belief that Christ will come again to judge the living and the dead is ultimately an act of hope that God will act in and through Christ to effect perfect justice. Michael Schmaus observes, "In the midst of the painful confusions of this life arising from culpable and inculpable injustices alike, therefore, we are able to look forward with trust to the time when everything will be made right in a final and unqualified way."[65] As we noted in the previous chapter, Jürgen Moltmann names this divine justice as God's creative justice. It reflects the righteousness of God that Jesus disclosed and effected in his public ministry, a righteousness that was practiced in his fellowship with the sinners and the sick. "The one who will come as Judge of the world is the one 'who bears the sins of the world' and who has himself suffered the suffering of the victims."[66] The justice revealed in Christ is neither strict retributive justice nor the calculations of a dispassionate bookkeeper; it is the saving justice of the God who is passionately committed to God's creation. The establishment of this perfect divine justice will entail the dissolution of evil—the defeat of all the forces that drain the life out of people and that wound God's good creation. And it will raise up and vindicate those who have been the innocent victims of human wrongdoing.

The symbol of the last judgment, while exhorting believers to respond wholeheartedly to the offer of God's grace, is ultimately a symbol that engenders hope. It invites us to cling to God as the Source of absolute goodness, the God whose goodness and love will be the final word in human history and the history of the cosmos. Belief in God's final judgment impels us to make memory of the saving deeds of God in history and in our own personal lives, lest we lose heart and be tempted to give up in our efforts on behalf of the reign of God. Benedict XVI asserts, "Only God can create justice. And faith gives us the certainty that he does so. The image of the Last Judgement is not primarily an image of terror, but an image of hope; for us it may even be the decisive image of hope."[67]

Luke Timothy Johnson and Hans Küng offer salutary reminders that belief in particular and general judgment does not provide for us a precise chronology or "itinerary" of God's dealings with the world. The images of this judgment found in the Bible and the theological tradition should not be taken as literal descriptions of the future. Küng asserts that the apocalyptic images and visions of the end of the world would be misunderstood if they were viewed as a kind of chronological revelation of information about the last things at the end of the world. We are not given "with infallible exactitude" the details of what will happen for the concrete shape of things to come.[68] Johnson points out that the propositions of the creed state *that* something is the case, not *how* it is the case. "The profession of Jesus as judge does not state how God through Christ will restore right relations in the world (that is, bring about justice), but it does state that God in Christ knows what those relations are and is powerfully at work to make them right."[69]

COSMOLOGICAL AND ESCHATOLOGICAL VISIONS OF THE FUTURE

Modern theologians must take into account the scientific discoveries about the origins and the future of the universe that have been made in the past hundred years. Concerning the origins of the universe, the work of Edwin Hubble (1889–1953), Father Georges Lemaitre (1984–1966), Arno Penzias (b. 1933), and Robert Wilson (b. 1936)—among many others—led to the development of the "big bang" theory of origins.[70] Hubble's study of the light waves from stars led to the conclusion that the stars are moving away from earth and moving faster in direct proportion to their distance. This finding led to the conclusion that the universe is expanding. Lemaitre proposed that the universe began with an explosion of a "primeval atom."[71] In 1964, Penzias and Wilson detected cosmic background radiation, which scientists had predicted would still be present because of the big bang.

Scientists tell us that the physical origins of the universe date back to about 13.8 billion years when, in a singular, barely decipherable moment, an unimaginably small, hot density of energy went through a period of rapid inflation.[72] From the very start, the physical constants and the initial cosmic conditions had to be exactly what they were in order for the universe to develop in the way it did, especially for life eventually to appear. Early in the first second of this event, the four fundamental forces of nature emerged: gravitation, electromagnetism, and the strong and weak nuclear forces. The nuclei of hydrogen and helium formed when protons and neutrons united. After hundreds of thousands of years, these nuclei bonded with electrons to form atoms. As the universe continued to expand, galaxies began to take shape, comprised originally of large clouds of hydrogen and helium. Stars were formed through processes of nuclear fusion that took place in pockets of gas that had collapsed, heated up and fragmented. Carbon, nitrogen, and oxygen, elements essential to the emergence of life, were formed in further nuclear reactions. With the supernova explosions of large stars, heavier elements were produced and spread throughout the universe, leading to the formation of additional stars and planets. Our solar system formed from a molecular cloud of gas about 4.6 billion years ago. About a billion years after the formation of the solar system, the first bacterial cells, lacking nuclei, appeared on earth. Physicist and theologian John Polkinghorne observes that there seems to have been a direction to this cosmogenesis, leading to the appearance of life:

> Although the universe appears to have been lifeless for the first eleven billion years of its existence, there is a real sense in which it was pregnant with the possibility of life from the very beginning. Only because the balance between the fundamental forces of gravity and electromagnetism is what it is and no different, have stars been able to burn for the billions of years that are necessary if they are to be able to fuel the development of life on one of their planets. Only because the laws of nuclear physics are what they are and no different, has the range of chemical elements necessary for carbon-based life been produced by the stars, from whose dead ashes we and all other living creatures here on Earth are made.[73]

Contemporary scientists predict that the universe as we know it will eventually end, though the manner of its ending is debated.[74] One theory posits an end to the expansion of the universe and a giant contraction, leading to a collapse back to an extremely small, dense, and hot state. Another theory, favored by many cosmologists, envisions the endless expansion of the universe, which will result in diminished energy and the inability to support life. It will lead to a state of entropy death. Polkinghorne explains that the universe itself, "on the largest possible scale on which we observe it, is balanced between the competing effects of the initial big bang (blowing matter apart) and the pull of gravity (drawing matter together). Our knowledge is not sufficiently accurate to enable us to be sure which tendency will ultimately win, but either way the observable universe is condemned to eventual futility."[75] Long before the demise of the universe, carbon-based life on earth will become extinct. Scientists predict that in about five billion years the sun will run out of its hydrogen fuel, swell up and become a red giant, engulfing the orbits of Venus and Mars and burning up planet Earth in the process.

The Jesuit astrophysicist William Stoeger discusses other possible catastrophes that Earth could undergo before being burnt by a swollen sun.[76] For example, he makes note of the well-known crater found in Yucatan, Mexico, which was formed about 65 million years ago when an asteroid at least ten kilometers in diameter crashed into the earth, releasing more than 100 million megatons of energy. There is solid evidence that this event caused or substantially contributed to a mass extinction during which the dinosaurs and other species disappeared. Stoeger notes that in at least three of the five major mass extinctions identified by scientists, there is significant evidence that asteroid or cometary impact was a contributing factor. He chronicles other possible planetary catastrophes as well, like comets crashing into earth and the collision of two neutron stars, which would release a huge amount of energy and form a black hole, destroying all life existing within a space of thousands of light years. These and other catastrophic events remain real possibilities for our planet. Stoeger argues that Christians must take these possibilities seriously:

> If we are to take the truth discovered by the sciences seriously, denying the scientific description of death and the more reliable scientifically supported accounts of eventual certain life-ending and earth-ending catastrophes is really not an option. Choosing that course leads us to reject unreasonably a great deal of overwhelming evidence concerning how life and its nurturing environments emerged, developed and are structured, as well as very well substantiated conclusions concerning past catastrophic events and the potential for such events in the future.[77]

Scientific predictions about the distant future of life and the universe itself are, then, quite sobering. What responses do these predictions elicit, in nonbelievers and believers? Robert John Russell discusses some of these responses.[78] There are those who view eschatology as irreconcilable with cosmology. Russell quotes a statement made by the Nobel Prize winning scientist Steven Weinberg, who speaks of a "hostile universe" and says, "It is even harder to realize that this present universe has evolved from an unspeakably unfamiliar condition, and faces a future extinction of endless cold or intolerable heat. The more the universe seems comprehensible, the more it also seems pointless."[79] Russell also refers to "physical cosmology," developed by Freeman Dyson, Frank Tipler, and John Barrow. These thinkers, in different ways, reduce human life to information processing. Russell states that for Tipler and Barrow, "if the rate of [information] processing could continually increase, an infinite amount of information could be processed (thus, they claim, constituting 'eternal life') even in the finite time remaining before the closed universe fries."[80] Russell also cites thinkers who argue that the findings of cosmology are simply irrelevant to eschatology because science and theology inhabit two separate worlds. Russell calls this approach a "dead end." The approach of the scientist and theologian Arthur Peacocke sets aside the questions of bodily resurrection and the redemption of nature, instead focusing on our personal movement toward and into God that begins in the present. Peacocke views our ultimate destiny as the beatific vision of God. Finally, Russell adduces various perspectives from process theologians, who envision an ultimate condition of "objective immortality" through God's memory of us. While some process theologians have also suggested a "subjective immortality" in which a person continues after death to be a center of experience within God, there are questions about how congruent such a view is with the philosophical system of Alfred North Whitehead. Russell concludes that "these [process] views cannot deal adequately with the bodily resurrection of Jesus, viz., the empty tomb traditions, nor respond to the challenge that science poses about the far future."[81]

Polkinghorne and Russell also attempt to address the challenges to Christian belief in bodily resurrection and the transformation of the cosmos posed by scientific cosmology. Polkinghorne locates the foundation of eschatological hope in the resurrection of Jesus from the dead. The pattern of what happened to Jesus is the pattern of what will happen for each person and for the cosmos itself. The dead Jesus is raised up to new life. The body of the risen Christ bears the marks of his passion but is also transformed. It is the same Jesus, but he is in a transfigured state. This means that the hope of Christians for the cosmos does not entail a second creation *ex nihilo*. It is not that God wipes the cosmic slate clean and starts again. Rather, the new creation is the divine redemptive transformation of the old creation. "The new is not a second creation *ex nihilo*; it is a resurrected world created *ex vetere*."[82]

This foundation leads Polkinghorne to emphasize the role that continuity and discontinuity play in Christian eschatology. The new creation for which Christians hope will have elements of continuity with the present creation and elements of newness that entail discontinuity. Polkinghorne suggests that theology will identify the nature of the discontinuities, while the nature of the continuities "are things on which science may hope to comment to some degree, and even contribute some modest insight into the form of coherent possibility."[83] He delineates three areas of continuity that have been illumined by the discoveries of scientists: the significance of relationality in a modern understanding of physical reality; the recognition that the concept of "information" of a pattern-forming kind must be added to the ideas of matter-energy; a dynamic view of physical reality in terms of open becoming rather than static being.

The notion of pattern-forming information plays a leading role in Polkinghorne's account of the eschatological fulfillment of the human person. As we saw in the first chapter, this pattern takes the place inhabited by the "soul" in traditional theological anthropology, and, like Aquinas on the soul, Polkinghorne speaks of this pattern as the form of the body. The carrier of continuity of the person "is the immensely complex information-bearing pattern in which [that] matter is organized."[84] This pattern is the carrier of a person's abiding and unique personal identity. Polkinghorne does not attribute intrinsic immortality to this pattern. The death of the person entails the real end of the information-bearing pattern. The Christian hope is that the pattern that is a human being will be held in the divine memory and that God in the eschatological future will re-embody the information-bearing pattern in a new environment of God's choosing—in the "matter" of the new creation. Polkinghorne envisages this ultimate fulfillment of the person as a dynamic existence that he describes as "everlasting," in contrast to a timeless experience of eternity. He states, "The beatific vision, then, will not be an atemporal experience of illumination but the unceasing exploration of the riches of the divine nature."[85]

In his discussion of the ultimate fulfillment of the cosmos, Polkinghorne also incorporates the elements of continuity and discontinuity. We have seen above that he thinks that science can indicate some of the continuities that will be found in the new creation. Polkinghorne says that the continuity between the old and new worlds will be expressed in a carryover of pattern. At the same time, Polkinghorne asserts that the redeemed universe will have a different physical "fabric" than the current creation. The universe as we experience it is adapted to sustaining the evolutionary exploration of potentiality. In this evolving world, transience is built into the physical fabric and thus death is the necessary cost of life. The matter-energy of the world to come will have a different character. "There will have to be a discontinuous change of physical law."[86] Here Polkinghorne again refers to the empty tomb and the bodily resurrection of Jesus, which is the source of our hope for the transformation of matter. He also alludes to the Eastern Christian idea of divinization (*theosis*)—participation in the life of God. He describes the redeemed new creation as, through the Cosmic Christ, being brought into a freely embraced and intimate relationship with the life of God.[87]

At the end of his book *The God of Hope*, Polkinghorne lists four summary propositions of eschatology: (1) If the universe is a creation, it must make sense everlastingly, and so ultimately it must be redeemed from transience and decay. (2) If human beings are loved by their Creator, they must have a destiny beyond their deaths. Every generation must participate equally in that destiny, in which it will receive the healing of its hurts and the restoration of its integrity, thereby participating for itself in the ultimate fulfillment of the divine mystery. (3) Insofar as present human imagination can articulate eschatological expectation, it has to do so within the tension between continuity and discontinuity. There must be sufficient continuity to ensure that individuals truly share in the life to come as their resurrected selves and not as new beings simply given old names. There must be sufficient discontinuity to ensure that the life to come is free from the suffering and mortality of the old creation.

(4) The only ground for such a hope is the steadfast love and faithfulness of God that is testified to by the resurrection of Jesus Christ.[88]

Robert John Russell builds on Polkinghorne's argument that the eschatological hope of Christians is grounded in belief in the bodily resurrection of Jesus. Thus, the transformation of the universe into a new creation will be analogous to what happened at Easter. It is a *creatio ex vetere* rather than a second *creatio ex nihilo.* Like Polkinghorne, Russell asserts that the new creation will entail elements of continuity and discontinuity with creation as we currently know it. He echoes Polkinghorne in arguing that science can offer an important perspective on the elements of continuity.[89]

Russell makes a significant contribution to the discussion through his reflections on the philosophical assumptions that are at work when considering the predictions made by scientists. He argues that scientific theories are descriptive, not prescriptive. One cannot assume that the events that science predicts *must* come to pass. His next move is to assert that "the processes of nature which science describes are the result of God's ongoing action as Creator and that their regularity is the result of God's faithfulness."[90] Thus God is free to act in new ways in human history and in the ongoing history of the cosmos. God did act in such a new way in raising Jesus Christ from the dead, and Christians believe that God will continue to act in new ways to bring about the new creation. Because God did act in a new way and continues to do so to bring about the new creation, we can say that scientific predictions about the end of the universe are "right but inapplicable." Russell declares, "In short, the future of the universe *would have been* what science predicts (i.e., freeze or fry) had God *not* acted at Easter and if God did not *continue* to act in the future."[91] God's action in raising Christ from the dead implies that God must have created the universe in such a way that it is transformable by God's action.

Russell offers some thoughts on the continuities and discontinuities characteristic of the new creation. It will not include natural evil. It will include processes of thermodynamics only to the extent that they contribute to natural good, not natural evil. The new creation will involve not only humanity but all the species and individual creatures that have been part of the history of life on earth. He asserts that "every moment in the history of the evolution of life, not just the end of historical time, must be taken up and transformed eschatologically by God into eternal life."[92] This will include the moments of suffering that have been so prevalent in human and cosmic history. The suffering of all of nature, including each species and each individual creature, "must be taken up into the voluntary suffering of Christ on the cross and through it the voluntary suffering of the Father."[93]

The view of final fulfillment proffered by Karl Rahner is grounded in his theology of grace and his Christology, which are intrinsically related. In our discussion of the Parousia, we saw that Rahner envisions the material cosmos as one day being subsumed into the fullness of God's self-communication to the cosmos. Rahner thinks of grace, that is, God's self-communication, as the reason for creation. God desires to give of self in love and so creates an evolving world that eventually produces conscious subjects who can freely accept God's loving self-bestowal. With regard to the motive of the incarnation, Rahner adopts the position of the medieval Franciscan theologian Duns Scotus, thus arguing that God would have become incarnate even if there had been no sin. The primary motive of the incarnation is God's desire to give of self in the most personal of ways. Once sin enters the picture, the incarnation takes on additional, redemptive, meaning. Rahner thinks of creation and incarnation not as two separate initiatives of God but "as two moments and two phases of the *one* process of God's self-giving and self-expression, although it is an intrinsically differentiated process."[94] In the incarnation, the Word of God became united not only with the isolated humanity of Jesus but with the matter of the universe itself. He claims that "the total reality of the world is *ipso facto* touched to its very roots by the incarnation of the Logos."[95] In the person and life of Jesus there is the unconditional and irrevocable self-communication of God (divinity) and the unconditional and irrevocable acceptance of the divine self-communication (humanity). Jesus, the incarnate Word of God, is "that historical person who appears in time and space and signifies the beginning of the absolute self-communication of God which is moving towards its goal, that beginning which indicates that this self-communication for everyone has taken place irrevocably and has been victoriously inaugurated."[96] Rahner explains that by this "beginning" he means the existence of God's self-communication that takes place *irrevocably*; he thinks that God's self-communication itself is coexistent with the whole spiritual history of the human race and of the world.

Rahner's vision of final fulfillment is also based on Christian belief in the resurrection of Jesus from the dead. He appeals to the tradition of Eastern Christian theology, which envisions the resurrection of Jesus as involving the transformation of human beings and of the whole creation.[97] Amid all of the diversity in creation, Rahner perceives a basic underlying unity. This fundamental unity means that the transfiguration of Jesus in the resurrection is an event for the whole world. It touches everyone. He describes the risen Christ as "the pledge and beginning of the perfect fulfillment of the world" and as the "representative of the new cosmos."[98] Rahner, then, speaks of the coming of the risen Christ and the end of the world in these words:

> The end of the world is, therefore, the perfection and total achievement of saving history which had already come into full operation and gained its decisive victory in Jesus Christ and in his resurrection. In this sense his coming takes place at this consummation in power and glory: his victory made manifest, the breaking through into experience, and the becoming manifest for experience too, of the fact that the world as a whole flows into his Resurrection and into the transfiguration of his body.[99]

For Rahner, then, the Christian vision of final fulfillment involves matter, not only spirit. This conviction is especially evident in his reflection "A Faith That Loves the Earth," which was mentioned in chapter 6.[100] Rahner begins by asserting that the Easter message is the most human message of Christianity. He observes that human beings are children of the earth, "too much children of the earth to be able to leave the earth behind completely."[101] Though the earth gives us much that is beautiful, it gives too little to satisfy us. Rahner then adduces Jesus's descent to the realm of the dead in his own death. Jesus reached the very center of earth so that he could infuse it forever with divine life. This means that the earth "is no longer a place of impermanence and death, because there *he* now is."[102] The fact that he is risen in his body means that he has begun to transfigure this world into himself. In his resurrection, Christ has not left the earth, since he still has his body, though now in a transfigured way. Rahner insists that Christians should love the earth. He likens the resurrection of Jesus to "the first erupting of a volcano, which shows that the fire of God is already burning inside the world and its light will eventually bring everything else to a blessed glow."[103] He is convinced that because of Easter the new forces of a transfigured world are already at work. Rahner concludes his meditation by declaring that since Easter "Mother Earth has brought forth only children that will be transfigured, for his resurrection is the beginning of the resurrection of all flesh."[104]

Elizabeth Johnson addresses eschatological themes in the context of constructing a theology of creation that is in dialogue with scientific findings about the origins of the universe.[105] Like Rahner, she emphasizes that what Christian eschatology says about the future of humanity and the cosmos is an extrapolation from the present experience of a faithful and gracious God. It does not pretend to be an eyewitness report from "the end." Thus, eschatological statements are wrapped in mystery. She states, "The logic of belief holds that if this absolute holy Mystery can create life, then this same holy Mystery in faithful love can rescue it from final nothingness."[106]

Johnson thinks that Christian theology must take the predictions about the far future of the universe given by scientific cosmology seriously. She expounds the theories about the demise of the universe and the ending of life on earth in a straightforward way. Johnson argues that Christian hope for a new, transfigured life with God does not deny these scenarios. "Its claim is based not on the potential of the finite world in itself to survive the final death, but on the character of God."[107] The language of eschatological hope is the language of courageous, abiding trust in the fidelity of God. Christian believers trust that "the Giver of life who created all beings out of nothing will still be there after the final devastation, holding fast to the beloved creation."[108]

At the end of chapter 4, we explored the position taken by Thomas Aquinas on the question whether plants and animals would participate in the new creation, and we noted Johnson's comment about it. Johnson appeals to the study of this issue by Paul Santmire.[109] Santmire proposes a symmetry/asymmetry framework in his exploration of Christian thinkers throughout history. He finds that a minority of Christian thinkers envision all living beings as included in the world's final transfiguration. There is symmetry in their thought between creation and redemption: God creates all things and will save all things from final annihilation. The majority of

Christian theologians, however, take an asymmetrical position in arguing that God creates all things but will not necessarily save all things. We saw that Thomas Aquinas is an example of this second position.

Johnson opts for symmetry in her consideration of this question. She argues that "a case can be made that for God to love the whole means to love every part."[110] All living creatures are part of the "flesh" of the world that the Word of God joined in the incarnation. The death and resurrection of Jesus offers hope of redemption for all flesh. The presence of the Creator Spirit who empowers all creation is also the power of resurrected life for all beings. With these principles in mind, Johnson says, "Given the personal presence of divine love to every creature in every moment, and the further revelation of the character of this love in the suffering and hope-filled story of Jesus Christ, there is warrant for holding that species and even individual creatures are not abandoned in death but taken into communion with the living God. Nothing is lost."[111] At the same time, Johnson acknowledges that redemptive fulfillment will be appropriate to each creature's own capacities.

It seems clear that there needs to be ongoing dialogue between theologians and scientific cosmologists on the future of humanity and the cosmos. The observations of Elizabeth Johnson about the nature and "logic" of Christian eschatological hope are helpful. There is no reason for theologians or ordinary Christians to deny well-reasoned scientific theories about the future of the universe and of life on earth, even while acknowledging that such theories may undergo significant modification in the future. If Christian hope for final fulfillment is grounded in belief in the resurrection of the crucified Jesus, this hope can encompass the eventual death of life on earth and the dissolution of the universe. Jesus really died. His human life ended. But God raised him from the dead into a new, transfigured life. God was powerful enough to bring life out of a brutal, oppressive death. Christians believe that the God who created the universe has power over the life of humans, planets and even the life of the universe. The Second Vatican Council, in *Gaudium et Spes*, said, "We know neither the moment of the consummation of the earth and of man [*sic*] nor the way the universe will be transformed. The form of this world, distorted by sin, is passing away, and we are taught that God is preparing a new dwelling and a new earth in which righteousness dwells, whose happiness will fill and surpass all the desires of peace arising in the hearts of men [*sic*]" (GS 39). As Vatican II said, there is much that we do not know about the future. But Christians cling to such a daring hope on the basis of their belief in the way God has acted in the past and in the way that God continues to act and to reveal Godself in the present. The God who created the universe because he wanted to give of self in love, who became human primarily because he sought union with his beloved creatures, who raised his incarnate Son from the dead, will in the end establish a "new" creation out of this "old" creation; it will be a dwelling suffused with God's unfathomable love.

EPILOGUE

Hope amid Suffering

In the exploration of the anthropological foundations of Christian eschatology, I noted that an intrinsic dimension of being human is to be confronted with the reality of suffering in one's own personal life and in the wider world. Much of the eschatological literature of the Bible and theology has been spawned by the experience of intense suffering. Christian eschatology must address the tragic history of suffering, which has scarred the life of every person, especially those who have lived in situations of deprivation and violence.

In that discussion of eschatology, I also asserted that the life of every person is driven by hope—"little hopes" and "bigger" hopes. In fact, the discipline of eschatology entails theological reflection on the language and vision of hope. We saw that Thomas Aquinas argued that we should hope for nothing less from God than God's very self. Despair, on the other hand, is based on a false view of God, one that denies that God grants pardon to sinners and brings salvation to people.

I conclude this study of Christian eschatology by offering a few modest reflections on the witness of Julian of Norwich, the fourteenth-century English anchoress and author of *Showings*.[1] Julian lived and wrote during a period of intense suffering in her society, and yet she authored a text that is suffused with hope to an extent found in few other Christian works. Her oft-quoted exclamation "All shall be well" is an eschatological statement that emerged from her personal encounter with the crucified and risen Christ.

Julian's theology is notoriously difficult to interpret. Edmund College and James Walsh, editors of the critical edition of *Showings*, remark, "Julian is hard going."[2] Denys Turner observes that her saying, "All shall be well" has been made a hackneyed platitude by some, in a way that glides over the complexities of her thought on evil, sin, and divine providence.[3] Still, it must be said that many modern readers have found inspiration and encouragement from reading *Showings*. As suggested above, this attraction may well come from her profound immersion in the mystery of sin and suffering, coupled with her insight into the joy and hope that God's love offers us.

HISTORICAL BACKGROUND

We know very few of the facts of Julian's life. Her given name was probably not Julian, as it was the custom of anchoresses to assume the name of the church to which their anchorhold was attached; in her case it was the church of Saint Julian in Norwich, England. Margery Kempe, another English spiritual writer, reports on a visit to Julian to seek her advice in either 1412 or 1413, noting that Julian was an expert in spiritual guidance.[4] Julian herself tells us that she was thirty-and-a-half years old when she had her seminal mystical experience, in May 1373. Thus, she must have been born near the end of 1342. Historians conclude that records indicating bequests made to a person named Julian, which date from 1413 to 1416, most likely refer to her, so she probably lived until at least the age of seventy-four. College and Walsh remark, "Had it not been that she was convinced that she was divinely commanded to write down her record of her visions, she might have been no more today than one among thousands of names of those who in medieval England lived as solitaries for the love of God, but of whom nothing else is known."[5]

Julian's work exists in two forms: a short text and a long text. Scholars conclude that the short text was written not long after the mystical experience on which it is based. The long text manifests sustained reflection and theological elaboration on this experience. In her reflection on one of her visions—that of the lord and his servant—Julian tells her readers, "For twenty years after the time of the revelation except for three months, I received inward instruction, and it was this: You ought to take heed to all the attributes, divine and human, which were revealed in this example, though this may seem to you mysterious and ambiguous."[6] Thus, it appears that she wrote the longer account of her showings in about 1393. Scholars debate about other details of Julian's life, especially at which stage of her life she undertook her vocation as an enclosed solitary and what she did before her enclosure.

The time in which Julian lived was a period of great tumult and profound human suffering. The Hundred Years War (1337–1453) between France and England dragged on in various phases, draining both countries of manpower and other resources and resulting in heavy taxation of the people. Because Norwich was a secure inland port (on the river Wensum) that was connected to London, it became an important center during this conflict and a crossroads of commerce. In England, peasants felt more and more disenfranchised until they finally revolted against the nobility in 1381, only to be brutally repressed. One of the leaders of this suppression was Julian's warlike and ostentatious bishop, Henry Despenser. In the life of the church, the papacy was exiled in Avignon (1309–1377) and, after its return to Rome, there was the scandalous period of the Great Western Schism (1378–1417), during which there were two and then three rival claimants to the papacy. Most significant, the Black Death ravaged Europe in intermittent waves, crossing over to London in the fall of 1348 and infecting the populace of Norwich in January of 1349.[7] This astoundingly virulent disease killed people within days or even hours of infection. While scholarly accounts of the death toll vary, most estimate that more than a third of the population of Europe perished in the Black Death. The impact on survivors was traumatic. Jane Maynard observes, "It is indeed clear from reading the chroniclers' accounts of the plague's devastation that those remaining alive survived a situation of unspeakable horror."[8]

Julian's work gives evidence of her acute awareness of the turmoil and suffering that must have been taking place outside the window of her anchorhold. With her eyes fixed on the suffering Christ, she engages in a sustained exploration of the mystery of sin and suffering. Her theology is the product of a person who spent much of her life alone with God. But it is not the thought of one who was unfamiliar with the outside world—with the realities of society, the church, and the suffering that ordinary people were facing. "It is clear from her book that Julian identified deeply with the suffering and brokenness of humanity, refusing to accept even the experience of God himself as a substitute for an answer for her urgent questioning about why all of this should be necessary."[9]

JULIAN'S EXPERIENCE OF CHRIST

Julian's theology is rooted in an extraordinary experience that she had a time of severe illness when she was thirty years old. A person of ardent devotion from her youth, Julian tells us of three graces that she specifically sought from God.[10] First, she desired a profound recollection of the passion of Jesus. She wanted to enter into the reality of Christ's passion as if she had been present at the crucifixion, even to the extent of having a vision of this event: "Therefore I desired a bodily sight, in which I might have more knowledge of our saviour's bodily pains, and of the compassion of our Lady and of all his true lovers who were living at that time and saw his pains, for I would have been one of them and have suffered with them."[11] Second, she wanted to experience a bodily illness of such severity that she would be convinced that she was going to die. She explains that she wished for such an illness because she "wanted to be purged by God's mercy, and afterwards live more to his glory because of that sickness."[12] She realized that these two desires were extraordinary, so she prayed that they would be granted to her only if they were in accordance with God's will. Third, she prayed for three "wounds": the wounds of true contrition, loving compassion, and longing with her will for God. She asked for the gift of these wounds without condition, trusting that this prayer was in accord with the teaching of the church.

Julian relates the experience of illness that occasioned her sixteen revelations ("showings") from God, though she focuses more on the revelations than on the details of her sickness. She reports that she became so ill that after three days a priest came to give her the last rites. She lingered for two more days and nights after receiving the sacraments. The priest set a crucifix before her eyes and instructed her to gaze upon it, saying to her, "I have brought the image of your saviour, look at it and take comfort from it."[13] While gazing on the crucifix, she experienced relief from her illness. Then she entered into a series of unusual spiritual experiences, beginning with the sight of blood streaming down the face of Jesus. Her descriptions of some of these showings are quite vivid, as when she depicts the way in which the flesh of Christ became dry in the midst of his suffering, causing him severe pain. Julian tells her readers that some of these showings were visual in form, others involved spiritual understanding, and others consisted of words from God (locutions) that were imprinted on her intellect. Though they vary in content, all of these showings relate to her immersion in the reality of the passion and her gradually deepening insight into the love of God revealed in the suffering Christ.

Julian manifests a deep yearning for complete identification with Jesus in his suffering, for authentic compassion in the sense of "suffering with" the crucified Christ. Reflecting on her experience, she writes, "For I wished that his pains might be my pains, with compassion which would lead to longing for God."[14] She perceives Mary as the exemplar for her own engagement with the suffering Christ. Commenting on the eighth revelation, Julian says, "Here I saw part of the compassion of our Lady, St. Mary; for Christ and she were so united in love that the greatness of her love was the cause of the greatness of her pain."[15] Because Mary had a greater love for her Son than has any human being, she suffered the most intense pains during his passion. Through this experience, Julian became convinced that contemplation of the suffering Christ was the most effective means of personal transformation, resulting in a more profound love of Christ. It was also the pathway to deepened insight into the mystery of God.

Julian says that she writes not just for vowed religious or for other anchoresses, but for all of her fellow Christians. She claims no special status because of the revelations, acknowledging that there are many in the church who have not had such experiences but who have more love for God than she does. As her work progresses, it becomes evident that her entry into the mystery of Christ's passion also entails an abiding concern for the suffering of humanity that was so palpable in her day. She asserts that in his passion Christ "saw and he sorrowed for every man's sorrow, desolation and anguish, in his compassion and love."[16] She proceeds to affirm of the risen Jesus, "And now he has risen again and is no longer capable of suffering, and yet he suffers with us."[17] The intimate relationship between the suffering Christ and suffering humanity becomes clearer to her as she considers the meaning of the allegory of the lord and the servant (see below). In her desire for recollection of the passion, Julian "is surely seeking greater solidarity with suffering humanity, identifying simultaneously with the suffering of Christ and of humankind, and thus able to mediate his compassion."[18]

The fact that Julian's teachings are grounded in an experience of visions raises the question of the authenticity of her theology and spirituality. In response to this concern, Grace Jantzen and Joan Nuth emphasize that these unusual experiences need to be situated within the overall context of her life and historical situation.[19] Nuth takes note of the predominance of visionary experiences among Christian mystics of the thirteenth and fourteenth centuries, especially in continental Europe. She avers that "visions gave validity to women's religious autonomy and authority in a day when these were not respected."[20] Moreover, Nuth emphasizes that Julian's focus is not on the visions themselves but on growth in understanding their meaning. Jantzen underlines Julian's disclaimer about any special prerogatives that might derive from her experience: "I am not good because of the revelations, but only if I love God better; and inasmuch as you love God better, it is more to you than to me."[21] For Julian, "what is truly important is not the fact of the experiences themselves but the deepened love of God which results from them and the insights communicated with them."[22] Julian's progress in developing contrition, compassion, and longing for God is the true measure of the validity of these experiences.

THE MEANING OF CHRIST'S PASSION

Julian's experience of the crucified Christ leads her to ponder the meaning and significance of his passion. She speaks of three ways of contemplating the passion.[23] The first is "to contemplate with contrition and compassion the cruel pain he suffered."[24] Julian echoes the common opinion of her day that in his passion Jesus suffered more than anyone else in human history. Because of the union of divinity and humanity in Jesus, he was given the strength to undergo the greatest possible suffering. Julian takes very seriously the physical dimensions of the passion of Jesus. The second way of meditation on the passion is to move beyond consideration of Christ's suffering to contemplate the love that motivated it. The third way is to consider prayerfully "the joy and bliss which make him take delight in it."[25] While consideration of the physical sufferings of Jesus is important to Julian, it becomes clear that the second and third ways of contemplating his passion offer the deepest insight into its meaning.

Julian envisions the passion of Jesus as the ultimate source of healing for a wounded humanity. The symbol of the blood of Jesus assumes prominence here. She observes that God has created bountiful waters on the earth for our physical needs and comfort. But "it is more pleasing to him that we accept for our total cure his blessed blood, to wash us of our sins, for there is no drink that is made which it pleases him so well to give us."[26] She perceives the wound in Jesus's side to be "large enough for all mankind that will be saved and will rest in peace and love."[27] The wounds that human beings suffer because of the effects of sin in the world are healed by the wounds that Jesus suffered in his passion. Jantzen observes that in Julian there is a "fine counterpoint" among the wounds of sin, the wounds of Christ, and her prayer for the three wounds of contrition, compassion, and longing with her will for God.[28]

Julian also meditates on the passion of Christ as the means of God's triumph over the powers of evil that oppress humanity. In her account of the fifth revelation, she reports that she was given insight into the malice of "the fiend"—the devil. But in this perception she also came to see the impotence of the devil. She says that God formed the saying "With this the fiend is overcome" in her soul.[29] While the devil still possesses unrelenting malice toward God and humanity, his power has ultimately been negated through the suffering of Christ. In fact, Julian maintains, God turns everything that God permits the devil to accomplish into joy for us and pain and shame for him. Further on in the long text, as Julian is reflecting on the sixteenth and final revelation, this theme of the defeat of the powers of evil is reprised. The message is personalized for her in the words, "You will not be overcome." Julian is assured that in spite of the difficulties of life, and despite her own sinfulness, the victory of God effected though the passion of Jesus means that for her and for her "fellow Christians" the redemptive love of God will have the final word. She writes, "He did not say: You shall not be troubled, you will not be belaboured, you will not be disquieted; but he said, You will not be overcome. God wants us to pay attention to these words, and always to be strong in faithful trust."[30] Julian wants her fellow Christians to concentrate not on the powers of evil but on the triumph of God's love over these powers through the crucified Christ.

The salient feature of Julian's reflection on the meaning of Christ's passion is her consistent emphasis that in the suffering Christ is revealed the depths of God's love for the human family. This theme is the leitmotif of her work and is repeated with many variations. She ponders the motivation behind Jesus's taking up the cross: "The love which made him suffer it [the passion] surpasses all his sufferings, as much as heaven is above earth; for the suffering was a noble, precious and honourable deed, performed once in time by the operation of love. And the love was without beginning, it is and shall be without end."[31] This is the governing principle in Julian's interpretation of Christ's passion. Nuth affirms, "Every detail of the passion deepened her understanding of the intimacy, depth and intensity of Christ's love for humanity."[32] Julian even experiences Jesus "asking" her if she is well satisfied that he suffered for her and assuring her that "if I could suffer more, I should suffer more."[33]

This interpretation of the passion is also reflected in Julian's meditation on the "spiritual thirst" of Jesus. Glossing the verse in the Johannine passion narrative, "I thirst" (John 19:28), Julian relates it to God's intense desire for us. While the God about whom Julian writes is indeed transcendent, her experience of God impels her to speak of "longing" in God as well as longing in Christ. Julian speaks of Christ's spiritual thirst, "which persists and always will until we see him on the day of judgment, for we who shall be saved and shall be Christ's joy and bliss are still here....Therefore this is his thirst and his longing for us, to gather us all here into him, to our endless joy, as I see it."[34] This thirst or longing is not only a characteristic of the human Jesus; Julian suggests that there is in God this same quality of thirst and longing, which comes from God's everlasting goodness.

Julian's conviction that the passion of Jesus is ultimately the revelation of divine love is also reflected in her use of maternal images for God and Jesus. She likens the suffering of Christ in his passion to the travail of a woman in childbirth, though she declares that the life brought about by Christ's suffering is enduring in a way that earthly life is not. She says that our earthly mothers bear us for pain and death, while "our true Mother Jesus, he alone bears us for joy and endless life."[35] She develops this birthing metaphor further: "So he carries us within him in love and travail, until the full time when he wanted to suffer the sharpest thorns and cruel pains that ever were or will be, and at last he died."[36] Julian compares the nourishment Christ offers us in the sacraments to the milk with which a mother feeds her child. She employs this maternal image for Jesus in an attempt to convey the strong and tender love that Christ has for every person—the same love that moved him to endure the cross. Julian even argues that the word applies to Jesus in a preeminent way: "This fair lovely word 'mother' is so sweet and kind in itself that it cannot be truly said of anyone or to anyone except of him and to him who is the true Mother of life and of all things."[37]

Jantzen asserts that while Julian speaks of sixteen revelations, "there was in the basic sense only one revelation, and that was the revelation of love."[38] Julian's perception of the divine love revealed in Jesus entails a redefinition of love:

> The passion itself is understood as love, as the supreme manifestation of the love of God. But this in turn brings with it a revision of the common understanding of what love means. It is true that love is the measure, but this is not any sentimental idea of love. The passion of Christ offers a principle for understanding what love really is: it is the standard by which love itself must be measured.[39]

SIN AND SUFFERING

It is in the context of Julian's experience of God's love revealed in the suffering Christ that we must situate her approach to sin and suffering, which are very closely related in her theology. The reader encounters a paradox here. On the one hand, Julian ponders the gravity of sin and its effects at great length. On the other hand, her experience of God convinces her that she and all Christians should concentrate more on God's redemptive grace than on sin. This is evident in her reflections on the parable of the lord and the servant in chapter 51 of the long text—a passage of critical importance.

Living during a period of protracted war, devastating plague, ecclesiastical scandal, and social unrest, Julian takes sin very seriously. Much of her reflection on the showings entails a call to conversion that she extends to her readers. Reflecting the traditional view of evil as a privation of the good, she claims that sin is not a substantial reality: "But I did not see sin, for I believe that it has no kind of substance, no share in being, nor can it be recognized except by the pain caused by it."[40] Sin is a defect. This belief rests on Julian's positive view of creation: creation is the good gift of a good Creator. In the same passage, however, Julian proceeds to say that "sin is the cause of all this pain." Julian does not distinguish between moral evil and natural/physical evil. She simply professes that sin is the cause of all that is disfigured in God's good creation. Sin is the cause of all woundedness and thus of all suffering. In the thirteenth showing she perceives that "Adam's sin was the greatest harm ever done or ever to be done until the end of the world."[41] Sin is "the sharpest scourge with which any chosen soul can be struck;"[42] it causes grief that can lead a person to the brink of despair. God wants us to recognize our sin so that we will not continue to fall and will seek forgiveness in a spirit of sincere contrition. In heaven we will see the extent and the gravity of the sins that we have committed. In this life, however, God permits us to see only a certain amount of our own sinfulness because "our sin is so foul and horrible that we should not endure to see it as it is."[43]

Julian's intense awareness of the overwhelming goodness of God and the destructive power of sin leads her to question why God did not prevent sin at the beginning of human history. She ponders this mystery for many years in light of her experience of Christ during her illness. She is convinced that "if there had been no sin, we should all have been pure and as like our Lord as he created us."[44] Thus, she says that she "often wondered why, through the great prescient wisdom of God the beginning of sin was not prevented."[45] She never discovers the answer to this mystery, instead experiencing God assuring her that in spite of the scourge of sin "all shall be well." The reader recognizes in Julian's persistent questioning her profound sensitivity to the effects of evil—especially the toll of human suffering—in the world in which she lived.

Julian's experience of God leads her to conclude that "sin is necessary."[46] The word "necessary" here is the translation of the Middle English word *behovely*. This term is given a range of meanings by modern scholars. Nuth argues that "necessary" is the nearest modern equivalent for the term, but it also carried with it the notion of "beneficial." Sin is beneficial because God is powerful enough to bring good out of it.[47] Nuth argues that Julian does not mean ontological necessity. "She means that sin is a fact of temporal human existence, universally affecting the whole human race, that must be accepted and endured."[48] Denys Turner says that the logical force of the word lay somewhere between that of the necessary and the contingent.[49] He likens it to a Latin term employed by medieval theologians: *conveniens*, which suggests "fittingness." Mysteriously, sin fits the "plot":

> Her general position concerning sin seems, in summary, to be the following: there is what we have to say about it, namely, first that it is behovely, that it is part of the plot, necessary if the true story of the divine love of Creation is to be told; and yet, second, each sin is freely done and might not have been, so that the existence of sin is a contingent fact. But how we are able to say both with consistency, *that* we cannot see, for we cannot in this life achieve the standpoint from within which their consistency can be comprehended, because we do not and could not know the sense the plot makes of it until the story is over.[50]

Julian's experience of God leads her to conclude that God protects us even in our sin and raises us up to a fulfillment that is more glorious than we would have enjoyed if there had been no sin. The traditional theme of *felix culpa* resounds throughout her work. This is clear from her discussion of the parable of the lord and the servant, which is Julian's gloss on the biblical story of the fall.

Julian experiences this story as a vision that is set before her eyes as part of the revelation given in her illness. After the vision leaves her, she is led to reflect on it for twenty years. The vision is of a lord sitting in state, whose beloved servant stands before him, eager to do the lord's bidding. In his haste to please his master, the servant dashes off, but he falls into a ditch and is injured. His greatest hurt is that he can no longer turn his face to look at his lord, "who was very close to him, in whom is all consolation."[51] Immersed in grief, the servant also loses touch with himself, with his own identity as a beloved servant. The lord imputes no fault to his servant, since the cause of his falling was his good will and his great desire to please his lord. Rather, the lord looks on his fallen servant with tenderness and pity. Seeing the harm and injuries that the servant has suffered in his efforts, the lord promises to reward the servant. As Julian explains it, the lord's "great goodness and his own honour require that his beloved servant, whom he loved so much, should be highly and blessedly rewarded forever, above what he would have been if he had not fallen, yes, and so much that his falling and all the woe he suffered from it will be turned into high, surpassing honour and endless bliss."[52] The wounds suffered by the servant in his fall will be turned into honors by his lord.

Julian realizes that aspects of this vision are not congruent with what she had been taught about the biblical story of the fall. Initially perplexed by this example, she continues to meditate upon it. Eventually, she comes to realize that the servant represents both Adam, that is, humanity, and Christ. Echoing the Pauline motif of Christ as the New Adam, Julian says that simultaneous with the fall of Adam was "the falling of [God's] dearly beloved Son," who "went down with Adam into hell, and by this continuing pity Adam was kept from endless death."[53] In a seminal passage, Julian declares, "In the servant is comprehended the second person of the Trinity, and in the servant is comprehended Adam, that is to say all men.... When Adam fell, God's Son fell; because of the true union that was made in heaven, God's Son could not be separated from Adam, for by Adam I understand all mankind."[54] Thus, for Julian an inseparable union exists between the Son of God and humanity from the very beginning of human history. When God looks at sinful human beings he sees Christ, the Son incarnate. God does not, then, assign blame to us for our sinfulness. God is not angry with human beings for their failures any more than God is angry with Christ. The Father "does not wish to assign more blame to us than to his beloved Son Jesus Christ."[55] Drawing upon the teaching about the church as the Body of Christ, Julian concludes that all humanity that will be saved through the incarnation and passion "is Christ's humanity, for he is the head, and we are his members, to which members the day and the time are unknown when every passing woe and sorrow will have an end, and everlasting joy and bliss will be fulfilled, which day and time all the company of heaven longs and desires to see."[56]

This account of the fall of humanity is markedly distinct from most classical versions, for example, Augustine's view of Adam's sin as a heinous crime of rebellion rooted in human pride. Julian's experience of the crucified Christ moves her to conclude that despite the gravity of sin and its consequences, there is no wrath in God. Though we deserve "pain, blame and wrath" because of our sin, "God is that goodness which cannot be angry, for God is nothing but goodness."[57] God is the One who invites us into friendship; thus "it is the most impossible thing which could be that God might be angry, for anger and friendship are two contraries."[58] Julian thinks that if God were ever angry with us, we would simply cease to be, since our very existence is completely dependent on the goodness and favor of the Creator. While we are often angry with ourselves and feel that God is angry with us, we are actually enveloped in the mercy of God. We are clothed in the love of God.

With this interpretation of God's attitude toward the sinner, it is understandable that Julian experiences God instructing her to focus on the atonement whenever she is tempted to become preoccupied with sin. She says that she was taught to "contemplate the glorious atonement, for this atoning is more pleasing to the blessed divinity and more honourable for man's salvation, without comparison, than ever Adam's sin was harmful."[59] Julian is also assured that God does not demand that we live completely free of sin. "He loves us endlessly, and we sin customarily, and he reveals it to us most gently."[60] Even in our sin God protects us in the divine love.

JOY AND HOPE IN SALVATION

It should be clear from what has already been said that in Julian's theology, salvation occupies the central place. She is acutely aware that sin has wounded God's good creation, and yet her strongest conviction is that God is at work in and through Christ to heal these wounds. Her theology, then, is suffused with hope. She consistently experiences God inviting her to trust in the divine presence and power, which is the source of healing for her and for all creation. Christians must keep their eyes focused on God's redemptive action in Christ; otherwise "we fall back upon ourselves, and then we find that we feel nothing at all but the opposition that is in ourselves, and that comes from the old root of our first sin."[61]

Julian repeatedly professes her adherence to the church's teaching about the possibility of final loss, of eternal separation from God. The reader receives the impression that she was afraid that her emphasis on God's faithful and redemptive love would lead to suspicion that she was espousing universalism. Julian observes, "And one article of our faith is that many creatures will be damned, such as the angels who fell out of heaven, who now are devils, and many men upon earth who die out of the faith of Holy Church, that is to say those who are pagans and die out of God's love."[62] She even desires a vision of hell and purgatory, asserting that she "believed steadfastly that hell and purgatory exist for the same ends as Holy Church teaches."[63] She is never given such a revelation, though an insight she gains through the fifth revelation about God's repudiation of the devil leads her to conclude that "every creature who is of the devil's condition in this life is no more mentioned before God and all his saints than is the devil."[64] This statement has an annihilationist "ring" to it.

While Julian confesses her agreement with church teaching on this matter, it is evident that she struggles with this doctrine. As she admits, it is not clear to her how all could be well if there are people who will be eternally condemned. In the account of her showings, she experiences God telling her about a "great deed" that will be done on the last day, which will make all things well. She writes, "This is the great deed ordained by our Lord God from without beginning, treasured and hidden in his blessed breast, known only to himself, through which deed he will make all things well. For just as the blessed Trinity created all things from nothing, just so will the same blessed Trinity make everything well which is not well."[65] Julian searches for insight into what this deed will be and how God will accomplish it, but she is told that it is a mystery that is not knowable to human beings in this life. She must simply trust in God's promise that it will take place, for what is impossible for human beings to conceive is not impossible for God to effect. Thus, she becomes convinced that she must hold both ends of the rope: her adherence to church teaching about the possibility of eternal loss and her trust in the great deed by which God will make all things well:

> And in this I was taught by the grace of God that I ought to keep myself steadfastly in the faith, as I had understood before, and that at the same time I should stand firm and believe firmly that every kind of thing will be well, as our Lord revealed at the same time. For this is the great deed which our Lord will do, and in this deed he will preserve his word in everything. And he will make well all which is not well. But what the deed will be and how it will be done, there is no creature who is inferior to Christ who

knows it, or will know it until it has been done, according to the understanding which I received of our Lord's meaning at this time.[66]

For Julian, the salvation that will be definitively established by God on the last day is a more abundant salvation in the wake of sin and the suffering that sin has caused. There is a level of fulfillment that we will experience that we would not have known if sin had never entered creation. Therefore, sin and suffering have a mysterious role to play in God's salvific work. This conviction is found throughout Julian's work, and it undergirds the hope that permeates it. Julian affirms that "grace transforms our dreadful falling into plentiful and endless solace; and grace transforms our shameful falling into high and honourable rising; and grace transforms our sorrowful dying into holy, blessed life." This transformation through grace is "so superabundant" that when we receive our eternal reward "there we shall thank and bless our Lord, endlessly rejoicing that we ever suffered woe; and that will be because of a property of the blessed love which we shall know in God, which we might never have known without woe preceding it."[67] Julian develops this idea near the end of *Showings* when she reflects on the vision we will be given at the time of judgment. At that time the mysteries now hidden in God will be revealed and no one will say, "Lord, if it had been so, it would have been well." Rather, Julian thinks, everyone will be moved to say that "because it is so, it is well; and now we see truly that everything is done as it was ordained by you before anything was made."[68]

What should one make of such a statement? Is this a simplistic answer to the question about why God allowed sin and suffering to enter creation in the first place and about the meaning of suffering in a creation loved so deeply by God? The terrible toll of human suffering in Julian's own day would seem to contradict such an answer. Julian's honest grappling with the reality of sin and suffering throughout her work seems inconsistent with a view that suggests that the reward of salvation will be so great that human beings will no longer lament the tragedies of human history. Grace Jantzen raises similar questions in her study of Julian, noting that "it seems wicked even to contemplate giving thanks for such tragic events as the Black Death and all the suffering this caused."[69] Jantzen contends that Julian can make such assertions only because she believes that there is an intrinsic link between the suffering caused by the presence of sin in the world and the experience of salvation in Christ. This intrinsic connection is the development of the "wounds" of contrition, compassion, and longing for God, which comes about in and through suffering.[70] Julian thinks that these qualities are essential for our reception of the gift of God's love and that they begin to take root in us when we experience sin and suffering in our lives. Without these three wounds "we could never be receptive to the delights of his [God's] love."[71] These are the wounds for which Julian prayed, and she considers them to be medicines for the soul by which we are healed and granted a more profound experience of the love of God. Julian is convinced that we will come to a more profound and integral fulfillment in God because we have passed through the experience of sin and suffering than we would have if there had been no sin and suffering.

Jantzen observes that "her [Julian's] assurance that all sin and pain will be rewarded and will bring about a good out of comparison to the pain itself is of great significance."[72] Nuth argues that Julian's teaching about salvation can be summarized thusly: "Her whole effort is to present to her troubled times the picture of a God who loves absolutely the whole creation which is itself an expression of divine love. Eschatological hope is not misplaced when it trusts that this love can bring all into eternal fulfillment."[73] For Julian this fulfillment consists ultimately in seeing "the blessed face" of God. We are destined in Christ to see God clearly, "face to his blessed face," and in that vision "no woe can remain, no well-being can be lacking."[74]

Julian's theology is sufficiently influenced by classical Christian thought to prevent her from asserting that the Creator is in any way dependent upon creatures. Nevertheless, the language that she uses manifests her conviction that we do make a difference to God. She speaks of God's delight and God's intense longing for us. For Julian, human happiness brings joy to God. "For it is God's will that we have true delight with him in our salvation and in it he wants us to be greatly comforted and strengthened, and so joyfully he wishes our souls to be occupied with his grace. For we are his bliss, because he endlessly delights in us; and so with his grace shall we delight in him."[75] Employing another metaphor, she asserts that we are God's crown: "For it was revealed that we are his crown, which crown is the Father's joy, the Son's honour, the Holy Spirit's delight, and endless marvelous bliss to all who are in heaven."[76] She makes her strongest statement in this regard when she claims that God "will never have his full joy in us until we have our full joy in him, truly seeking his blessed face."[77] While God is God and we are creatures, utterly dependent upon God for our very existence, God has freely entered into such a deep and enduring relationship with us that our destiny makes a difference to God. Drawing on the societal relationships of her own day, Julian often speaks of God's "courteous" or "familiar" love. Like a person of royal status who humbles herself or himself to associate with a mere servant, treating the servant as a friend, so God has lowered Godself to enter into a relationship of familiar friendship with us. This is a free action of God that has its source in divine love. As one who has become "familiar" with us, God has a stake in our fulfillment.

Julian's account of the showings granted to her by God does not provide a complete eschatology. Questions and lacunae remain. For example, her suggestion that in the vision afforded us in heaven we will no longer lament the evils of human history is questionable. It is virtually impossible that those in heaven will look back on the horrors of the Black Death (or the Shoah) and "say with one voice: Lord, blessed may you be, because it is so it is well."[78] Believers may imagine, rather, that fulfillment in God will leave appropriate "space" for lament over the tragedies of history and the suffering of countless victims. In our survey of Christian eschatology, we have seen that some theologians imagine the work of reconciliation and forgiveness continuing in eternal life. If one looks at Julian's theology as a whole, especially her emphasis on God's profound compassion in Christ, it seems that she would eschew any simplistic reconciliation with the pain and sorrow suffered by so many through the centuries.

What makes Julian's thought compelling to many people today is her sustained emphasis on the superabundance of God's love, which she consistently affirms even in the context of the intense suffering that was taking place all around her. In the final chapter of the long text, she says that she had wondered about the meaning of the showings, and she articulates the "answer" that was given her in this way: "What, do you wish to know your Lord's meaning in this thing? Know it well, love was his meaning."[79] As we have seen, Julian's is not a sentimental understanding of God's love; the light of divine charity shines for her through the prism of the suffering Christ. She recognizes that the redemptive love of God revealed and made effective in Christ was a costly love, costly even for God. But

Julian's experience of God convinced her that this divine love is more real and more powerful than the evil and suffering that plague the world.

Julian's contention that there is no wrath in God may ignore the important biblical theme of the wrath of God against sin. Though she does make mention of divine judgment, it may be that she does not give it the treatment that it deserves. And her conception of human frailty may underestimate the malice that often resides in the human heart. Nevertheless, her experience of God's intense love for a wounded humanity becomes the foundation of a theology that is permeated with hope. While her mantra "All shall be well" may sound shrill to the ears of people who are enduring inexplicable suffering, her vision is not a Pollyanna optimism. Rather it is a genuine expression of the theological virtue of hope, since it is grounded in her firm belief in the desire and the power of God to heal a fractured world. And for Julian, God does not just promise healing at the end of life, but draws near in the present to embrace the suffering person with a depth of compassion that gives new life.

NOTES

PREFACE

1. Preface I for Masses for the Dead, *The Roman Missal*, English translation according to the Third Typical Edition.

2. Jeannine Hill Fletcher, "Eschatology," in *Systematic Theology: Roman Catholic Perspectives*, ed. Francis Schüssler Fiorenza and John Galvin, 2nd ed. (Minneapolis: Fortress Press, 2011), 622.

3. Pope Benedict XVI, Encyclical Letter *Spe Salvi* (On Christian Hope), 2007, 2.

4. Fletcher, "Eschatology," 622.

5. Cited by Thomas O'Meara, OP, *Life beyond Death: A Traveler's Guide for Christians* (Saint Louis: The Catholic Health Association, 2019), 3. The French original is Congar, "Fins derniers," *Revue des sciences philosophiques et théologiques* 33 (1949): 463–84.

6. O'Meara, *Life beyond Death*, 3.

7. Zachary Hayes, *Visions of a Future: A Study of Christian Eschatology* (Wilmington, DE: Michael Glazier, 1989), 11–13.

8. Hayes, *Visions of a Future*, 11–12.

9. See, among others, Denis Edwards, *Deep Incarnation: God's Redemptive Suffering with Creatures* (Maryknoll, NY: Orbis Books, 2019). Edwards builds on the concept of "deep incarnation" first articulated by the Danish theologian Niels Gregersen.

10. Charles Taylor, *A Secular Age* (Cambridge, MA: Harvard University Press, 2007), passim.

11. See Ryan Burge, *The Nones: Where They Came From, Who They Are, and Where They Are Going* (Minneapolis: Fortress Press, 2021).

12. Gerhard Lohfink, *Is This All There Is? On Resurrection and Eternal Life*, trans. Linda Mahoney (Collegeville, MN: Liturgical Press, 2018).

13. International Theological Commission, "Some Current Questions in Eschatology," 1992, section 9.

14. Among his many writings, see Jürgen Moltmann, *In the End—the Beginning: The Life of Hope*, trans. Margaret Kohl (Minneapolis: Fortress Press, 2004).

15. Moltmann, *In the End—the Beginning*, 121.

16. Karl Rahner, "The Eternal Significance of the Humanity of Jesus for Our Relationship with God," *Theological Investigations*, vol. 3, *Theology of the Spiritual Life*, trans. Karl-H and Boniface Krüger (London: Darton, Longman and Todd, 1967), 35–46, at 37.

17. Carmen Nanko-Fernández, "Performative Theologies," in *The Wiley Blackwell Reader in Practical Theology*, ed. Bonnie J. Miller-McLemore (Oxford: John Wiley and Sons, 2019), 79–89, at 88.

18. Nanko-Fernández, "Performative Theologies," 87.

19. Nanko-Fernández, "Performative Theologies," 88.

20. Lohfink, *Is This All There Is?*, 61.

21. Dermot Lane, *Keeping Hope Alive: Stirrings in Christian Theology* (New York: Paulist Press, 1996), 19.

22. Lane, *Keeping Hope Alive*, 19.

23. See, for example, Terence Nichols, *Death and Afterlife: A Theological Introduction* (Grand Rapids, MI: Brazos Press, 2010). Nichols includes a chapter on near death experiences, concluding that readers will have to decide for themselves how best to interpret this phenomenon.

24. Rahner, "The Hermeneutics of Eschatological Assertions," in *Theological Investigations*, vol. 4, *More Recent Writings*, trans. Kevin Smyth (London: Darton, Longman and Todd, 1966), 323–46; *Foundations of Christian Faith: An Introduction to the Idea of Christianity*, trans. William Dych (New York: Crossroad, 1978), 431–34.

25. Rahner, *Foundations of Christian Faith*, 432.

26. Moltmann, *In the End—the Beginning*, 87.

27. Rahner, "The Hermeneutics of Eschatological Assertions," 332.

28. Rahner, *Foundations of Christian Faith*, 434.

29. Rahner, *Foundations of Christian Faith*, 434.

30. Benedict XVI, *Spe Salvi*, 13.

31. Lane, *Keeping Hope Alive*, 18; see Denzinger-Schönmetzer 806.

1. ANTHROPOLOGICAL FOUNDATIONS

1. Dermot Lane, *Keeping Hope Alive* (New York: Paulist Press, 1996), 38; quoting Rahner, "Theology and Anthropology," in *Theological Investigations*, vol. 9, *Writings of 1965–67* (London: Darton, Longman and Todd, 1972), 45.

2. Lane, *Keeping Hope Alive*, 38.

3. Anne Clifford, "Creation," in *Systematic Theology: Roman Catholic Perspectives*, 2nd ed., ed. Francis Schüssler Fiorenza and John Galvin (Minneapolis: Fortress Press, 2011), 210.

4. See Claus Westermann, *Genesis: A Practical Commentary*, trans. David Green (Grand Rapids, MI: Eerdmans, 1987), 20–21.

5. Daniel Horan, *Catholicity & Emerging Personhood: A Contemporary Theological Anthropology* (Maryknoll, NY: Orbis Books, 2019), 37–38.

6. Horan, *Catholicity & Emerging Personhood*, 38.

7. Horan, *Catholicity & Emerging Personhood*, 23.

8. Niels Gregersen, "*Cur Deus Caro*: Jesus and the Cosmic Story," *Theology and Science* 11 (2013): 375.

9. Gregersen, "*Cur Deus Caro*," 387.

10. John Haught, *Science and Faith: A New Introduction* (New York: Paulist Press, 2012), 160.

11. Augustine of Hippo, *Confessions*, I, 1, trans. Henry Chadwick (New York: Oxford University Press, 1991).

12. For a helpful treatment of this section of the *Summa Theologiae*, see Brian Davies, *The Thought of Thomas Aquinas* (New York: Oxford University Press, 1992), chapter 12.

13. Thomas Aquinas, *Summa Theologiae* 1–2, question 2.

14. Aquinas, ST 1–2, 2, 8; quoted in Davies, *Thought of Thomas Aquinas*, 229.

15. Aquinas, ST 1, 62,1; Davies, *Thought of Thomas Aquinas*, 230.

16. Here I draw on my discussion of Rahner in *Jesus and Salvation: Soundings in the Christian Tradition and Contemporary Theology* (Collegeville, MN: Liturgical Press, 2015), 154–5. See Rahner, *Foundations of Christian Faith*, 178–202.

17. Rahner, "Natural Science and Reasonable Faith," in *Theological Investigations*, vol. 21, *Science and Theology*, trans. Hugh Riley (New York: Crossroad, 1988), 33.

18. Rahner, "Natural Science and Reasonable Faith," 36.

19. Denis Edwards, *Christian Understandings of Creation: The Historical Trajectory* (Minneapolis: Fortress, 2017), 214.

20. Denis Edwards, *How God Acts: Creation, Redemption and Special Divine Action* (Minneapolis: Fortress, 2010), 44.

21. See Rahner, *Foundations of Christian Faith*, 31–35. For a clear discussion of Rahner's position, see Elizabeth Johnson, *Abounding in Kindness: Writings for the People of God* (Maryknoll, NY: Orbis Books, 2015), 25–30.

22. Rahner, *Foundations of Christian Faith*, 32.

23. Rahner, *Foundations of Christian Faith*, 33.

24. Johnson, *Abounding in Kindness*, 28.

25. Rahner, *Foundations of Christian Faith*, 38.

26. Rahner, *Foundations of Christian Faith*, 194-95; see Edwards, *Christian Understandings of Creation*, 216–17.

27. Rahner, "A Faith That Loves the Earth," in *The Mystical Way in Everyday Life: Sermons, Prayers and Essays*, ed. Annemarie Kidder (Maryknoll, NY: Orbis Books, 2010), 53.

28. Gustavo Gutiérrez, *A Theology of Liberation: History, Politics and Salvation*, trans. Sister Caridad Inda and John Eagleson (Maryknoll, NY: Orbis Books, 1973), 151.

29. Lane, *Keeping Hope Alive*, 30–31.

30. Lane, *Keeping Hope Alive*, 32; see Teilhard de Chardin, *Human Energy* (New York: Harcourt Brace Jovanovich, 1936/1978), 63.

31. Lane, *Keeping Hope Alive*, 34.

32. Pope Francis, *Laudato Si'*, 65; *CCC*, 357.

33. Pope Francis, *Laudato Si'*, 70.

34. Pope Francis, General Audience, November 25, 2013; in *The Church of Mercy: A Vision for the Church* (Chicago: Loyola Press, 2014), 28.

35. Pope Francis, *Laudato Si'*, 240.

36. Elizabeth Johnson, "Communion of Saints and Mary," in Fiorenza and Galvin, *Systematic Theology*, 455.

37. Congregation for the Doctrine of the Faith, "Letter of the Sacred Congregation of the Doctrine of the Faith on Certain Questions Concerning Eschatology," (May 17, 1979), 3. The final phrase in the statement, "though deprived for present of the complement of its body" (*interim tamen complemento sui corporis carens*), was not in the original publication of the letter found in *Osservatore Romano* (July 23, 1979) but is found in the version of the letter of the *Acta Apostolicae Sedis* (71, 1979, 939).

38. *Catechism of the Catholic Church*, 362–68.

39. For a discussion of Protestant views on theological anthropology, see Hans Schwarz, *Eschatology* (Grand Rapids, MI: Eerdmans, 2000), 261–80.

40. Lane, *Keeping Hope Alive*, 40.

41. Lane, *Keeping Hope Alive*, 40.

42. See especially Joseph Ratzinger, *Eschatology: Death and Eternal Life*, trans. Michael Waldstein (Washington, DC: CUA Press, 1988). The German original was published in 1977. Of particular importance is the afterword to the English edition, 261–74.

43. Ratzinger, *Eschatology*, 257.

44. John Polkinghorne, *The God of Hope and the End of the World* (New Haven, CT: Yale University Press, 2002), 105–11.

45. Polkinghorne, *The God of Hope*, 105–6.

46. Polkinghorne, *The God of Hope*, 107.

47. Ratzinger, *Eschatology*, 154.

48. Ratzinger, *Eschatology*, 259.

49. Terence Nichols, *Death and Eternal Life: A Theological Introduction* (Grand Rapids, MI: Brazos Press, 2010), 129–132.

50. Nichols, *Death and Eternal Life*, 130.

51. Gutiérrez, *A Theology of Liberation*, 33–37; see Ryan, *Jesus and Salvation*, 136–37.

52. For the main lines of Rahner's theology of freedom, see *Foundations of Christian Faith*, 35–39; 93–106.

53. Rahner, "Eternity from Time," in *Theological Investigations*, vol. 19, *Faith and Ministry*, trans. Edward Quinn (New York: Crossroad, 1983), 175.

54. Rahner, *Foundations of Christian Faith*, 98; italics in the original.

55. Rahner, *Foundations of Christian Faith*, 102.

56. Rahner, *Foundations of Christian Faith*, 103; italics in the original.

57. Ratzinger, *Eschatology*, 216.

58. International Theological Commission, "Some Current Questions on Eschatology," 10.3.

59. John R. Sachs, "Current Eschatology: Universal Salvation and the Problem of Hell," *Theological Studies* 52 (1991): 227–54, especially 246–54.

60. Sachs, "Current Eschatology," 247; italics in the original.

61. Sachs, "Current Eschatology," 251; italics in the original.

62. Pope Francis, *Laudato Si'*, 66.

63. Irenaeus of Lyons, *Against Heresies* 4,38, 3; quoted in Brian Daley, *The Hope of the Early Church: A Handbook of Patristic Eschatology* (Grand Rapids, MI: Baker Academic, 1991), 29.

64. Augustine of Hippo, Treatise "On Nature and Grace," chapter 62 (liii); in *Saint Augustine: Anti-Pelagian Writings*, vol. 5 of *The Nicene and Post-Nicene Fathers*, trans. Benjamin Warfield (Grand Rapids, MI: Eerdmans, 1971).

65. See Rahner, *Foundations of Christian Faith*, 106–14.

66. Rahner, *Foundations of Christian Faith*, 108.

67. Rahner, *Foundations of Christian Faith*, 109.

68. Rahner, *Foundations of Christian Faith*, 110.

69. John Thiel, *Icons of Hope: The "Last Things" in Catholic Imagination* (Notre Dame, IN: University of Notre Dame Press, 2013), 52.

70. See Ryan, *God and the Mystery of Human Suffering: A Theological Conversation across the Ages* (New York: Paulist Press, 2011). See also, Ryan, "God's Presence in Our Suffering," in *Incarnate Grace: Perspectives on the Ministry of Catholic Health Care*, ed. Charlie Bouchard (Saint Louis: Catholic Health Association of the United States, 2017), 102–21.

71. Elizabeth Johnson, *Ask the Beasts: Darwin and the God of Love* (London: Bloomsbury, 2014), 184.

72. Denis Edwards, *The God of Evolution: A Trinitarian Theology* (New York: Paulist Press, 1999), 36.

73. Phil Zylla, *The Roots of Sorrow: A Pastoral Theology of Suffering* (Waco, TX: Baylor University Press, 2012), 58–69.

74. Zylla, *The Roots of Sorrow*, 63.

75. See Daniel Harrington, *Why Do We Suffer? A Scriptural Approach to the Human Condition* (Franklin, WI: Sheed & Ward, 2000).

76. Walter Brueggemann, *Israel's Praise: Doxology against Idolatry and Ideology* (Philadelphia: Fortress Press, 1984), 143.

77. See Thomas Aquinas, *Summa Theologiae*, 2–2, questions 17–18. See the discussion in Brian Davies, *The Thought*.

78. Aquinas, *Summa Theologiae*, 2–2. 17. 2.

79. Aquinas, *Summa Theologiae* 2–2. 20. 1

80. Lane, *Keeping Hope Alive*, 60.

81. John MacQuarrie, *Christian Hope* (New York: Crossroad, 1978), 13.

82. MacQuarrie, *Christian Hope*, 13.

83. Edward Schillebeeckx, *Church: The Human Story of God*, trans. John Bowden (New York: Crossroad, 1990), 5.

84. Schillebeeckx, *Church: The Human Story of God*, 5–6.

85. Jürgen Moltmann, *In the End—the Beginning: The Life of Hope*, trans. Margaret Kohl (Minneapolis: Fortress Press, 2004), 87.

2. THE HOPE OF ISRAEL

1. Zachary Hayes, *Visions of a Future: A Study of Christian Eschatology* (Wilmington, DE: Michael Glazier, 1989), 40. Note that some scholars, like Bill Arnold, caution against giving too broad a meaning to eschatology. See Bill T. Arnold, "Old Testament Eschatology and the Rise of Apocalypticism," in *The Oxford Handbook of Eschatology*, ed. Jerry L. Walls (New York: Oxford University Press, 2008), 24.

2. John MacQuarrie, *Christian Hope* (New York: Crossroad, 1978), 33.

3. Here I draw on the reflection of the Genesis texts given by Hayes in *Visions of a Future*, 18–22. Hayes makes use of the analysis given by Mircea Eliade in *Cosmos and History: The Myth of the Eternal Return*.

4. Hayes, *Visions of a Future*, 19.

5. Arnold, "Old Testament Eschatology," 25.

6. Hayes, *Visions of a Future*, 21–22.

7. K. A. Kitchen, "Exodus," in *The Anchor Bible Dictionary*, vol. 2, ed. David Noel Freedman (New York: Doubleday, 1992), 701.

8. Here I draw on my observations from *Jesus and Salvation: Soundings in the Christian Tradition and Contemporary Theology* (Collegeville, MN: Liturgical Press, 2015), 6.

9. Walter Brueggemann, "The Book of Exodus," in *The New Interpreter's Bible: A Commentary in Twelve Volumes*, vol. 1 (Nashville: Abingdon Press, 1994), 736–7.

10. See Bernhard Anderson, *Understanding the Old Testament*, 4th ed. (Englewood Cliffs, NJ: Prentice-Hall, 1986), 483–84. See also Ryan, *Jesus and Salvation*, 7–8.

11. See the discussion of Israel's royal ideology by Leslie Hoppe in "Messiah," in *The Collegeville Dictionary of Pastoral Theology*, ed. Carroll Stuhlmueller (Collegeville, MN: Liturgical Press, 1996), 619–20.

12. Marinus de Jonge, "Messiah, in *The Anchor Bible Dictionary*, vol. 4, ed. David Noel Freedman (New York: Doubleday, 1992), 779.

13. Quoted by Marinus de Jonge, "Messiah," 783.

14. de Jonge, "Messiah," 781.

15. In this section I draw on observations that I have made in *Jesus and Salvation*, 16–19; and *God and the Mystery of Human Suffering: A Theological Conversation across the Ages* (New York: Paulist Press, 2011), 20–27.

16. N. T. Wright, *The Resurrection of the Son of God* (Minneapolis: Fortress Press, 2003), 99.

17. Hans Schwarz, *Eschatology* (Grand Rapids, MI: Eerdmans, 2000), 36.

18. Wright, *The Resurrection of the Son of God*, 99.

19. Wright, *The Resurrection of the Son of God*, 100.

20. Dianne Bergant, "Salvation," in Stuhlmueller, *Collegeville Dictionary of Biblical Theology*, 868.

21. Kent Harold Richards, "Death," in Freedman, *Anchor Bible Dictionary*, 2:110.

22. Theodore Lewis, "Dead, Abode of the," in Freedman, *Anchor Bible Dictionary*, 2:102.

23. Wright, The Resurrection of the Son of God," 88–89.

24. Terence Nichols, *Death and Afterlife: A Theological Introduction* (Grand Rapids, MI: Brazos Press, 2010), 20.

25. Lewis, "Dead, Abode of the," 104.

26. John J. Collins, "Day of the Lord," in Stuhlmueller, *Collegeville Pastoral Dictionary of Biblical Theology*, 199–200, at 199. See also Richard H. Hiers, "Day of the Lord," in Freedman, *Anchor Bible Dictionary*, 2:82–83.

27. Hiers, "Day of the Lord," 82.

28. Hiers, "Day of the Lord," 83.

29. Hiers, "Day of the Lord," 83.

30. Collins, "Day of the Lord," 199.

31. Arnold, "Old Testament Eschatology," 29.

32. Joseph Ratzinger, *Eschatology: Death and Eternal Life*, trans. Michael Waldstein (Washington, DC: CUA Press, 1988), 87.

33. Wright, *The Resurrection of the Son of God*, 104.

34. Wright, *The Resurrection of the Son of God*, 107.

35. See Ratzinger, *Eschatology: Death and Eternal Life*, 88.

36. Ratzinger, *Eschatology: Death and Eternal Life*, 89.

37. Nichols, *Death and Afterlife*, 23.

38. Wright, *The Resurrection of the Son of God*, 117.

39. Wright, *The Resurrection of the Son of God*, 120.

40. Wright, *The Resurrection of the Son of God*, 110.

41. Wright, *The Resurrection of the Son of God*, 113.

42. See Robert Doran, "1 and 2 Maccabees," in *The Jerome Biblical Commentary for the Twenty-First Century*, 3rd ed., ed. John J. Collins, Gina Hens-Piazza, Barbara Reid, OP, and Donald Senior, CP (London: T & T Clark, 2021), 570–73.

43. Doran, "1 and 2 Maccabees," 616.

44. John Macquarrie, *Christian Hope* (New York: Seabury, 1978), 40.

45. Doran, "1 and 2 Maccabees, 625.

46. See Karina Martin Hogan, "Wisdom of Solomon," in Collins et al., *Jerome Biblical Commentary*, 754–57.

47. Ratzinger, *Eschatology*, 91.

48. See Wright, *Resurrection of the Son of God*, 168.

49. Joanne McWilliam Dewart, *Death and Resurrection*, Message of the Fathers of the Church 22 (Wilmington, DE: Michael Glazier, 1986), 23.

50. Ratzinger, *Eschatology*, 91.

51. Wright, *Resurrection of the Son of God*, 175.

52. Macquarrie, *Christian Hope*, 41.

53. Wright, *Resurrection of the Son of God*, 127.

54. Ratzinger, *Eschatology*, 89.

55. John Collins, "Apocalyptic Eschatology in the Ancient World," in Walls, *Oxford Handbook of Eschatology*, 46. Collins cites the work of scholars from the Society of Biblical Literature.

56. Collins, "Apocalyptic Eschatology in the Ancient World," 47.

57. Brendan Byrne, *Paul and the Economy of Salvation: Reading from the Perspective of the Last Judgment* (Grand Rapids, MI: Baker Academic, 2021), 14–15.

58. Wright, *Resurrection of the Son of God*, 162.

59. Daniel Harrington, *Why Do We Suffer? A Scriptural Approach to the Human Condition* (Franklin, WI: Sheed & Ward, 2000), 71.

60. Collins, "Apocalyptic Eschatology in the Ancient World," 47. Here Collins quotes Adela Yarbro Collins, "Introduction: Early Christian Apocalypticism," *Semeia* 36 (1986): 7.

61. I draw here on my earlier work in *God and the Mystery of Human Suffering*, 44–45, which in turn relies on the analysis of Daniel Harrington in *Why Do We Suffer?*, 78–81.

62. Byrne, *Paul and the Economy of Salvation*, 27.

63. Ernst Käsemann coined this phrase in "The Beginnings of Christian Theology," *New Testament Questions of Today*, 102.

3. NEW TESTAMENT ESCHATOLOGY

1. John Meier, "The Historical Jesus," in *The Jerome Biblical Commentary for the Twenty-First Century*, 3rd ed., ed. John J. Collins, Gina Hens-Piazza, Barbara Reid, OP, and Donald Senior, CP (London: T & T Clark, 2021), 149–50.

2. Meier, "The Historical Jesus," 150.

3. Meier, "The Historical Jesus," 150.

4. See Gerhard Lohfink, *Jesus and Community*, trans. John Galvin (Philadelphia: Fortress Press, 1984), 11.

5. Meier, "The Historical Jesus," 150.

6. N. T. Wright, *Jesus and the Victory of God* (Minneapolis: Fortress Press, 1996), 199–203.

7. Meier, "The Historical Jesus," 151.

8. Elizabeth Johnson, *Creation and the Cross: The Mercy of God for a Planet in Peril* (Maryknoll, NY: Orbis Books, 2018), 75.

9. See Meier, "The Historical Jesus," 151.

10. Meier, "The Historical Jesus," 151.

11. Raymond Brown, *Introduction to New Testament Christology* (New York: Paulist Press, 1994), 66n88.

12. Meier, "The Historical Jesus," 153.

13. Meier, "The Historical Jesus," 155.

14. Wright, *Jesus and the Victory of God*, 176.

15. Johnson, *Creation and the Cross*, 81.

16. Meier, "The Historical Jesus," 152.

17. Wolfgang Schrage, in Erhard Gerstenberger and Wolfgang Schrage, *Suffering*, trans. John E. Steely (Nashville: Abingdon Press, 1980), 265.

18. Brown, *Introduction to New Testament Christology*, 64, Similarly, Wright observes that Jesus never performed mighty works in order to impress. Rather, he saw these actions as part of the inauguration of the sovereign and healing rule of Israel's covenant God. See *Jesus and the Victory of God*, 191.

19. Brown, *Introduction to New Testament Christology*, 64–65.

20. Meier, "The Historical Jesus," 152.

21. Schrage, *Suffering*, 263–64.

22. M. Shawn Copeland, *Knowing Christ Crucified: The Witness of African American Religious Experience* (Maryknoll, NY: Orbis Books, 2018), 57–58.

23. Copeland, *Knowing Christ Crucified*, 58.

24. Copeland, *Knowing Christ Crucified*, 58.

25. See Meier, "The Historical Jesus," 157–58.

26. Meier, "The Historical Jesus," 160.

27. Meier, "The Historical Jesus," 160.

28. Meier, "The Historical Jesus," 160.

29. The work of Heinz Schürmann is often cited: *Begegnung mit dem Wort*, ed. J. Zmijewski (Bonn, 1980), 273–309.

30. Brown, *Introduction to New Testament Christology*, 49.

31. Gerald O'Collins, *Christology: A Biblical, Historical, and Systematic Study of Jesus*, 2nd ed. (New York: Oxford University Press, 2009), 76.

32. O'Collins, *Christology*, 76.

33. Meier, "The Historical Jesus," 160. See also Meier, "The Eucharist at the Last Supper: Did It Happen?" *Theology Digest* 42 (1995): 335–51.

34. Meier, "The Historical Jesus," 160.

35. Donald Senior, *The Passion of Jesus in the Gospel of Mark* (Wilmington, DE: Glazier, 1984), 125.

36. Daniel Harrington, *The Gospel of Matthew*, Sacra Pagina series, vol. 1 (Collegeville, MN: Liturgical Press, 1991), 407.

37. Harrington, *The Gospel of Matthew*, 400.

38. Brian Robinette, *Grammars of Resurrection: A Christian Theology of Presence and Absence* (New York: Crossroad, 2009), 7.

39. Gerhard Lohfink, *Is This All There Is? On Resurrection and Eternal Life*, trans. Linda Maloney (Collegeville, MN: Liturgical Press, 2018), 132.

40. Raymond Brown, "The Resurrection of Jesus," in *The New Jerome Biblical Commentary* (Englewood Cliffs, NJ: Prentice-Hall, 1990), 1375.

41. Brown, "The Resurrection of Jesus," 1375. In this remark, Brown does not reckon with the tradition about Mary Magdalene.

42. John Galvin, "Jesus Christ," in *Systematic Theology: Roman Catholic Perspectives*, ed. Francis Schüssler Fiorenza and John Galvin, 2nd ed. (Minneapolis: Fortress Press, 2011), 293; see also Raymond Collins, *First Corinthians*, Sacra Pagina, vol. 7 (Collegeville, MN: Liturgical Press, 1999), 531. Collins says that most scholars are convinced that it originated in a Palestinian context.

43. N. T. Wright, *The Resurrection of the Son of God* (Minneapolis: Fortress Press, 2003), 321.

44. Collins, *First Corinthians*, 532.

45. Wright, *The Resurrection of the Son of God*, 322.

46. Robinette, *Grammars of Resurrection*, 95.

47. Robinette, *Grammars of Resurrection*, 72.

48. Robinette, *Grammars of Resurrection*, 96.

49. Robinette, *Grammars of Resurrection*, 97, citing Kasper, *Jesus the Christ* (New York: Paulist Press, 1976), 139.

50. O'Collins, *Christology*, 105.

51. Kasper, *Jesus the Christ*, 139–40.

52. Galvin, "Jesus Christ," 303.

53. O'Collins, *Christology*, 103–10.

54. O'Collins, *Christology*, 104.

55. O'Collins, *Christology*, 107.

56. O'Collins, *Christology*, 107.

57. O'Collins, *Christology*, 108.

58. Jeannine Hill Fletcher, "Eschatology," in Fiorenza and Galvin, *Systematic Theology*, 624. Fletcher cites the 1992 document of the International Theological Commission, "Some Current Questions in Eschatology."

59. Donald Senior, *1 & 2 Peter*, New Testament Message Series, vol. 20 (Wilmington, DE: Michael Glazier, 1920), 3. See also Senior's commentary on First Peter in *1 Peter, Jude and 2 Peter*, Sacra Pagina Series, vol. 15 (Collegeville, MN: Liturgical Press, 2003).

60. Patricia McDonald, "The View of Suffering Held by the Author of 1 Peter," in *The Bible on Suffering*, ed. Anthony Tambasco (New York: Paulist Press, 2001), 177.

61. Senior, *1 & 2 Peter*, 6.

62. Lohfink, *Is This All There Is?*, 123.

63. Collins, *First Corinthians*, 548.

64. Collins, *First Corinthians*, 567.

65. Frank Matera, *Resurrection: The Origin and Goal of the Christian Life* (Collegeville, MN: Liturgical Press 2015), 106.

66. Mario Inzulza, SJ, "The Parousia: A Suitable Symbol for a Renewed Eschatological, Cosmic Narrative" (STD diss., Boston College School of Theology and Ministry, July 2018), 199.

67. In his doctoral dissertation, Mario Inzulza, SJ catalogues many of these interpretations. See Inzulza, "The Parousia," 196–246.

68. Matera, *Resurrection*, 109.

69. Sheila McGinn, "Romans," in Collins et al., *Jerome Biblical Commentary*, 1566.

70. Matera, *Resurrection*, 109.

71. McGinn, "Romans," 1566.

72. Inzulza, "The Parousia," 110.

73. Inzulza, "The Parousia," 121–27.

74. Inzulza, "The Parousia," 121.

75. Inzulza, "The Parousia," 127.

76. Brendan Byrne, *Paul and the Economy of Salvation: Reading from the Perspective of the Last Judgment* (Grand Rapids, MI: Baker Academic, 2021), 229.

77. Christopher Rowland, "The Eschatology of the New Testament Church," in *The Oxford Handbook of Eschatology*, ed. Jerry Walls (New York: Oxford University Press, 2008), 60.

78. Rowland, "The Eschatology of the New Testament Church," 61.

79. Adela Yarbro Collins, "Revelation," in Collins et al., *Jerome Biblical Commentary*, 1855.

80. Yarbro Collins, "Revelation," 1857.

81. Yarbro Collins, "Revelation," 1880.

82. Frank Matera, *New Testament Christology* (Louisville, KY: Westminster John Knox Press, 1999), 212.

83. See Matera, *New Testament Christology*, 202.

84. Rowland, "The Eschatology of the New Testament Church," 65–68.

85. The term *apokatastasis* refers to the restoration of all creatures to their original union with God. See Daley, *Hope of the Early Church*, 292. It

is one form of Christian universalism. The term is found in the New Testament in Acts 3:21.

4. ESCHATOLOGY IN THE EARLY CHURCH AND MIDDLE AGES

1. My exposition in this section of the chapter is heavily dependent on two studies of early Christian eschatology: Joanne McWilliam Dewart, *Death and Resurrection*, vol. 22 of Message of the Fathers of the Church (Wilmington, DE: Michael Glazier, 1986), and Brian Daley, *The Hope of the Early Church: A Handbook of Patristic Eschatology* (Grand Rapids, MI: Baker Academic, 1991).

2. Daley, *The Hope of the Early Church*, 25.

3. Irenaeus of Lyons, *Adversus Haereses*, V.14.1; cited in Dewart, *Death and Resurrection*, 93.

4. Irenaeus of Lyons, *Adversus Haereses*, V.12.6; cited in Dewart, *Death and Resurrection*, 94.

5. Irenaeus of Lyons, *Adversus Haereses*, IV.18.5; cited in Dewart, *Death and Resurrection*, 96.

6. Irenaeus of Lyons, *Adversus Haereses*, V.14.2; cited in Daley, *Hope of the Early Church*, 31.

7. Tertullian, *De Resurrectione Carnis*, 1; cited in Dewart, *Death and Resurrection*, 100.

8. Tertullian, *De Resurrectione Carnis*, 14; cited in Dewart, *Death and Resurrection*, 106.

9. Tertullian, *De Resurrectione Carnis*, 8; cited by Dewart, *Death and Resurrection*, 105.

10. Dewart, *Death and Resurrection*, 122.

11. Origen, *On First Principles*, I.vi.4; cited by Dewart, *Death and Resurrection*, 126.

12. Origen, *On First Principles* II.x.3; cited in Dewart, *Death and Resurrection*, 129.

13. Origen, *Psalms, fragment*; cited in Dewart, *Death and Resurrection*, 134.

14. Daley, *The Hope of the Early Church*, 61.

15. Augustine, Sermon 362.xviii.21.

16. Augustine, *The City of God*, 13.20, trans. Marcus Dods (New York: Modern Library, 1950).

17. Augustine, *Fortunatus*, 22; cited by Dewart, *Death and Resurrection*, 174.

18. Augustine, *Literal Commentary on Genesis* XII.35–36; cited by Dewart, *Death and Resurrection*, 182.

19. Augustine, *The City of God*, 22.24.

20. See Jacques Dupuis and Josef Neuner, ed. *The Christian Faith in the Doctrinal Documents of the Catholic Church*, 6th ed. (New York: Alba House, 1995), n. 18.

21. Dupuis and Neuner, *The Christian Faith*, n. 2302; Denzinger-Schönmetzer, n. 540.

22. Denziger-Schönmetzer 801; see Dupuis and Neuner, *The Christian Faith*, n. 20.

23. Robert Wilken, *The Spirit of Early Christian Thought* (New Haven, CT: Yale University Press, 2003), 158–61.

24. Wilken, *The Spirit of Early Christian Thought*, 159.

25. Wilken, *The Spirit of Early Christian Thought*, 161.

26. Daley, *The Hope of the Early Church*, 221 (italics in the original).

27. Augustine, *The City of God*, 20.9.

28. Tertullian, *De Corona*, 3.2; cited by John Baldovin, "Mass Intentions: The Historical Development of a Practice," part 1, *Theological Studies* 81, no. 4 (December 2020): 873.

29. Baldovin, "Mass Intentions," 874.

30. Baldovin, "Mass Intentions," 875.

31. Cited in Baldovin, "Mass Intentions," 876.

32. Here I draw on the citation and discussion of this work in Jacques LeGoff, *The Birth of Purgatory*, trans. Arthur Goldhammer (Chicago: University of Chicago Press, 1984), 49–50.

33. *The Passion of Perpetua and Felicitas*, quoted by LeGoff, *The Birth of Purgatory*, 49.

34. LeGoff, *The Birth of Purgatory*, 46–47.

35. Augustine, *Confessions*, trans. Henry Chadwick (Oxford: Oxford University Press, 1991), book 9, xvi, 27.

36. Augustine, *Confessions*, book 9, xiii, 35.

37. Augustine, *Confessions*, book 9, xiii, 37.

38. Augustine, *The Care to Be Taken for the Dead*, 1,1 and 3; cited in *The Hope of Eternal Life*, Lutherans and Catholics in Dialogue XI, ed. Lowell Almen and Richard Sklba (Minneapolis: Lutheran University Press, 2011), n. 223.

39. Augustine, *Enchiridion* 29.110; cited by Daley, *Hope of the Early Church*, 140.

40. Almen and Sklba, *The Hope of Eternal Life*, n. 221.

41. Dewart, *Death and Resurrection*, 20.

42. Dewart, *Death and Resurrection*, 64. Dewart points out that sometimes Justin writes as if the kingdom and the punishment of the unjust will be eternal.

43. Justin, *Dialogue*, 80; cited in Dewart, *Death and Resurrection*, 64.

44. Dewart, *Death and Resurrection*, 97.

45. Irenaeus of Lyons, *Adversus Haereses* V.34.3; cited by Dewart, *Death and Resurrection*, 99.

46. Irenaeus of Lyons, *Adversus Haereses* V.35.2–36.1; cited by Dewart, *Death and Resurrection*, 99.

47. Daley, *The Hope of the Early Church*, 31; quoting *Adversus Haereses* V.32.1.

48. Daley, *The Hope of the Early Church*, 133; quoting Augustine, Sermon 259.

49. Augustine, *The City of God*, 20.9.

50. Augustine, *The City of God*, 20.9.

51. Daley, *Hope of the Early Church*, 134.

52. In this section I draw on my discussion in Ryan, *Jesus and Salvation*, 67–69.

53. J. Patout Burns, "The Economy of Salvation: Two Patristic Traditions," *Theological Studies* 37(1976): 598–619.

54. Burns, "The Economy of Salvation," 599.

55. See John R. Sachs, "Apocatastasis in Patristic Theology," *Theological Studies* 54(1993): 617–640, at 618. Sachs cites *Stromateis* 7,6.34.4 and 7,16.102.5.

56. Daley, *Hope of the Early Church*, 47.

57. Sachs, "Apocatastasis in Patristic Theology," 621. Sachs cites *Contra Celsum* 7.72 among many other texts.

58. Sachs, "Apocatastasis in Patristic Theology," 625. There is ambiguity in Origen's thought about the salvation of the devil and the demons. Sachs points especially to Origen's *Letter to Friends in Alexandria*, in which Origen denies having taught the conversion and redemption of the demons.

59. Sachs, "Apocatastasis in Patristic Theology," 627–28.

60. Sachs, "Apocatastasis in Patristic Theology," 629. Sachs cites *Oration* 16.8.

61. Sachs, "Apocatastasis in Patristic Theology," 630.

62. Sachs, "Apocatastasis in Patristic Theology," 631. Sachs cites *Oration* 33.9.

63. Daley, *Hope of the Early Church*, 84.

64. Gregory of Nyssa, *Life of Moses*, 2.239; quoted by Daley, *Hope of the Early Church*, 88.

65. See Sachs, "Apocatastasis in Patristic Theology," 636.

66. Gregory of Nyssa, *On the Making of Man*, 16.16–18, in *Nicene and Post-Nicene Fathers*, Second Series, vol 5: *Gregory of Nyssa: Dogmatic Treatises, etc.*, ed. Philip Schaff and Henry Wace, trans. H. A. Wilson (Peabody, MA: Hendrickson Publishers, 1995), 406.

67. Gregory of Nyssa, *Address on Religious Instruction*, 26, in *Christology of the Later Fathers*, ed. Edward Hardy (Philadelphia: Westminster Press, 1954), 304.

68. Daley, *Hope of the Early Church*, 85.

69. Burns, "The Economy of Salvation," 609.

70. Augustine, *The City of God*, 21.17.

71. Augustine, *Enchiridion on Faith, Hope and Love*, ch. 99.

72. Augustine, *Enchiridion on Faith, Hope and Love*, ch. 103.

73. See Daley, *Hope of the Early Church*, 188–90; Sachs, "Apocatastasis in Patristic Theology," 638–39.

74. Daley, *Hope of the Early Church*, 190.

75. Sachs, "Apocatastasis in Patristic Theology," 640.

76. Daley, *Hope of the Early Church*, 223.

77. Daley, *Hope of the Early Church*, 219–24.

78. LeGoff, *The Birth of Purgatory*, 290.

79. For biographical information about Joachim, see M. F. Laughlin, "Joachim of Fiore," *The New Catholic Encyclopedia*, 2nd ed. (Detroit: Thomson Gale, 2003), 876–77. See also Bernard McGinn, *The Calabrian Abbot: Joachim of Fiore in the History of Western Thought* (New York: MacMillan, 1985), 1–47. I draw heavily on McGinn's work in my presentation of the thought of Joachim.

80. So McGinn, *The Calabrian Abbot*, 22.

81. McGinn, *The Calabrian Abbot*, 190.

82. McGinn, *The Calabrian Abbot*, 113.

83. McGinn, *The Calabrian Abbot*, 192.

84. DS 803–806; Neuner, *The Christian Faith*, 317–20.

85. McGinn, *The Calabrian Abbot*, 175.

86. Thomas Aquinas, *Summa Theologiae* 1, 39,5 and 1–2, 106,4.

87. Hans Schwarz, *Eschatology* (Grand Rapids, MI: Eerdmans, 2000), 327; Schwarz cites Bloch, *The Principle of Hope*, 2:510.

88. See the discussion in Almen and Sklba, *The Hope of Eternal Life*, nn. 159–66.

89. Almen and Sklba, *The Hope of Eternal Life*, n. 163.

90. Daley, *Hope of the Early Church*, 140.

91. Augustine, *The City of God*, 21,26.

92. LeGoff, *The Birth of Purgatory*, 70.

93. LeGoff, *The Birth of Purgatory*, 88.

94. Gregory the Great, *Dialogues*, 4, 41; quoted in Almen and Sklba, *The Hope of Eternal Life*, n. 171.

95. Gregory the Great, *Dialogues* 4, 47; Almen and Sklba, *The Hope of Eternal Life*, n. 172.

96. Gregory the Great, *Dialogues* 4, 57; see Daley, *Hope of the Early Church*, 214 and LeGoff, *The Birth of Purgatory*, 91.

97. I follow LeGoff in this section, *The Birth of Purgatory*, 167–68. See also LeGoff, "Le Purgatoire Entre L'Enfer et Le Paradis," *Le Maison Dieu* 144 (1980): 103–38.

98. LeGoff, *The Birth of Purgatory*, 165. LeGoff cites Peter the Chanter's *Summa de Sacramentis et Animae Consiliis.*

99. Denzinger-Schönmetzer 856; Dupuis and Neuner, *The Christian Faith*, n. 26.

100. LeGoff, "Le Purgatoire," 117–26.

101. LeGoff, *The Birth of Purgatory*, 289.

102. LeGoff, *The Birth of Purgatory*, 293.

103. John Thiel, *Icons of Hope: The "Last Things" in Catholic Imagination* (Notre Dame, IN: University of Notre Dame Press, 2011), 83.

104. Thiel, *Icons of Hope*, 86.

105. Jeannine Hill Fletcher, "Eschatology," in *Systematic Theology: Roman Catholic Perspectives*, ed. Francis Schlüssler-Fiorenza and John Galvin (Minneapolis: Fortress Press, 2011), 629.

106. Here I draw on the work of two authors in particular: Brian Davies, *The Thought of Thomas Aquinas* (Oxford: Clarendon Press, 1992); Thomas O'Meara, *Thomas Aquinas: Theologian* (Notre Dame, IN: University of Notre Dame Press, 1997).

107. Aquinas, *Summa Theologiae* I–II, 17, 2.

108. Aquinas, *Summa Theologiae* II–II, 18, 4, ad 2.

109. Aquinas, *Summa Theologiae* III, 54,2. See the discussion in Davies, *The Thought of Thomas Aquinas*, 340–41.

110. Aquinas, *Compendium Theologiae*, ch. 236; cited in Davies, *The Thought of Thomas Aquinas*, 340.

111. Davies, *The Thought of Thomas Aquinas*, 340.

112. Aquinas, *Summa Theologiae* III, 56, 1; cited in Davies, *The Thought of Thomas Aquinas*, 342.

113. Aquinas, *Summa Theologiae* III, 57, 6; cited in Davies, *The Thought of Thomas Aquinas*, 343.

114. Terence Nichols, *Death and Afterlife: A Theological Introduction* (Grand Rapids, MI: Brazos Press, 2010), 67.

115. Aquinas, *Super primam epistolam ad Corinthios lectura*, 15; cited in Davies, *The Thought of Thomas Aquinas*, 216.

116. Aquinas, *Summa Theologiae* I, 76, 1, ad 6; cited in Davies, *The Thought of Thomas Aquinas*, 217. In book 4 of his *Summa Contra Gentiles*, Aquinas says that it is contrary to the nature of the soul to be without the body; SCG 4, 79, 10.

117. Aquinas, *Compendium Theologiae*, ch. 153; cited in Davies, *The Thought of Thomas Aquinas*, 219.

118. Aquinas, *Summa Theologiae* III, *Supplement*, 69, 2. See also *Summa Contra Gentiles* 4, 91.

119. Aquinas, *Summa Theologiae* III, *Supplement*, 69, 6.

120. LeGoff, *The Birth of Purgatory*, 268.

121. Aquinas, *Summa Contra Gentiles*, trans. Charles O'Neil (University of Notre Dame Press, 1975), 4, 91, 6.

122. Aquinas, *Summa Theologiae* III, *Supplement*, 71,2.

123. Aquinas, *Summa Theologiae* III, *Supplement*, q. 91. See also *Summa Contra Gentiles* 4, 97,5. Elizabeth Johnson discusses Aquinas's treatment of this question in *Ask the Beasts: Darwin and the God of Love* (London: Bloomsbury, 2014), 229.

124. Aquinas, *Summa Theologiae* III, *Supplement* 91, 1.

125. Johnson, *Ask the Beasts*, 229.

126. Aquinas, *Summa Theologiae* III, *Supplement*, 91,5.

127. Johnson, *Ask the Beasts*, 230.

5. FROM THE HIGH MIDDLE AGES TO THE TWENTY-FIRST CENTURY

1. Jared Wicks, "The Intermediate State: Patristic and Medieval Doctrinal Development and Recent Receptions," in *The Hope of Eternal Life: Lutherans and Catholics in Dialogue XI*, ed. Lowell Almen and Richard Sklba (Minneapolis: Lutheran University Press, 2011), 133–75.

2. Wicks, "The Intermediate State," 134.

3. Augustine, *The City of God*, 13,8; cited in Wicks, "The Intermediate State," 138–39.

4. Gregory the Great, *Dialogues*, 4, 26; cited in Wicks, "The Intermediate State," 143.

5. Wicks, "The Intermediate State," 151.

6. Wicks, "The Intermediate State," 152.

7. Wicks, "The Intermediate State," 158.

8. Wicks, "The Intermediate State," 159.

9. Wicks, "The Intermediate State," 160.

10. Denzinger-Schönmetzer 1000; Jacques Dupuis and Josef Neuner, ed., *The Christian Faith in the Doctrinal Documents of the Catholic Church*, 6th ed. (New York: Alba House, 1995), n. 2305.

11. DS 1000; Dupuis and Neuner, *The Christian Faith*, n. 2305.

12. DS 1002; Dupuis and Neuner, *The Christian Faith*, n. 2307.

13. Joseph Ratzinger, *Eschatology: Death and Eternal Life*, trans. Michael Waldstein (Washington, DC: CUA Press, 1988), 138.

14. See Wicks, "The Intermediate State," 171.

15. Here Wicks (171–72) cites Medard Kehl, *Dein Reich komme. Eschatologie als Rechenschaft über unsere Hoffnung* (Kevelaer: Topos, 2003), 270–72.

16. See Dupuis and Neuner, *The Christian Faith*, nn. 2308–10; Lowell Almen and Richard Sklba, eds., *The Hope of Eternal Life*, Lutherans and Catholics in Dialogue XI (Minneapolis: Lutheran University Press, 2011), nn. 174–76.

17. Almen and Sklba, *The Hope of Eternal Life*, n. 174.

18. DS 1304; Dupuis and Neuner, n. 2308. A similar statement about purgatory had been made by the Second Council of Lyons in 1274 in its *Profession of Faith of Michael Palaelogus* (DS 856; Dupuis and Neuner 26).

19. DS 1305; Dupuis and Neuner, n. 2309.

20. DS 1820; Dupuis and Neuner, n. 2310.

21. DS 1820; Dupuis and Neuner, n. 2310.

22. DS 998; cited in Almen and Sklba, *The Hope of Eternal Life*, n. 178.

23. Martin Luther, "Ninety-Five Theses," in *Martin Luther: Selections from His Writings*, ed. John Dillenberger (Garden City, NY: Doubleday, 1961), thesis 27, 493.

24. See Hans Schwarz, *Eschatology* (Grand Rapids, MI: Eerdmans, 2000), 297–98; also Almen and Sklba, *The Hope of Eternal Life*, nn. 43–44.

25. Martin Luther, *Predigten des Jahres 1533*, in WA 17/-20 as cited in Schwarz, *Eschatology*, 298.

26. Schwarz, *Eschatology*, 298.

27. See Jaroslav Pelikan, *Reformation of Church and Dogma (1300–1700)*, vol. 4 of *The Christian Tradition* (Chicago: University of Chicago Press, 1984), 136–37.

28. Luther, *The Smalcald Articles*, in *The Book of Concord*, 295, as cited in Schwarz, *Eschatology*, 359.

29. Almen and Sklba, *The Hope of Eternal Life*, n. 183.

30. Almen and Sklba, *The Hope of Eternal Life*, n. 184.

31. Apology, Article XII, 148, as cited in Almen and Sklba, *The Hope of Eternal Life*, n. 184.

32. Almen and Sklba, *The Hope of Eternal Life*, n. 191.

33. *Luther's Works*, vol. 37, ed. Robert H. Fischer (Philadelphia: Muhlenberg Press, 1961), 369, as cited in Almen and Sklba, *The Hope of Eternal Life*, n. 229.

34. Almen and Sklba, *The Hope of Eternal Life*, n. 232.

35. Almen and Sklba, *The Hope of Eternal Life*, n. 232.

36. Luther, *Weimar Ausgabe* 18:6, cited in Almen and Sklba, *The Hope of Eternal Life*, n. 233.

37. Almen and Sklba, *The Hope of Eternal Life*, n. 237.

38. *Augsburg Confession*, article 24, *Creeds of the Churches*, ed. John Leith, 3rd ed. (Louisville, KY: John Knox Press, 1982), 73.

39. Almen and Sklba, *The Hope of Eternal Life*, n. 120.

40. Schwarz, *Eschatology*, 328.

41. Almen and Sklba, *The Hope of Eternal Life*, n. 143.

42. Jürgen Moltmann, *The Coming of God: Christian Eschatology*, trans. Margaret Kohl (Minneapolis: Fortress Press, 1996), 100.

43. John Calvin, *Institutes of the Christian Religion* (1559), trans. Henry Beveridge (Grand Rapids, MI: Eerdmans, 1989), III.5.6.

44. Pelikan, *Reformation of Church and Dogma (1300–1700)*, 218.
45. Calvin, *Institutes of the Christian Religion (1559)*, III.23.2.
46. Calvin, *Institutes of the Christian Religion (1559)*, III. 23.1.
47. Pelikan, *Reformation of Church and Dogma (1300–1700)*, 222.
48. In this section, I draw on the analysis of Schwarz, *Eschatology*, 107–134.
49. Albrecht Ritschl, *Instruction in the Christian Religion*, n. 5, as quoted in Schwarz, *Eschatology*, 107.
50. Schwarz, *Eschatology*, 107–8.
51. Schwarz, *Eschatology*, 109.
52. Schwarz, *Eschatology*, 112.
53. Albert Schweitzer, *The Quest of the Historical Jesus*, ed. John Bowden (Minneapolis: Fortress Press, 2001), 327. See the discussion of Schweitzer in Jürgen Moltmann, *The Coming of God: Christian Eschatology*, trans. Margaret Kohl (Minneapolis: Fortress Press, 1996), 8–10.
54. Schweitzer, *The Quest of the Historical Jesus*, 347.
55. Moltmann, *The Coming of God*, 9.
56. Peter Phan, "Roman Catholic Theology," in *The Oxford Handbook of Eschatology*, ed. Jerry Walls (Oxford: Oxford University Press, 2008), 221.
57. Schwarz, *Eschatology*, 125.
58. Schwarz, *Eschatology*, 125.
59. Rudolf Bultmann, *History and Eschatology: The Presence of Eternity*, The Gifford Lectures (Edinburgh: University of Edinburgh, 1955).
60. Bultmann, *History and Eschatology*, 151.
61. Moltmann, *The Coming of God*, 20–21.
62. Moltmann, *The Coming of God*, 21.
63. Moltmann, *The Coming of God*, 21.
64. Karl Rahner, "The Hermeneutics of Eschatological Assertions," *Theological Investigations*, vol. 4, *More Recent Writings*, trans. Kevin Smyth (London: Darton, Longman and Todd, 1966), 323–46. See the discussion of this essay by Phan, "Roman Catholic Theology," 222–26.
65. Rahner, "The Hermeneutics of Eschatological Assertions," 326.
66. Rahner, "The Hermeneutics of Eschatological Assertions," 327.
67. Rahner, "The Hermeneutics of Eschatological Assertions," 330.
68. Rahner, "The Hermeneutics of Eschatological Assertions," 331.
69. Rahner, "The Hermeneutics of Eschatological Assertions," 332.
70. Rahner, "The Hermeneutics of Eschatological Assertions," 333.
71. Phan, "Roman Catholic Theology," 222.
72. Rahner, "The Hermeneutics of Eschatological Assertions," 337.
73. Rahner, "The Hermeneutics of Eschatological Assertions," 343.
74. Rahner, "The Hermeneutics of Eschatological Assertions," 343–344.
75. Rahner, "The Hermeneutics of Eschatological Assertions," 345.

76. Brian Robinette argues that by "de-apocalypticizing" eschatology Rahner has restricted its meaning primarily to only one of its grammatical modes—the grammar of fulfillment. Because of this, he cannot adequately account for the "prophetic and political magnitude of resurrection language." Robinette, *Grammars of Resurrection: A Christian Theology of Presence and Absence* (New York: Crossroad, 2009), 196.

77. Karl Rahner, *Foundations of Christian Faith: An Introduction to the Idea of Christianity*, trans. William Dych (1978; repr. New York: Crossroad, 2013), 432–33.

78. Phan, "Roman Catholic Theology, 216.

79. Carl Peter, "The Last Things and *Lumen Gentium*," *Chicago Studies* 24, no. 2 (1985): 215–37, at 231.

80. Peter, "The Last Things," 235.

81. See Gustavo Gutiérrez, *The God of Life*, trans. Matthew O'Connell (Maryknoll, NY: Orbis Books, 1989), 118–39.

82. Phan, "Roman Catholic Theology," 218.

83. Karl Rahner, "Basic Theological Interpretation of the Second Vatican Council," in *Theological Investigations*, vol. 20, *Concern for the Church*, trans. Edward Quinn (New York: Crossroad, 1981), 77–89.

84. James Nickoloff, introduction to *Gustavo Gutiérrez: Essential Writings* (Maryknoll, NY: Orbis Books, 1996), 3–4.

85. Gustavo Gutiérrez, *The God of Life*, trans. Matthew O'Connell (Maryknoll, NY: Orbis Books, 1991), 101.

86. Gutiérrez, *The God of Life*, 102.

87. Gutiérrez, *The God of Life*, 102.

88. Gutiérrez, *The God of Life*, 109.

89. Puebla, n. 1142; *The God of Life*, 115.

90. Gutiérrez, *The Truth Shall Make You Free: Confrontations*, trans. Matthew O'Connell (Maryknoll, NY: Orbis Books, 1990), 30.

91. Gutiérrez, *The Truth Shall Make You Free*, 30.

92. Gutiérrez, *The God of Life*, 14.

93. Gutiérrez, *The God of Life*, 14.

94. Gutiérrez, *A Theology of Liberation*, trans. Sister Caridad Inda and John Eagleson (Maryknoll, NY: Orbis Books, 1973), 153.

95. Gutiérrez, *A Theology of Liberation*, 177; emphasis in the original.

96. Congregation for the Doctrine of the Faith, "Instruction on Certain Aspects of the 'Theology of Liberation,'" *Origins* 14, no. 13 (1984): 193–204; "Instruction on Christian Freedom and Liberation," *Origins* 15, no. 44 (1986): 713–28.

97. CDF, "Instruction on Certain Aspects of the 'Theology of Liberation,'" IX, 3.

98. CDF, "Instruction on Christian Freedom and Liberation, 58.

99. CDF, "Instruction on Christian Freedom and Liberation, 60.

100. CDF, "Instruction on Christian Freedom and Liberation," 60.

101. CDF, "Instruction on Christian Freedom and Liberation," 60.

102. Robinette, *Grammars of Resurrection*, 195–211.

103. Robinette, *Grammars of Resurrection*, 196.

104. Robinette, *Grammars of Resurrection*, 207–8.

105. Mario Inzulza, SJ, "The Parousia: A Suitable Symbol for a Renewed Eschatological, Cosmic Narrative" (STD diss., Boston College School of Theology and Ministry, 2018).

106. Inzulza, "The Parousia," 94. Inzulza cites Lyotard, *The Postmodern Condition*, xxiii–xxiv.

107. Inzulza, "The Parousia," 91.

108. Inzulza, "The Parousia," 96.

109. Inzulza, "The Parousia," 91.

110. John Thiel, *Icons of Hope: The "Last Things" in Catholic Imagination* (Notre Dame, IN: University of Notre Dame Press, 2013), 5.

111. Thiel, *Icons of Hope*, 9. Thiel refers especially to Rahner's essay, "The Life of the Dead," in *Theological Investigations*, 4:347–354.

112. Thiel, *Icons of Hope*, 12.

6. THE DESTINY OF THE INDIVIDUAL

1. Dermot Lane, *Keeping Hope Alive: Stirrings in Christian Theology* (New York: Paulist Press, 1996), 43.

2. Karl Rahner, *On the Theology of Death*, vol. 2 of *Quaestiones Disputatae*, trans. W. J. O'Hara (New York: Herder & Herder, 1961).

3. Martin Heidegger, *Being and Time*, trans. J. MacQuarrie and Edward Robinson (New York: Harper & Row, 1962).

4. Karl Rahner, "Christian Dying," in *Theological Investigations*, vol. 18, *God and Revelation*, trans. Edward Quinn (New York: Crossroad, 1983), 230.

5. See Rahner, "Proving Oneself in Time of Sickness," in *Theological Investigations*, vol. 7, *Further Theology of the Spiritual Life*, trans. David Bourke (New York: Herder & Herder, 1977), 275–84.

6. Rahner, *On the Theology of Death*, 38.

7. As we will see further on, contemporary theologians like Elizabeth Johnson point out that death was part of the evolutionary process long before humans arrived on the scene.

8. Rahner, "On Christian Dying," in *Theological Investigations*, 7:285.

9. Gisbert Greshake, "Towards a Theology of Dying," *The Experience of Dying*, *Concilium*, vol. 94, ed. Norbert Greinacher (1974), 88.

10. Greshake, "Towards a Theology of Dying," 88.

11. Elisabeth Kübler-Ross, *On Death and Dying* (New York: MacMillan, 1969), 13.

12. Denzinger-Schönmetzer, 540.

13. Jürgen Moltmann, *In the End—the Beginning: The Life of Hope*, trans. Margaret Kohl (Minneapolis: Fortress Press, 2004), 47.

14. Brian Robinette, *Grammars of Resurrection: A Christian Theology of Presence and Absence* (New York: Crossroad, 2009), 23.

15. Gerhard Lohfink, *Is This All There Is? On Resurrection and Eternal Life*, trans. Linda Maloney (Collegeville, MN: Liturgical Press, 2018), 132.

16. International Theological Commission, "Some Current Questions in Eschatology," (1992), n. 1.

17. Thomas Aquinas, *Summa Theologiae*, 3, *Supplement* 76,1; see also *Summa Theologiae* 3,54,2.

18. Elizabeth Johnson, *Ask the Beasts: Darwin and the God of Love* (London: Bloomsbury, 2014), 208.

19. Karl Rahner, "The Festival of the Future of the World," in *Theological Investigations*, 7:183.

20. Rahner, "The Festival of the Future of the World," 183.

21. Karl Rahner, "A Faith that Loves the Earth," in *The Mystical Way in Everyday Life: Sermons, Prayers and Essay*, ed. Annemarie Kidder (Maryknoll, NY: Orbis Books, 2010), 55.

22. Rahner, "A Faith That Loves the Earth," 56.

23. Karl Rahner, "The Eternal Significance of the Humanity of Jesus for Our Relationship with God," in *Theological Investigations*, vol. 3, *Theology of the Spiritual Life*, trans. Karl-H. and Boniface Kruger (London: Darton, Longman and Todd, 1967), 35–46.

24. Rahner, "Eternal Significance of the Humanity of Jesus," 41.

25. Rahner, "Eternal Significance of the Humanity of Jesus," 43.

26. Rahner, "Eternal Significance of the Humanity of Jesus," 44.

27. *Catechism of the Catholic Church*, n. 997. The CCC describes the "when" of the resurrection as "at the last day," or "at the end of the world" in n. 1001.

28. See Gisbert Greshake and Jacob Kremer, *Resurrectio Mortuorum: Zum theologischen Verständnis der leiblichen Auferstehung* (Darmstadt: Wissenschaftliche Buchgesellschaft, 1986), 158–61; 255–76.

29. Greshake, *Resurrectio Mortuorum*, 257.

30. Lohfink, *Is This All There Is?*, 180.

31. Lohfink, *Is This All There Is?*, 220.

32. Karl Rahner, "The Intermediate State," in *Theological Investigations*, vol. 17, *Jesus, Man and the Church*, trans. Margaret Kohl (New York: Crossroad, 1981), 119–20.

33. Karl Rahner, *Foundations of Christian Faith: An Introduction to the Idea of Christianity*, trans. William Dych (New York: Crossroad, 1978/2013), 435–36.

34. Rahner, *Foundations of Christian Faith*, 442.

35. Michael Schmaus, *Dogma 6: Justification and the Last Things* (Kansas City, MO: Sheed & Ward, 1977), 196–98; 226–33.

36. Schmaus, *Dogma 6*, 197. Further along in this same volume (232–33), Schmaus speaks of the vision of God and the resurrection of the dead occurring in different phases. He claims that this consideration does not differ fundamentally from the theory of resurrection in death. There seems to be some lack of clarity here.

37. Joseph Ratzinger, *Eschatology: Death and Eternal Life*, trans. Michael Waldstein (Washington, DC: CUA Press, 1988), 148–49.

38. Ratzinger, *Eschatology*, 149.

39. Ratzinger, *Eschatology*, 267.

40. Ratzinger, *Eschatology*, 184.

41. Congregation for the Doctrine of the Faith, "Letter on Certain Questions Concerning Eschatology," *Origins* 9, no. 9 (1979): 131–33.

42. International Theological Commission, "Some Current Questions in Eschatology, 1992.

43. International Theological Commission, "Some Current Questions in Eschatology," 1992, 2.1.

44. International Theological Commission, "Some Current Questions in Eschatology," 1992, 5.4.

45. Lane, *Keeping Hope Alive*, 154.

46. Lane, *Keeping Hope Alive*, 159.

47. *Catechism of the Catholic Church*, n. 1022.

48. Schmaus, *Dogma 6*, 235.

49. Thomas O'Meara, *Life beyond Death: A Traveler's Guide for Christians* (St. Louis: The Catholic Health Association, 2019), 37.

50. O'Meara, *Life beyond Death*, 37.

51. Zachary Hayes, *Visions of a Future: A Study of Christian Eschatology* (Wilmington, DE: Michael Glazier, 1989), 110–11.

52. Ratzinger, *Eschatology*, 206.

53. Lohfink, *Is This All There Is?*, 152.

54. Moltmann, *In the End—the Beginning*, 141.

55. Pope Benedict XVI, *Spe Salvi*, 2007, n. 47.

56. Congregation for the Doctrine of the Faith, "Letter on Certain Questions Concerning Eschatology."

57. *Catechism of the Catholic Church*, n. 1030.

58. *Catechism of the Catholic Church*, n. 1032.

59. International Theological Commission, "Some Current Questions in Eschatology," 1992, n. 8.1.

60. Jeannine Hill Fletcher, "Eschatology," in *Systematic Theology: Roman Catholic Perspectives*, 2nd ed., ed. Francis Schlüssler Fiorenza and John P. Galvin (Minneapolis: Fortress Press, 2011), 634.

61. Rahner, *Foundations of Christian Faith*, 442.

62. Karl Rahner, "Purgatory," in *Theological Investigations*, vol. 19, *Faith and Ministry*, trans. Edward Quinn (New York: Crossroad, 1983), 185.

63. Rahner, "Purgatory," 190–91.

64. Pope Benedict XVI, *Spe Salvi*, n. 46.

65. Pope Benedict XVI, *Spe Salvi*, n. 46.

66. Pope Benedict XVI, *Spe Salvi*, n. 47.

67. Pope Benedict XVI, *Spe Salvi*, n. 47.

68. Lane, *Keeping Hope Alive*, 148.

69. Lowell Almen and Richard Sklba, ed., *The Hope of Eternal Life: Lutherans and Catholics in Dialogue XI* (Minneapolis: Lutheran University Press, 2011), n. 207.

70. I owe the use of this image of rehabilitation for purgatory to a committed and very insightful lay Catholic named Maureen Hackett.

71. Lohfink, *Is This All There Is?*, 237–39.

72. Lohfink, *Is This All There Is?*, 238.

73. Lohfink, *Is This All There Is?*, 239.

74. Pope Benedict XVI, *Spe Salvi*, n. 48.

75. Pope Benedict XVI, *Spe Salvi*, n. 48.

76. Pope Benedict XVI, *Spe Salvi*, n. 48.

77. Almen and Sklba, *The Hope of Eternal Life*, nn. 219–78.

78. Almen and Sklba, *The Hope of Eternal Life*, n. 245.

79. Almen and Sklba, *The Hope of Eternal Life*, n. 274.

80. Andrew Louth, "Eastern Orthodox Eschatology," in *The Oxford Handbook of Eschatology*, ed. Jerry Walls (New York: Oxford University Press, 2008), 239–40.

81. Louth, "Eastern Orthodox Eschatology," 240.

82. Louth, "Eastern Orthodox Eschatology," 240.

83. DS 1000.

84. DS 1001.

85. Aquinas, *Summa Contra Gentiles*, III, 63.

86. Aquinas, *Summa Theologiae*, I, 12,5. Neil Ormerod notes that Aquinas was aware of the difficulties that this teaching posed, as this knowledge could be misconstrued as being divine. Aquinas acknowledged that it must not be understood as though the divine essence were in reality the form of our intellect: "The meaning is that the proportion of the Divine essence to our intellect is as the proportion of form to matter" (*Summa Theologiae*, III Supplement, 92,1). See Ormerod, "'And We Shall See Him Face to Face': A Trinitarian Analysis of the Beatific Vision," *Theological Studies* 82, no. 4 (2021): 647n2.

87. Aquinas, *Summa Theologiae*, I,12,6.

88. Aquinas, *Summa Theologiae*, I,12,7.

89. Aquinas, *Summa Contra Gentiles* III,63,10.

90. Ormerod, "And We Shall See Him Face to Face," 646–62.

91. Ormerod, "And We Shall See Him Face to Face," 660.

92. Ormerod, "And We Shall See Him Face to Face," 661.

93. John Thiel, *Icons of Hope: The "Last Things" in Catholic Imagination* (Notre Dame, IN: University of Notre Dame Press, 2013), especially 27–55.

94. Thiel, *Icons of Hope*, 43.

95. Thiel, *Icons of Hope*, 40.

96. Thiel, *Icons of Hope*, 54.

97. See Karl Rahner, "The Eternal Significance of the Humanity of Jesus for Our Relationship with God," in *Theological Investigations*, 3:35–46. See also Rahner, "Why and How Can We Venerate the Saints?" *Theological Investigations*, 8:3–23.

98. Rahner, "Why and How Can We Venerate the Saints?," 12.

99. Rahner, "Eternal Significance of the Humanity of Jesus," 44.

100. Gerald O'Collins, "In the End, Love," in *Faith in the Future: Studies in Christian Eschatology*, ed. John Galvin (New York: Paulist Press, 1994), 25–42.

101. O'Collins, "In the End, Love," 35.

102. Pope Benedict XVI, *Spe Salvi*, n. 12.

103. Ratzinger, *Eschatology*, 235.

104. DS 1002.

105. International Theological Commission, "Some Current Questions in Eschatology" (1992), 10.3.

106. John R. Sachs, "Current Eschatology: Universal Salvation and the Problem of Hell," *Theological Studies* 52 (1991): 227–54.

107. Ratzinger, *Eschatology*, 205–6.

108. Karl Rahner, "Guilt, Responsibility, Punishment within the View of Catholic Theology," in *Theological Investigations*, vol. 6, *Concerning Vatican Council II*, trans. Karl-H. and Boniface Kruger (New York: Seabury, 1974), 214–15.

109. Rahner, *Foundations of Christian Faith*, 443.

110. Rahner, *Foundations of Christian Faith*, 444.

111. Hans Urs von Balthasar, *Dare We Hope "That All Men Be Saved?"* trans. David Kipp and Lothar Krauth (San Francisco: Ignatius Press, 1988).

112. Hans Urs von Balthasar, *Mysterium Paschale: The Mystery of Easter*, trans. Aidan Nichols (San Francisco: Ignatius Press, 2000), 164.

113. Hans Urs von Balthasar, *The Von Balthasar Reader*, ed. Medard Kehl and Werner Löser (New York: Crossroad, 1982), 153.

114. Sachs, "Current Eschatology," 246.

115. Hans Küng, *Eternal Life? Life after Death as a Medical, Philosophical, and Theological Problem*, trans. Edward Quinn (Garden City, NY: Doubleday, 1985), 141.

116. Küng, *Eternal Life?*, 141.

117. Küng, *Eternal Life?*, 140.

118. Moltmann, *In the End—the Beginning*, 140.

119. Moltmann, *In the End—the Beginning*, 143.

120. Moltmann, *In the End—the Beginning*, 143.

121. Moltmann, *In the End—the Beginning*, 143.

122. Edward Schilebeeckx, *Church: The Human Story of God*, trans. John Bowden (New York: Crossroad, 1990), 136–139.

123. Schillebeeckx, *Church*, 137.

124. Schillebeeckx, *Church*, 137.

125. Schillebeeckx, *Church*, 138.

126. Sachs, "Current Eschatology," 246–54.

127. Sachs, "Current Eschatology," 247.

128. Sachs, "Current Eschatology," 252.

129. Sachs, "Current Eschatology," 251.

130. Sachs, "Current Eschatology," 251; emphasis in the original.

131. For a discussion of Gregory's eschatology, see Andrew Klager, "Orthodox Eschatology and St. Gregory of Nyssa's *De Vita Moysis*," in *Compassionate Eschatology: The Future as Friend*, ed. Ted Grimsrud and Michael Hardin (Eugene, OR: Cascade Books, 2011), 230–52.

132. International Theological Commission, "The Hope of Salvation for Infants Who Die without Being Baptized," *Origins* 36, no. 45 (April 26, 2007): 725–46.

133. Pope Innocent III, letter to Humbert, archbishop of Arles, *Maiores Ecclesiae Causas*, DS 780.

134. ITC, "The Hope of Salvation," n. 23; see Thomas Aquinas, *De Malo*, q.5, a.3.

135. ITC, "The Hope of Salvation," introductory paragraphs.

136. ITC, "The Hope of Salvation," n. 87.

137. ITC, "The Hope of Salvation," n. 96.

138. *Catechism of the Catholic Church*, n. 1261.

139. USCCB, *Order of Christian Funerals*, n. 255.

7. CORPORATE AND COSMIC FULFILLMENT

1. Susan Wood, "Communal and Sacramental Dimensions of Eschatology," in *The Hope of Eternal Life: Lutherans and Catholics in Dialogue XI*, ed. Lowell Almen and Richard Sklba (Minneapolis: Lutheran University Press, 2011), 181. Here Wood draws on the work of Henri de Lubac in "Sanctorum Communio," in *Theological Fragments*, trans. Rebecca Balinski (San Francisco: Ignatius Press, 1989), 19. See also Elizabeth Johnson, "Communion of Saints and Mary," in *Systematic Theology: Roman Catholic Perspectives*, 2nd ed., ed. Francis Schüssler Fiorenza and John Galvin (Minneapolis: Fortress Press, 2011), 433.

2. Wood," Communal and Sacramental Dimensions of Eschatology," 182.

3. Johnson, "Communion of Saints and Mary," 433.

4. Pope Francis, *Gaudete et Exsultate*, 6–9.

5. Pope Francis, *Gaudete et Exsultate*, 6.

6. Pope Francis, *Gaudete et Exsultate*, 7.

7. Karl Rahner, "All Saints," in *Theological Investigations*, vol. 8, *Further Theology of the Spiritual Life, 2*, trans. David Bourke (New York: Crossroad, 1977), 25.

8. Rahner, "All Saints," 25–26.

9. Rahner, "All Saints," 29.

10. Johnson, "Communion of Saints and Mary," 454.

11. Johnson, "Communion of Saints and Mary," 435.

12. Johnson, "Communion of Saints and Mary," 437.

13. Rahner, "All Saints," 27.

14. Rahner, "All Saints," 27.

15. Johnson, "Communion of Saints and Mary, 442–43.

16. Johnson, "Communion of Saints and Mary," 443.

17. Johnson, "Communion of Saints and Mary," 450–51.

18. Johnson, "Communion of Saints and Mary," 450.

19. Johnson, "Communion of Saints and Mary," 451.

20. Pope Paul VI, apostolic letter *Marialis Cultus*, For the Right Ordering and Development of Devotion to the Blessed Virgin Mary (1974), 37.

21. Edward W. Fasholé-Luke, "Ancestor Veneration and the Communion of Saints," in *New Testament Christianity for Africa and the World*, ed. Mark E. Glasswell and Edward W. Fasholé-Luke (London: SPCK, 1974), 214. For a study of the role of ancestor veneration in African eschatology, see Ibigbolade S. Aderibigbe, *Contextualizing Eschatology in African Cultural and Religious Beliefs* (New York: Routledge, 2020), especially 61–67.

22. Fasholé-Luke, "Ancestor Veneration and the Communion of Saints," 220.

23. Johnson, "Communion of Saints and Mary," 455.

24. DS 30.

25. DS 150.

26. DS 801.

27. Karl Rahner, "The Resurrection of the Body," in *Theological Investigations*, vol. 2, *Man in the Church*, trans. Karl-H. Kruger (Baltimore: Helicon Press, 1963), 213.

28. Karl Rahner, "He Will Come Again," in *Theological Investigations*, vol. 7, *Further Theology of the Spiritual Life*, trans. David Bourke (New York: Herder, 1971), 177. This is the English translation of the verse to which Rahner refers. The Revised NAB reads, "This Jesus who has been taken up

from you into heaven will return in the same way as you have seen him going into heaven."

29. Rahner, "He Will Come Again," *Theological Investigations*, 7:178.

30. Rahner, "He Will Come Again," *Theological Investigations*, 7:179.

31. Karl Rahner, "God Who Is to Come," in *Prayers for a Lifetime*, ed. Albert Raffelt (New York: Crossroad, 1984), 149–56.

32. Rahner, *Foundations of Christian Faith*, 445.

33. Rahner, *Foundations of Christian Faith*, 445–46.

34. Michael Schmaus, *Dogma 6: Justification and the Last Things* (Kansas City, MO: Sheed & Ward, 1977), chapter 15.

35. Schmaus, *Dogma 6*, 177.

36. Joseph Ratzinger, *Eschatology: Death and Eternal Life*, trans. Michael Waldstein (Washington, DC: CUA Press, 1988), 202.

37. Ratzinger, *Eschatology*, 202.

38. Ratzinger, *Eschatology*, 203.

39. Ratzinger, *Eschatology*, 203.

40. Gerhard Lohfink, *Is This All There Is? On Resurrection and Eternal Life*, trans. Linda Maloney (Collegeville, MN: Liturgical Press, 2017), 211–20.

41. Lohfink, *Is This All There Is?*, 211.

42. Lohfink, *Is This All There Is?*, 219.

43. In this section I draw on my discussion of Moltmann in *God and the Mystery of Human Suffering: A Theological Conversation across the Ages* (New York: Paulist Press, 2011), 206–208.

44. Jürgen Moltmann, *The Coming of God: Christian Eschatology*, trans. Margaret Kohl (Minneapolis: Fortress Press, 1996), 23.

45. Jürgen Moltmann, *In the End—the Beginning*, trans. Margaret Kohl (Minneapolis: Fortress Press, 2004), 87.

46. Jürgen Moltmann, *The Church in the Power of the Spirit*, trans. Margaret Kohl (New York: Harper & Row, 1977), 58.

47. Jürgen Moltmann, *The Way of Jesus Christ: Christology in Messianic Dimensions*, trans. Margaret Kohl (San Francisco: HarperSan Francisco, 1990), 139.

48. Moltmann, *The Way of Jesus Christ*, 32.

49. Moltmann, *The Way of Jesus Christ*, 32.

50. Moltmann, *The Way of Jesus Christ*, 314.

51. Moltmann, *The Coming of God*, 105.

52. Zachary Hayes, *Visions of a Future: A Study of Christian Eschatology* (Wilmington, DE: Michael Glazier, 1989), 162.

53. Hayes, *Visions of a Future*, 163.

54. Luke Timothy Johnson, *The Creed: What Christians Believe and Why It Matters* (New York: Doubleday, 2003), 192–206.

55. Johnson, *The Creed*, 200.

56. Hayes, *Visions of a Future*, 173.

57. Ratzinger, *Eschatology*, 207.

58. Moltmann, *In the End—the Beginning*, 144.

59. John Thiel, *Icons of Hope: The "Last Things" in Catholic Imagination* (Notre Dame, IN: University of Notre Dame Press, 2013), 149–52.

60. Thiel, *Icons of Hope*, 149.

61. Thiel, *Icons of Hope*, 150.

62. Thiel, *Icons of Hope*, 151.

63. Thiel, *Icons of Hope*, 151.

64. Pope Benedict XVI, encyclical *Spe Salvi*, 41.

65. Schmaus, *Dogma 6*, 203.

66. Moltmann, *In the End—the Beginning*, 142.

67. Pope Benedict XVI, *Spe Salvi*, 44.

68. Hans Küng, *Eternal Life? Life after Death as a Medical, Philosophical and Theological Problem*, trans. Edward Quinn (New York: Doubleday, 1985), 209.

69. Johnson, *The Creed*, 204–5.

70. See Laurie Brink, OP, *The Heavens Are Telling the Glory of God: An Emerging Chapter for Religious Life, Science, Theology and Mission* (Collegeville, MN: Liturgical Press, 2022), 80–83.

71. Georges Lemaitre, *The Primeval Atom: An Essay on Cosmogony* (New York: Van Nostrand, 1950), 78; cited by Brink, *The Heavens Are Telling the Glory of God*, 82.

72. In this section, I am dependent on the summaries provided by a number of scientists and theologians. See John Haught, *Making Sense of Evolution: Darwin, God and the Drama of Life* (Louisville, KY: Westminster John Knox Press, 2010); Denis Edwards, *How God Acts: Creation, Redemption and Special Divine Action* (Minneapolis: Fortress Press, 2010); John Polkinghorne, *Belief in God in an Age of Science* (New Haven, CT: Yale University Press, 1998); Thomas Berry, *The Great Work: Our Way into the Future* (New York: Three Rivers Press, 1999). I am also indebted to the explanations and insights given to me by Dr. Anthony Mahowald, Emeritus Professor of Biology at the University of Chicago.

73. John Polkinghorne, *The God of Hope and the End of the World* (New Haven, CT: Yale University Press, 2002), 4–5.

74. Here I draw on my comments in *Jesus and Salvation*, 160.

75. John Polkinghorne, "Eschatology: Some Questions and Some Insights from Science," in *The End of the World and the Ends of God*, ed. John Polkinghorne and Michael Welker (Harrisburg, PA: Trinity Press, 2000), 31.

76. William Stoeger, SJ, "Scientific Accounts of Ultimate Catastrophes in Our Life-Bearing Universe," in Polkinghorne and Welker, *The End of the World and the Ends of God*, 25.

77. Stoeger, "Scientific Accounts of Ultimate Catastrophes," 19–20.

78. Robert John Russell, "Cosmology and Eschatology," *The Oxford Handbook of Eschatology*, ed. Jerry Walls (New York: Oxford University Press, 2008), 567–70.

79. Steven Weinberg, *The First Three Minutes: A Modern View of the Origin of the Universe* (New York: Basic Books, 1977), 154–55; cited by Russell, "Cosmology and Eschatology," 567.

80. Russell, "Cosmology and Eschatology," 568.

81. Russell, "Cosmology and Eschatology," 570.

82. Polkinghorne, "Eschatology," 30.

83. Polkinghorne, "Eschatology," 30.

84. Polkinghorne, *The God of Hope*, 105–6.

85. Polkinghorne, "Eschatology," 40.

86. Polkinghorne, "Eschatology," 39.

87. Polkinghorne, *The God of Hope*, 116.

88. Polkinghorne, *The God of Hope*, 148–49.

89. Russell, "Cosmology and Eschatology," 572–73.

90. Russell, "Cosmology and Eschatology," 573.

91. Russell, "Cosmology and Eschatology," 573–74 (italics in the original).

92. Robert John Russell, "Resurrection, Eschatology, and the Challenge of Big Bang Cosmology," *Interpretation* 70, no. 1 (2016): 57.

93. Russell, "Resurrection, Eschatology, and the Challenge of Big Bang Cosmology," 57.

94. Karl Rahner, *Foundations of Christian Faith: An Introduction to the Idea of Christianity*, trans. William Dych (New York: Crossroad, 1978/2013), 197.

95. Karl Rahner, "Christology in the Setting of Modern Man's Understanding of Himself and of the World," in *Theological Investigations*, vol. 11, *Confrontations 1* (Baltimore: Helicon Press, 1966), 219. This passage is cited in Denis Edwards, *Deep Incarnation: God's Redemptive Suffering with Creatures* (Maryknoll, NY: Orbis Books, 2019), 90. Edwards's discussion of Rahner's theology of incarnation is very helpful.

96. Rahner, *Foundations of Christian Faith*, 193.

97. Karl Rahner, "Dogmatic Questions on Easter," in *Theological Investigations*, vol. 4, *More Recent Writings*, trans. Kevin Smyth (New York: Crossroad, 1982), 21–33. Edwards discusses this essay in *Deep Incarnation*, 95–96.

98. Rahner, "Resurrection," in *Encyclopedia of Theology: The Concise Sacramentum Mundi*, ed. Karl Rahner (New York: Seabury Press, 1975), 1442. See Edwards, *Deep Incarnation*, 96.

99. Karl Rahner, "The Resurrection of the Body," in *Theological Investigations*, 2:213.

100. Karl Rahner, "A Faith That Loves the Earth," in *The Mystical Way in Everyday Life: Sermons, Prayers and Essays*, ed. Annemarie Kidder (Maryknoll, NY: Orbis Books, 2010), 52–58. This article was originally published in the journal *Geist und Leben*.

101. Rahner, "A Faith That Loves the Earth," 53.

102. Rahner, "A Faith That Loves the Earth," 55.

103. Rahner, "A Faith That Loves the Earth," 56.

104. Rahner, "A Faith That Loves the Earth," 58.

105. See especially *Ask the Beasts: Darwin and the God of Love* (London: Bloomsbury, 2014) and *Creation and the Cross: The Mercy of God for a Planet in Peril* (Maryknoll, NY: Orbis Books, 2018).

106. Johnson, *Ask the Beasts*, 213.

107. Johnson, *Ask the Beasts*, 220.

108. Johnson, *Ask the Beasts*, 221.

109. Paul Santmire, *The Travail of Nature: The Ambiguous Promise of Christian Theology* (Minneapolis: Fortress, 1985).

110. Johnson, *Ask the Beasts*, 230.

111. Johnson, *Ask the Beasts*, 231.

EPILOGUE: HOPE AMID SUFFERING

1. In this chapter I draw on the chapter on Julian in my book *God and the Mystery of Human Suffering: A Theological Conversation across the Ages* (New York: Paulist Press, 2011), chapter 5.

2. Edmund Colledge and James Walsh, introduction to *Showings* (New York: Paulist Press, 1978), 2.

3. Denys Turner, *Julian of Norwich: Theologian* (New Haven, CT: Yale University Press, 2011), 18.

4. Colledge and Walsh, introduction to *Showings*, 18. See *The Book of Margery Kempe*, ed. W. Butler-Bowden (Oxford: Oxford University Press, 1944), 54–56.

5. Colledge and Walsh, introduction to *Showings*, 19.

6. *Showings*, LT 51/270.

7. Jane Maynard, *Transfiguring Loss: Julian of Norwich as a Guide for Survivors of Traumatic Grief* (Cleveland: Pilgrim Press, 2006), 60–61.

8. Maynard, *Transfiguring Loss*, 62,

9. Grace Jantzen, *Julian of Norwich: Mystic and Theologian* (New York: Paulist Press, 1988), 46.

10. *Showings*, ST 1/125–27; LT 2/177–78.

11. *Showings*, LT 2/178.

12. *Showings*, LT 2/178.

13. *Showings*, LT 3/180.

14. *Showings*, LT 3/180.
15. *Showings*, LT 18/210.
16. *Showings*, LT 20/213.
17. *Showings*, LT 20/214.
18. Jantzen, *Julian of Norwich*, 61. In his study of Julian's thought, Christopher Abbott argues that Julian's perspective deepens and matures as she reflects on her experience. Abbott asserts that "in reconstructing her relation to the figure of Christ crucified Julian narrates her own movement from pious individualism to an inclusive compassion rooted in her developed understanding of Christ's identification with the Church." See *Julian of Norwich: Autobiography and Theology*, Studies in Medieval Mysticism, vol. 2 (Cambridge: D. S. Brewer, 1999), at 77.
19. Jantzen, *Julian of Norwich*, 77–85; Joan Nuth, *Wisdom's Daughter: The Theology of Julian of Norwich* (New York: Crossroad, 1991), 12–16.
20. Nuth, *Wisdom's Daughter*, 15. Nuth cites the work on visionary mystics by Elizabeth Petroff, *Medieval Women's Visionary Literature* (Oxford: Oxford University Press, 1986).
21. *Showings*, LT 9/191.
22. Jantzen, *Julian of Norwich*, 80.
23. *Showings*, LT 20–22/214–18. See Nuth, *Wisdom's Daughter*, 138–41.
24. *Showings*, LT 20/214.
25. *Showings*, LT 23/218.
26. *Showings*, LT 12/200.
27. *Showings*, LT 24/210.
28. Jantzen, *Julian of Norwich*, 172.
29. *Showings*, 13/201.
30. *Showings*, LT 68/315.
31. *Showings*, LT 22/217.
32. Nuth, *Wisdom's Daughter*, 43.
33. *Showings*, 22/216.
34. *Showings*, 31/230.
35. *Showings*, LT 60/298.
36. *Showings*, LT 60/298.
37. *Showings*, LT 60/298–99.
38. Jantzen, *Julian of Norwich*, 91.
39. Jantzen, *Julian of Norwich*, 91–92.
40. *Showings*, LT 27/225.
41. *Showings*, 29/228.
42. *Showings*, 39/244.
43. *Showings*, LT 78/332.
44. *Showings*, LT 27/224.
45. *Showings*, LT 27/224.
46. *Showings*, LT 27/225.

47. Nuth, *Wisdom's Daughter*, 129.
48. Nuth, *Wisdom's Daughter*, 121.
49. Turner, *Julian of Norwich: Theologian*, 205.
50. Turner, *Julian of Norwich: Theologian*, 66–67.
51. *Showings*, LT 51/267.
52. *Showings*, LT 51/269.
53. *Showings*, LT 51/271.
54. *Showings*, LT 51/274.
55. *Showings*, 51/275.
56. *Showings*, LT 51/276.
57. *Showings*, LT 46/259.
58. *Showings*, LT 49/264.
59. *Showings*, LT 29/228.
60. *Showings*, LT 82/338.
61. *Showings*, LT 47/261.
62. *Showings*, LT 32/233.
63. *Showings*, LT 33/234.
64. *Showings*, LT 33/234.
65. *Showings*, LT 32/232–33.
66. *Showings*, LT 32/233.
67. *Showings*, LT 48/263.
68. *Showings*, LT 85/341.
69. Jantzen, *Julian of Norwich*, 186.
70. Jantzen, *Julian of Norwich*, 186–87.
71. Jantzen, *Julian of Norwich*, 187.
72. Jantzen, *Julian of Norwich*, 189.
73. Nuth, *Wisdom's Daughter*, 169.
74. *Showings*, LT 72/320.
75. *Showings*, LT 23/218–19.
76. *Showings*, LT 51/278.
77. *Showings*, LT 72/320.
78. *Showings*, LT 85/314.
79. *Showings*, LT 86/342.

SCRIPTURE INDEX

SUBJECT INDEX